MIDAS AND 1000 COWS

MIDAS AND 1000 COWS

An Entrepreneur's Crazy Journey to
Making Millions

BILL LEWIS

www.midasand1000cows.com

Copyright © 2016 Bill Lewis

All Rights Reserved

ISBN-13: 97-1537713168
ISBN-10: 1537713167

This book is a work of fiction. The names, characters, places and incidents are products of the writer's imagination or have been used fictitiously and are not to be construed as real. Any resemblance to persons, living or dead, actual events, locales or organizations is entirely coincidental.

DEDICATION

To my children, Stephen and Jane, who are forever in my mind,
and
To all the brave souls who have had the courage to support and encourage me, and to work alongside me on endeavors that others thought crazy, foolhardy, and often challenging. To those who have shared my belief that we were attempting to do the achievable, not the seemingly impossible. And to those who joined me as we created, adapted, toiled, and persevered as we reached the pinnacle of our chosen Everest. You all know who you are.

ACKNOWLEDGMENTS

I must express my thanks to some special people who demonstrated patience and calm counsel, while helping me to bring my ideas and the story to reality.

I mention Aisake Vulkadavu, who first persuaded me to think seriously about writing a book and convinced me that I could achieve something outstanding and Adam Mortimer, who has been my Mentor and Coach, and who has tirelessly provided advice and has given me inspiration when I was 'blocked' and guidance when I was 'on a roll'.

The book would have been littered with grammatical inconsistencies and errors if it was not for the diligence of David Connolly who proof read and edited the manuscript, and gave me back a publishable script. Thank you Gentlemen

Table of Contents

FOREWORD xiii
PREFACE xv
INTRODUCTION 1
CHAPTER ONE (AND MORE) 5
ABOUT BILL LEWIS 293
RESOURCES 295

FOREWORD

In the vast sea of books and other media on entrepreneurship, start-ups, personal development and motivation, Bill Lewis has achieved a remarkable feat of providing readers with a substantial resource, which will have far more impact and be far more reaching than the size of the book would suggest.

To start, the dramatic story of Midas's journey takes the reader face to face with the realities of investing personal money into a start-up and the consequences of failure. It highlights personal vulnerabilities, which many of us will instantly relate to, and then Bill explains why things are as they are. By introducing the Law of Attraction, he brings into the narrative a thousand years of secrets, which have been known to those who have had phenomenal success. He also explains the reasons why many people – ordinary people, business people, young and not so young – succeed or fail at a particular endeavor and what can be done about it.

The story about Midas is a human drama, a story of failure grasped from the jaws of success, and the fight back. Midas is the classic hero of a millennia of adventure stories. Midas, had he lived five hundred years ago, would have been a man who braved the uncharted waters of oceans and walked across mountain ranges to cartograph the lands beyond.

But the uniqueness of the book is the way in which storytelling is used, to the full, to teach the realities of business start-ups, and why some businesses fail while some succeed. It tells of the special characteristics of the modern-day warrior, the entrepreneur. It shows how heroes and heroines of the digital world are fighting the battle fought by those who went before – with the same tenacity and determination.

In any drama there are the characters, the cast, who play key roles in the journey the hero is undertaking; Midas and One Thousand Cows, is no exception. Some of the cast of characters will be appear in the network of the reader as he or she embarks on the business start-up adventure. The importance of the cast in the story, in the success or otherwise of the business endeavor is thrown into sharp relief in the pages that follow. The lessons are immeasurable.

A significant addition, of outstanding value, Bill Lewis has included a great section of resources for the entrepreneur in the final part of the book – highlighting media and sources of inspiration and information that is immediately available to anyone seeking answers to almost every question that the story of Midas will illicit. It would be a person of limited intellect or minimal perceptive abilities who would not be moved to think of how they would deal with the problems that confronted Midas and where they would seek answers.

Bill Lewis's undoubted talents, business pedigree and entrepreneurial experience, and his ability as a first-class storyteller, is manifestly apparent from the novel and the resources addition.

I applaud the experience, insight, and efforts that have gone into creating a book that will change people's lives and create a lasting resource. In addition, this is a classic 'cannot-put-down' novel that will have you turning every page in eager anticipation of the next episode and the next challenge; it will continue to test you, the reader, to solve the issues that Midas faces.

Joe Vitale

PREFACE

My life thus far has been interesting, fascinating, challenging, and not without adventure. In business I have had considerable success, tempered with some quite spectacular failures. I have never been afraid to step outside the norm, to take a risk, to accept a challenge, and to believe that the impossible is possible. For having that mindset, from wherever it came, I feel humbled and grateful. My journey through life has been influenced by many wonderful people: friends, colleagues, mentors, and figures who I respect and who I would aspire to be like. I have always pursued opportunity and I thank those that have allowed me, and encouraged me, to pass through the portal of chance, to see what I could make of the land on the other side. On my journey I have learned many lessons, and as I look at the range of publications, books, and information about entrepreneurship, I remain convinced that I have something of value to contribute, however small – something that the budding entrepreneur will find useful, something which the executive or businessman will find inspiring, something all readers will find entertaining. Midas and 1000 Cows is fiction, based on fact. Midas and his adventures are an amalgam, a montage, of events, experiences, and trials that have been experienced by many people. Today, right now, similar events, experiences, and trials are the subject of someone's thoughts, anguish, dreams, elation, and /or celebration, somewhere in the world.

In reading reviews of books on entrepreneurship I often found that the reader wanted to feel as though they had, in their hands, something based on real experience and not academic research, something based on events in the trenches, not in the classroom.

That is not to say that academia does not have a lot to contribute to the subject of entrepreneurship, indeed it has; many noble and reputable business schools are providing outstanding courses on entrepreneurship. There are scholarly works that are worthy of study, and I have included reference to two of these in the resource section at the end of the book.

Nevertheless, I would argue that there is room for a different, lighter, more interesting, and – maybe – dramatic way of imparting the reality of life as an entrepreneur. If there are ideas that reveal themselves in the story that follows that you can use, please take advantage of them. If there are ideas that would not use, please put them to one side; they may be useful at some stage in the future.

The parts of the story that relate to Midas's personal development may resonate with some readers. However, the book is not intended to be an erudite treatise on the psychological make-up required to be an entrepreneur, nor is it an in-depth course on personal development. Rather it is intended to highlight the impact of one's upbringing and personal life and how these factors can play a significant part in the context of business challenges, outcomes, and success. As a result, if you find that something in the realms of your personal mindset is worthy of further study, some pointers and references are found in the resource section at the end of the book.

I have enjoyed writing about Midas's journey. I hope that you will enjoy and benefit from the tales of the unexpected and the manner in which lessons and secrets are revealed.

Midas's journey spans nearly a decade and therefore it has been necessary to leave out parts to focus on the highlights and events which provide context, character, flavor, meaning and real outcomes. I hope that continuity, as it is provided, will allow the reader to remain engaged and enjoy exploring, thinking, and considering what they would or wouldn't have done if they were Midas. And, in the process of self-reflection, become more able to enhance their own journey – wherever it takes them.

MIDAS AND 1000 COWS

INTRODUCTION

Storytelling has been the method of teaching for two thousand years; only in the last century has the educational establishment developed newer and different (better?) ways of teaching. Yet, storytelling inspires purposeful reflection; it makes the process of learning more intimate and human. The listener or the reader is offered the opportunity to connect to the story's characters, or see the world literally from within someone else's persona. Stories affect our emotions and make us laugh, cry, fear, and get angry—evoking different reactions from a simple textbook or presentation, however good and relevant the content. Also, no matter how organized or detailed a textbook might be, there's something about the shape of a story — the evolving narrative, the problem, the search for a solution, the resolution—that resonates with our desire to learn and explore, to associate and be part of a journey, Midas's Journey.

For these reasons, I have adopted a novel to share my extensive experiences as an entrepreneur and to both introduce, share, and teach certain aspects of entrepreneurship and, more importantly, to challenge the readers to ask themselves, "What would I do in those circumstances?" or, maybe, to evoke them to cry out, "Don't do that!"

Midas is a thirty-something guy, in a job that he hates. He is offered the chance to escape. His decision impacts the next ten years of his life. He roller coasts through business ventures, travels across the world, and has to confront the fact that others do not believe and behave as he expects. He is also challenged to explore himself.

In this book a reader will learn:
- How to turbo-charge success by understanding the personal dynamics of mental preparedness and acquired business skills

- To identify the influences that impact a person's risk profile and sources of success and failure
- To recognize the importance of taking inspired action and stepping where others fear to tread
- How the stages of evolution of a business, from creation to funding to IPO are traversed, and how necessary it is to pivot, (change focus and strategy) to constantly build the dimensions of successful business
- Why mentors and influential figures are a gift beyond value on the entrepreneur's journey.

In the story, Midas is faced with innumerable situations that stretch and challenge him; he has to make decisions that may prove to be catastrophic, if wrong, or may open the door to phenomenal and unexpected success.

He is tested by events that all of us face each day – to start a business or not, decisions on a market and a position, on a critical hire and a mitigating strategy, on the need to develop and apply the creative and persuasive skills, the tasks of stepping through the funding ladder from self-funding, crowd-funding, intermediate sources of funds, and to – for some – the Silicon Valley VC.

Midas finds that politics are a vital ingredient, to be ignored at your peril. He finds that employing people has a multi-sided dimension and in ways that he did not anticipate. He is befriended by a mentor who helps him on a journey to consider himself, as well as his business ambitions, and teaches him how the two relate; the value is inestimable.

In the end, Midas finds that no matter what you achieve, the world has another challenge waiting.

There are no right answers nor are there prescriptions in this book. The journey teaches how entrepreneurs find success, and the price they have to pay; whether you are prepared to pay that price, is for you to decide. There are ideas that have worked, for some; there are failures. There are situations which you may have approached and solved in a different way and that's ok; and there is a taste of what it is in real life to be an entrepreneur in a world of opportunity and creativity.

Not everyone is going to be Elon Musk, Steve Jobs, Oprah Winfrey, or Warren Buffet. Some people may be like Midas, seeking fame and fortune and a successful life by creating something that someone wants, and creating wealth for themselves, their employees, and their shareholders, without demanding of themselves to be a billionaire.

As the novel closes, the reader is led to a substantial resource section, included in final part of this book and at a companion web site (www.midasand1000cows.com), which features:

- A summary of the philosophies a modern day Vince Lombardi. Sir David Brailsford, Performance Director of Team Sky, UK, who has been referred to as Britain's own Vince Lombardi, is the man behind some of the most celebrated British sporting stories of this century, and
- A substantial reference resource highlighting videos, web sites, books, and other resources that the fledgling entrepreneur, and more experienced colleagues, should access on a regular basis.

The story, the lessons, the philosophies, and the reading and reference list, provide a significant reservoir of knowledge and experience that any new or experienced entrepreneur can access to expand, build, and develop their personal capacity and business capability.

A Final Word. During Midas's journey a character called Nestor appears, usually without warning. Nestor's apparent ability to make an appearance at any time, in any place, may seem disconcerting, or just too much of a coincidence. Do not let this distract you; this is a novel, after all. I invite you to think of Nestor as the genie in Aladdin's Lamp, Midas's Alter Ego, or his Deus ex Machina – with seemingly supra natural powers – you are well advised to take note of what he says.

All that remains is for you to enjoy Midas's story of "An Entrepreneur's Crazy Journey to Making Millions".

ONE

Like many 30-year-olds, Midas obsessed about his health and fitness as he fought the conflicting demands of a heavy workload, travel schedule, and a less than healthy diet. He sought to compensate by a daily routine of exercise; he knew that it took a strong will to build and maintain exercise as a habit. He worked hard at it.

He stepped from the front door of his apartment block, a redbrick two-story building on Du Page Street. He had left his live-in girlfriend in bed. It was 6.00am. He gulped in the crisp, dry, early morning air as he turned left to start his seven-mile morning run. This was his routine when he was at home: exercise before the rigors of the day took over.

After a few yards, he broke into a half-sprint to wake his limbs and increase his breathing. He headed along the street towards the City Church. This was downtown Elgin, IL, an outer suburb of Chicago, USA. Nothing much happened in Elgin, and even less at 6.00am. The street was deserted.

At the church he made a left and then a right to cut through a car park and hit the Leisure Trail along the Fox River.

He paid little attention to the water; he was on autopilot. He turned left again and followed the river for the next two miles, his feet hitting the tarmac with a steady rhythm. Ahead he saw Route 20, crossing over the Trail. He would pass under the highway's fifty-foot-high span and branch South East; he would then jog steadily for another seven or eight minutes until he hit the old railway tracks another half a mile on.

Today, he was not going under the bridge. He was barred from the track by a police incident truck, doors open, with blue lights flashing.

Emerging from the truck, a police officer approached him with his hand held out.

"That's as far as you go." He was definite in his statement. "The area is closed until we tell you. You're gonna have to turn around and head back" The cop nodded his head in the direction that Midas had come; his hand had dropped from the halting gesture to rest on his pistol.

Midas looked past the cop and he could see a fire truck and fleet of city ambulances with their rear doors open, all parked on the far side of the bridge, almost out of view. Medics and firemen were running back and forth; each time they left their vehicles, they would run into the forest that lay beneath the highway.

"What's happened?"

"Head on back, nothing for you to see." There was a very definite tone to the cop's voice.

Midas retraced his steps. He tried to imagine what had happened.

The highway, way above him, was busy, even at this early hour. But now he could tell there was a tailback and he could just make out the red flashing lights of a fleet of fire trucks and tenders way above him.

On that road, he thought, *moments before, there were tired overnight drivers heading for a breakfast stop as the dawn started to break; trucks passing though the city in convoy to destinations further south; families on holiday, who had set off in the early hours, kids sleeping on the back seat.*

His mind was active and frustrated with the lack of knowing, *what had happened? Did a car leave the highway? Did someone jump? How many?*

His mind was visualizing now, he saw the picture of a limp, torn body in the trees; pieces of luggage broken open and the detritus of a serious accident hanging from branches of the dense wooded banks of the highway, that would have broken the fall of any vehicle leaving the highway by exiting over the parapet on the far side of the highway. All of these images fleeted across his mind. Without information, the mind creates its own scenarios.

It was a bad start to the day for someone. *Who?*

He looked up at the sound of a helicopter. WGN-TV were already heading to the scene; he would see what he was barred from seeing on the morning news.

Midas returned to his apartment. His first action was to open the fridge. He was a soymilk fan and took a half-pint bottle and drained it. He headed to the bathroom, threw his running gear on the bathroom floor and got into the shower, his mind switching his thoughts to the day ahead.

His title at work was Program Director. He excelled at implementing very large technology systems. Leading multi-disciplinary teams – large teams, sometimes over one hundred people – on one major endeavor, this was his forte. He was good at his job; his clients' team members endorsed that view, as did his clients. He was in demand. But he had just one problem.

That problem was a guy everyone knew as Gravel – gravel, as in sharp, small stones that hurt your feet. In Midas's case, Gravel was his boss, and he caused Midas grief and pain, every day.

Gravel was a micromanager. You know the kind: the boss that has to know every minute detail of every action, for every client, of every co-worker; and once known, they interfere. And Gravel constantly interfered. Midas was good at making decisions and typically made outstanding and clever decisions, but Gravel usually changed that or overruled him. Gravel's stock-in-trade was his regular attempts to bully, and to erode the confidence of Midas and his staff.

His thoughts this morning were no different from every other morning. He hated his job. He hated Gravel.

When, when am I going to get out of this?

He asked himself a hundred, no, a thousand times.

He came out of the shower and his girlfriend was still not up. She had begun to shout from the bedroom about being late, about not having enough money to buy new clothes, about the utility bills still needing to be paid, her credit card being maxed out, and sometimes Midas could not comprehend how, on a decent salary, she was always struggling.

He was still trying to figure out how he got into this relationship. He had known Pat for about a year. She worked at the casino about a mile away from his apartment. He remembered how he was dating her, and one night she came back to his place and stayed the night.

She stayed over a couple of nights later, and then announced that she wanted to stay – longer. She meant, move in. Before Midas realized what had happened, he had a live-in girlfriend.

She was Filipino by origin, and was a loud, Goth-like figure. Midas was not small, he stood six-two and was lithe and athletic, but she was big, noisy, demanding, and belligerent. She was extravagant with Midas's money. She commanded more space than her five-foot-six heavy frame occupied.

She had taken control of his life and apartment. She intimidated and threatened, her voice seeming to have two settings – loud and obscene. There were times when the relationship was good, but Midas was trying to figure out the last time it was when he felt he experienced the 'good'.

Lately, she had taken to criticizing Midas for a myriad of reasons: his job wasn't good enough, he didn't earn enough, his apartment was too small, and he didn't have a car,

Not only was he sick of his job, but he was also now sick of this relationship.

As he set off for his twenty-minute walk to his office, he was unaware that today was going to be anything but usual. The great universe had a surprise in store.

TWO

Some forty-five minutes later, Midas slumped into his chair in his cube, in his concrete and glass office on South Riverside Drive. His office was in a bland commercial development, in a nondescript part of town. His cubicle was grey, his desk was light grey, and his Mac laptop blended with this color scheme. The wall behind him was midgray, with the carpets black and grey. Only the white ceiling added some contrast to this rain-colored scene.

Today Gravel was on holiday, and Midas might just get some peace and quiet, and be able to concentrate on what he liked to do best – plan out his next major program and run a number of virtual program reviews.

But coffee first.

He walked down to the coffee machine. Pressing the button, black liquid poured into his grey plastic cup. Corporate identity grey was insidious. *The coffee was passable at least,* Midas thought, as he made his way back to his desk.

He sat and flicked open his laptop; he didn't immediately start work. He just sipped his coffee, his mind wandering. He was thinking about how he came to be in Elgin, how he came to be where he is. His mind drifted back to his parents, Dick and Winifred.

Dick and Winifred were born in North Wales, UK. They had grown up in a small town. Both came from staunch, working-class families, who knew their place in society, troubled no one, went to church, and proceeded through their life as though it was an immutable, ordained journey. In 1956, Dick was working as a laborer for a military contractor in the UK. He had been sent on a long-term contract to the USA and had eventually become an accidental immigrant. At the outset, he had no intention of staying in North America, but when the contract ended, he was offered a job in the military-civilian complex outside Chicago where he had been working for two years. Winifred travelled to join him.

They settled in Will County and led a generally contented and uneventful life. They had enough income to get by, but nothing was left over for luxuries or extravagance. They travelled regularly to the city to attend the First United Methodist Church at 77 West Washington Street, an institution located on 'Methodist Corner' since the mid-nineteenth century. This provided continuity to their Christian Methodist upbringing in North Wales.

Outside Dick and Winifred's home, as time marched forward into the mid-60's, the world was in the grips of a revolution of love, freedom and expression. Old norms were being overturned and established barriers torn down. However, for this quiet Methodist couple, the world did not change; it continued in its own peaceful way; the bible was read, church was the center of their life, and they kept to themselves.

A decade further on, in the mid 70's, Midas comes into the world. As his mother would often tell Midas, and repeat to those who could be bothered to listen, she had a 'terrible birth', and Midas was such a weak child and not as strong as other boys; he was lucky to have survived. It was as though whatever pain and suffering had been wrought on his mother was Midas's responsibility. This was an admonishment that would weigh heavily on the young boy for years to come.

At home Midas had lived in a pious space; there was no alcohol, no smoking, no profanity, and television was frowned upon. Sundays were a day of rest, intended only for food, bible reading, and worship; he too was dragged along to church to attend Sunday school, where he was indoctrinated in the Methodist faith.

He was an only child; he missed his brother who had apparently died shortly after childbirth some two years before Midas was born. He was brought up in a strict Methodist household, told to speak only when he was spoken to, and to 'know his place'. By the time he had reached his teens he was a seething, frustrated young man who had difficulty in creating relationships, was frequently bullied and taunted, and yet he believed that he was destined to 'make something' of himself.

He watched his parents grow old, with very little to show for decades of hard labor and doffing the cap to bosses and authority figures. They still went to church, and it seemed that religion, which held no meaning for Midas, was their source of comfort. They missed their old country and, in the years to come, would die still yearning to return to Wales.

Midas was determined that the same fate, a life of corporate servitude with nothing to show but a stooped frame and failing eyesight, would not befall him. Ironically, at age seventeen, in a bid to leave the confines and constraints of his home and environment, he had applied to join the bastion of servitude, rank, and structure – the Military. But, by good grace, he had been rejected on medical grounds.

This was the time when Midas first realized he suffered from amblyopia; a condition where the vision in one eye is negligible due to a misalignment of the eye, or other debilitation, which was not treated in the childhood years. As there was no money in the household for expensive remedial surgery, he adapted to his normality. He vaguely remembered having glasses and eye patches when he was young, which he regularly abandoned either because they were an inconvenience, or because they made him the subject of taunts and attacks. In junior school, being bespectacled and eye-patched frequently led to him being beaten up for no reason other than his tormentors saw him as 'different' and 'weak'.

His strategy for survival was to seek his own company and avoid mixing; he became a classic loner, a role he was to adopt through his high school years, mixing as much as was necessary but avoiding confrontation. He read and studied when others played football; he cycled and ran when others went to bars and movies; and he made his own way through adolescence, frequently falling foul of his father's constrained views of how he should behave, as any rebellious teen is wont to do.

He applied to, and gained acceptance at University. He worked and studied and paid his way. In 1998, he graduated with honors in Computer and Management Sciences, from the University of Chicago. His parents, now in their twilight years, were proud of him; he could get 'a good job' which would secure his lifelong future; they still retained the misplaced notion that a job for life was the best security that one could have.

After a series of technology-related jobs after University graduation, Midas had been headhunted by a small Systems Engineering business that had its headquarters in the unlikely location of Elgin, due to the CEO and President both living in the city. There were over one hundred staff spread around the country.

Midas had remembered he had been told, upon joining, that he was employee number one hundred and thirty-two. He had been with the company for three years, advancing to larger and more complex projects and programs in a regular upward trajectory. Today, he was one of the most senior program managers in the business – a testimony to his technical skill, work ethic, and determination to succeed.

THREE

It was about 10 AM when his phone rang. He looked at the screen displaying a number he didn't recognize. Normally, he didn't answer calls he did not recognize, he would end the call. But today, for whatever reason, he decided to answer.

"This is Midas, who is this?"

"Hi, my name is Jenny, I work for a Hedrick and Struggles. We are head hunting and senior recruitment consultants. I would like to talk to you. Do you have a moment? Is it convenient?"

I shouldn't have answered this call, Midas thought. *Another recruitment company trying to sell me resources.*

"Yes," he answered, making his annoyance clear in his tone.

"I represent KPMG; you will, of course have heard of them."

"Yes," Midas had heard of one of the biggest names in consulting.

Jenny continued, "I believe that we may have something that will interest you."

"Really, I am listening," Midas remained unconvinced,

"They have a new practice area, a new business sector – a program management practice – and we've been told that you have some good experience and a great track record in this field."

"Yeah," responded Midas, skeptical as to why a company like KPMG, one of the big five, would want someone like him.

"Can we arrange coffee?" asked the Jenny.

"Sure, when?"

"I live and work from my place in Elmhurst, that's not too far from you. How about after work today"

Midas thought for a moment. That was a forty-minute drive, and he did not have a car.

Jenny sensed his hesitation, she added, "You can grab a taxi if you want, we'll pay."

"Yeah, OK, that will help. That works."

Jenny responded, "Ok to meet then. There's a Starbucks at West North Avenue, I will send you the details. How about six?"

"I can't do six; seven works," replied Midas,

"OK, seven it is"

The rest of the day passed uneventfully – lunch at his desk, client calls, couple of project meetings, and it was okay. Midas was feeling positive when he left the office; no aggravation from Gravel, and some good feedback from clients.

He had reckoned it was 40 minutes to Elmhurst.

The taxi he had booked earlier was outside the office at six-twenty. He climbed in. It was one of the regular drivers who Midas knew. Not having a car, Midas had gotten to know the local drivers, and this evening it was Joe, a big-hearted veteran, long retired from the Marines. Joe still imagined he was on call for the military and carried a weapon on his person, as well as a grab bag of his personal possessions in the front of his cab. He would tell Midas countless times, "You never know when you are going to get the call, I told 'em I am ready any time, just call. They have my number."

It was seven o'clock as Joe dropped Midas at the Starbucks Jenny had nominated.

Midas went in and ordered a double macchiato. Minutes later, he was sitting by the window, looking out at the highway.

Moments later, Jenny walked through the door and joined him. She was short, late twenties, casual, in jeans and red polo top. She had a black leather jacket and woolen scarf, topped off with a black ski hat. She was not as Midas had imagined a top-flight exec recruitment consultant to be, but then he wasn't sure what or whom he was expecting.

Jenny held out her hand and smiled. "Hi Midas, great you could come so quickly. Hey, you look like your LinkedIn photo."

Midas had been an early adopter of LinkedIn, and he often used it to source his teams. Today, in 2007, it was slowly becoming the de facto source of professional record.

She had the email printed out that he saw earlier; it was the outline of the position on offer. It was a Program Director, with the responsibility and the chance to start and build a new department, a new service, for KPMG, based from the city offices. They talked for a while.

It was clear to Midas that the job was a fantastic opportunity. It was demanding, exciting, and absolutely gelled with his background. He was certain that he could do it.

Forty minutes later, Joe was parked outside the Starbucks, waiting for Midas.

Midas came out of the coffee shop and said good-bye to Jenny, with a feeling of elation and a big smile on his face; he almost wrenched the rear door of the taxi door off its hinges in his excitement.

"Hey, steady there!" Joe shouted, "I have to take this back to the depot in one piece. Can't have you wrecking the car."

"Sorry," muttered Midas, still smiling to himself.

He got back to his apartment and pushed the key into the lock. As he was about to turn the key the door opened, and a Goth apparition almost felled him.

In a flurry of black and highly colored chiffon, Pat screamed out of the door, with a "Gotta go, get out of my way!" She pushed Midas to one side.

He had no time to say anything about the meeting.

On second thoughts, I think it is better to keep quiet right now, just in case, Midas thought. *I don't know if we are even going to be together much longer.*

FOUR

Midas had woken up to an empty bed beside him once again. He had been out for his run, come back and showered.

It was 8:00am, and over a bagel and coffee Midas was conversing with himself.

Where was she going last night in such a hurry? Who was she with?

He was eating breakfast and scanning his phone for messages. It was not the first time his live-in girlfriend had disappeared for the night without saying anything.

His mind was churning over the question. *Do I care?*

On previous occasions when Pat returned, any question as to her whereabouts was usually met with "None of your sodding business," and then a continued torrent of abuse about something unrelated would follow.

He was getting tired of the dysfunctional relationship.

Maybe he would ask again later when he came back from work tonight, that's if she was at home!

Midas settled into his cube and checked his mail.

Amazing! There was an invitation to visit KPMG for an interview. The interview was to be tomorrow, in the afternoon. It was downtown Chicago, so that would be a full day out of the office.

He suddenly found that he was really excited. Secretly, he was pleased that he might get out of the clutches of Gravel.

As he left the office, he stopped by Gravel's office. He pushed the door open and looked inside. Gravel grunted as he looked up

"Don't you know to knock?"

"Yeah," sighed Midas, "It was open."

"Maybe," Gravel, looked back at his papers, ignoring Midas.

"I am going to a medical tomorrow. I'll work from home."

"I guess you're going to check to see if you're alive," scowled Gravel.

Midas shrugged and stepped back out of the Gravel's office. There was no point in saying anything more.

Late the following morning, Midas stepped out of his apartment into the bright sunshine. He squinted as he looked up. *Sunshine, maybe that's prescient*, he thought.

His appointment was at 2.00pm, at East Randolph Street, in downtown Chicago. It was an easy journey. He walked ten minutes to Elgin station and then made the one-hour and twenty-minute metro ride to Union Station. He then changed to the Blue Line and ten minutes later, he was at Randolph and Columbus. A one-minute walk took him to KPMG's office.

He looked ahead of himself to the corporate tower. He stepped through the revolving doors. Already Midas was feeling intimidated as he walked across the marble expanse of the reception lobby. He pressed for the elevator and moments later, he stepped into the KPMG reception, which he noted was about five-times larger than their largest meeting room in his very grey office complex.

"Hi Midas, I was expecting you," said the tall, young, smartly dressed man behind an expanse of heavy teak reception desk. "Step this way, please."

Midas was shown into a conference room. He was wearing his best pair of chinos with loafers, and a smart button-down shirt, but he was starting to feel underdressed.

The wall of glass from floor to ceiling overlooked the whole of downtown and the city beyond. Midas felt his loafers sinking in the pile of the carpet and saw that when he dropped his backpack on the floor that too made an indentation. *Plush, very plush*, he thought

Moments later, two guys about Midas's age came in; they were casually but smartly dressed. They introduced themselves as Paul, from talent recruitment, and Jonathan, from consulting strategy. They sat down and exchanged pleasantries as coffee was brought in, with china cups. *Of course*, thought Midas.

The conversation about Midas, the firm's plans, including the opportunity for program management and business transformation to be integrated with technical delivery, was detailed and lengthy. After about ninety minutes Paul, from talent recruitment, drew the meeting to a close and asked Midas to wait. Paul and Jonathan stepped out of the conference room.

Ten minutes later, Jonathan returned with another guy, tall, casually dressed in expensive looking slacks and shirt, hair neatly trimmed, and rimless glasses which Midas thought certainly did not come from a downtown Supersavers but more likely from a very upmarket Gucci collection. *I guess he's from Boston, very Ivy League*, thought Midas.

The new guy was introduced as James, the partner who would have the responsibility for the new business unit that, if he were successful, Midas would head. The ensuing conversation and discussion was animated, excited, and heated at the same time. It went on for about sixty minutes before James made his exit and Jonathan showed Midas to the elevator. As they parted, Jonathan said, "I hope to see you again, very soon."

Midas travelled back to Elgin. He felt drained and excited at the same time, a dazed expression on his face. His mind was overactive.

When he got back to his apartment, Pat was at home. She was lounging on the sofa wrapped in a red quilted housecoat of gigantic proportions. She looked at him with surprise.

"What are you doing here at this time?"

"I have been downtown."

"What have you bought for me?" she asked.

"Nothing, it wasn't that kind of visit," replied Midas.

"Typical," she snorted. "You go all the way downtown and you don't bring anything back to this hellhole. I can't buy anything here."

Midas poured himself a glass of Soymilk. He mentioned a discussion at KPMG to Pat, who was now engrossed in some trashy program on the TV, as though it was a passing event, just an exploratory discussion; he added it would probably go nowhere.

Pat nodded, said nothing, eyes glazed by the reality show she was watching.

In the next few days Midas wrestled and wrestled and wrestled with the thought of the meetings. He thought of the smart dudes; he saw their offices from the outside; he looked at the website; he looked at their clients.

He thought to himself, this is too big, this is too cool, KPMG – Big Five? But it was right, the next step, and he was ready.

FIVE

The following day there was a mail in his inbox. It was from Jenny. KPMG wanted to offer him the role of Director of Program Management, on a salary that was multiple of what he had now.

Midas read the offer letter once. What should he do? Should he grab this opportunity by the throat, shake it and embrace it? Should he love this opportunity? Should he be joyous about it? Send an acceptance reply immediately and order a bottle of champagne to celebrate?

Midas was surprised at his degree of nonchalance. He read and re-read the letter many times. But the more he read it, the more he realized that he was becoming increasingly depressed.

Midas thanked Jenny and said he needed a short time to think about it. Jenny was understanding, and said she could wait, but not to be too long before he replied.

That night he told Pat about the job, and a possible move. At once she was elated, joyous, and excited. She was shouting, "So fantastic!"

The new apartment, the car, she was seeing it all. This was her 'get into her real live reality program' of her own. The world now was only a happy place. She could see the world was starting to open up, no more scraping and scrimping.

The Fox River Trail was dry, and Midas was running with his mind in a daze. He didn't see the river this morning. He didn't see the trees. His eyes were downcast; he was looking at the tarmac. His feet were pounding the hard surface as he swirled in turmoil.

As he ran, he could hear his father: "Don't change jobs too often, it's not good for you. You are not going to move forward in your career if you keep changing your job. Keep it. Keep it steady; don't hop and change. And stay away from those rich people; they use you, and spit you out."

He was struggling now. He was at this desk. His mind was blank. He was writing back to the recruiter and KPMG. What to write?

He hit the keys – it was short and to the point. He closed his laptop and walked to the coffee machine. He grasped the edge of the machine. He could not believe what he had written. He could not dream of how his life could become.

Midas's email was short and to the point, he said "Thanks, but no thanks".

He turned the job down

That evening he went home and could not figure out how he was going to tell Pat. The new apartment, new car, it was to be a reality show come to life for her. All their dreams, her dreams, postponed for another time – until later, later, later.

His decision was met with intense anger, rage, shouting, screaming, and almost fighting. In the end, she pulled on the door of the apartment as though she wanted to tear it from its hinges and bolted through the door. Midas heard her screaming as she ran out of the building

"You're a loser, Midas; you're worse than a loser! Damn. Why am I with a loser? You're worse than my father and he was no good! "

SIX

Several weeks had passed since the day that Midas turned his back on the world of plenty, the world of a new opportunity. He was still at his grey desk.

He had just collected his grey coffee cup when Gravel stormed past.

"I want to see you, NOW! Not tomorrow, NOW!"

Midas walked down to Gravel's office. Gravel was red in the face. He was standing, and he was gripping his desk as though he was scared the desk would fly away if he let go.

"Midas! You're a bastard. After all I've done for you, after I take care of you, and give you opportunity. Believe me, believe me, I know you went to that interview. I know they wanted to steal you away from here – that's not loyalty, is it?"

The conversation was one-sided, a tirade and a verbal storm of expletives, invectives, and insults screamed from Gravel's mouth in a torrent of abuse.

This was an exchange that Midas would not forget. Their already tortuous relationship could never ever be repaired.

Midas went back to his cube. He threw his laptop into his backpack and left the office. He went back to his empty apartment. Pat was at work.

He walked to the sofa, threw the quilted housecoat, which gave off a stale odor, onto the floor, and then sat down with his head buried in his hands. He was asking himself what had possessed him to throw away an offer of a lifetime?

Was he not good enough? Were the echoes of his childhood, of not being strong enough, of not being 'like other boys', still festering deep in his subconscious, crippling his self-confidence, wrecking his self-esteem?

Was it the status that a position with KPMG, as a Director of Program Management, would confer, that scared him? Did he feel he was not good enough? Was it his father's message about people should not want to be 'above their station in life', gnawing at him from deep in the vaults of his childhood memories, from parental programming all those years ago?

He could not figure it out.

The following morning Gravel told Midas, "I want to see your report on the Exxon project now." Midas did as he was asked, and emailed in the report. This was one of Midas's showcase projects. It was a massive project with nearly one hundred staff, being delivered against record timescales. Without naming the client, he had enjoyed sharing the challenges and solutions, and progress on the project with James and Jonathan at KPMG, and receiving their approbation.

Ten minutes later he got Gravel's response. "My office now," was all the email said.

Midas saw Gravel's face. It was like watching a carousel of expressions, a fixed stare, a smile, a cynical grin, and a sarcastic grunt of victory. Then he spoke.

"What's the rubbish you've just given me?"

This project was probably the best-managed in the business, but Gravel nitpicked his way through the deadlines, the deliverables, and a copy of the application code Midas's team had written.

"It's all crap! I have never seen a project that is so bad in all my years!" Gravel was now screaming. "Deadlines missed, change notices not recorded, over-budget, it is worse than I have seen from an intern…"

By now Gravel was standing, thumping the desk and getting redder and redder in the face. He stopped for a moment, put his fingers on some papers in his desk and looked down at them. The silence was deafening.

Slowly he looked up. He was squinting, leering, and then, he raised his hand and slammed it down on top of the pile of papers.

"These reports are not worth a dime, not worth the time it took to print out this garbage. YOU'RE FIRED. Get out!"

Midas went back to his desk. As he approached, two of the security guys were already there. He could see that he had been set up. Gravel had already sent for them. The report review was a farce, a charade.

They wore grey; grey uniforms, in a grey place. "Ok Midas, grab your laptop, and your things, come with us. They marched him into the security office, took his laptop from him and ten minutes later handed it back – clean. All evidence of the last three years' work, of hundreds of thousands of dollars earned, of countless hours booked, and deadlines met, wiped away, gone into a corporate digital oblivion.

Minutes later Midas was out of the front door, and three hours later, having walked for miles around the city, drank coffee in a couple coffee shops, he arrived home – in the middle of the day. Never before had he been known to arrive home before evening.

Pat had returned from her shift at the casino.

She looked at him, "What are you doing home at this time?"

"I quit?"

"Really?"

"Yes"

"No. You were fired." Forty minutes before Midas had walked through the door, one of Midas's co-workers had already called Midas at his home, and blurted out the story to Pat.

She stood with her hands on her full hips, feet apart, with her face contorted with disgust, "I told you you're a loser. I'm leaving."

She continued ranting and raving, calling Midas every conceivable adjective that could describe him as being a loser and worthless,

Then she was out of the front door in no time. Midas had not seen the travel bag and the backpack already packed and positioned by the front door

As she exited she shouted over her shoulder, "If you want me, I'm not coming back." With that, she had gone.

Midas looked in the mirror in the hallway as he pushed the front door closed – no job, no girlfriend, and a bottle for a companion for the foreseeable future.

SEVEN

Midas was unemployed. He was settling into a dangerous routine.

Each day he would drift from caffeine to alcohol and back again. He would smoke a couple of joints before he went downtown to his newly frequented bar, which he would hit up in the early evening. Sometimes he stayed an hour, sometimes longer, whatever the mood dictated. He had neither commitments nor anyone to go home to.

Today was a regular day. He reached the bar at around 7:00pm. He would stay until he felt like he could face the loneliness of the night, and then would make his way back to his apartment.

The bar was not crowded. He got his drink and made his way to a booth. He sat down and held his drink in front of him, in a way that he felt secure, as though if he let go, the table, the glass, and the drink would fall over.

These days, he was not running; he was drinking. He was not thinking: he was reflecting.

Then a voice said, "Hey, buddy, mind if I sit down here? The place is crowded."

Midas nodded

"My name is... Well, they call me Nestor, what's yours?"

Midas nodded in a perfunctory manner. "I'm Midas."

"Let's drink to Midas," said Nestor.

Midas wasn't sure that he was in a particularly talkative mood and couldn't quite figure out why this guy had come and sat down at his table. He looked around; the bar was not crowded, a few booths and tables were occupied and there were other places where this guy could sit. He shrugged his shoulders.

Nestor looked different from the usual people one would normally run into in this joint. First of all, he was little bit older than the regular crowd. He was of an indeterminate age, wore a relaxed style, was tanned, balding, and weighed around one eighty pounds. *His tweed jacket is brown, worn, weathered and probably expensive*, Midas thought to himself. Nestor wore the jacket over a black polo neck, atop black jeans and black brogues. He had a maroon silk handkerchief in the top pocket of his jacket. *He's a cross between an aged hippy and an English country gent*, Midas smiled inwardly. But hey, what the hell, he appeared to be friendly enough.

"So what do you do Nestor, and what kind of name is that?"

Nestor looked across the table and smiled, "Hey, thanks for asking, I have spent an age travelling, kinda helping, advising, and, well, I guess I am a mentor. But I took some time off; I used to get a bad rap. I'm back in the groove again now." He laughed.

"Go on," said Midas, "bad rap for what?"

"I used to be very boastful. Sure, I am wise and clever and astute, people tell me that, but I was boastful, and although people asked me for my thoughts, ideas, and wisdom, they used to chide me about the way I talked about myself. Well, I soon learned. Humility is valuable. If you can have wisdom and humility people will listen to you, and ask you for sagely advice. If you are boastful, they think everything you say is BS, even when it is not."

Nestor looked into his glass, and then looked up. "Well, that's what I learned as I went through university."

"Which university is that?" asked Midas.

"Life, of course," laughed Nestor.

"What do you mean, life?"

"The University of Life," answered Nestor. "Do you know it is the greatest university that is available to you? I tell everyone there is a vast storehouse: information, knowledge, experience, and ideas from great thinkers, great achievers, philosophers, writers, painters, artists – it's all there, all you need to do is to look.

"What I learned has changed me, my mind, my life, and that of many other people too."

"That so? So, what have you learned?" asked Midas

"I know it sounds crazy and unbelievable at first, but you, and I mean anyone, can achieve pretty much whatever they desire if they believe they can do it."

Nestor continued, "Desire and belief are an unstoppable combination. You see, you have the talent Midas, to do anything you want, if only you believe. Just like me, just like other people.

"There are hundreds, if not thousands, of sportsmen and women who achieve great things – achieve performances which other people think impossible. And why? How? Belief. Belief, Midas, belief."

Nestor was intense, eyes wide open, and gesticulating with his hands. He was clearly stating something in which he had an unstoppable faith – it was in his very actions and voice.

Nestor continued, "Someone called Napoleon Hill, and by the way, you should read some of his books – great genius on how we can reach our potential – once said, 'What the mind can conceive, the mind can achieve'.

"It happens in all walks of life, not just sportspeople and explorers and adventurers. Let me tell you a story.

"One day, a good friend of mine decided that he wanted to play the guitar. He had never played before, never even picked a guitar up in his life. He believed he could become a great guitar player. So, he found himself a teacher. He learned, he practiced, and practiced, and practiced; he had discipline. As a result, within a year, he cut his own album, which does not gather dust, nor has it bombed – it sells.

"You see, his motivation was that he wanted to give people pleasure and have pleasure in playing. He had desire, belief and discipline – and wanted to give. You see I have added a two other factors, discipline and a desire to give. Please remember that.

"How about you, Midas? That's the name! So, are you like your namesake? Do you attract money?"

Midas laughed. "You've got to be joking. Anyway, money is not important to me really."

"Really, what is important to you?"

"Well, I think right now, a job would be important; or doing something which brought me some money," replied Midas

"But you just said money wasn't important."

"I have some." Then Midas told him of the argument with Gravel, his girlfriend leaving, and all the other issues that had come to haunt him over the past few weeks. He then looked at Nestor. "So, what's it to you?"

"Nothing," replied Nestor, "but I've been there, I've been where you have been, where you are. I was even further down the ladder than you are now. I got back up, and I am successful. It took time. But our paths were similar when you get right down to it."

"Yeah, so why are you here?" asked Midas.

Nestor replied, "The Universe works in strange ways."

Nestor looked reflective for a moment, as though he was in a different time. He shook his head, smiled enigmatically, and continued, "You know, the bar was half-empty when I came in for a drink. I took my drink from the bar and something told me to come and sit down here. Things happen for a reason."

"Yeah, I've heard that before," grunted Midas.

Midas looked at the half-empty bar, at his glass, at the man opposite him. *Strange…* he thought.

Nestor remained silent.

Then Midas spoke "OK, as you are so interested, I'll tell you where I am right now. I have this idea to start a business. Yeah, I know, I will make myself some money. I was good at what I did before, and instead of making money for the likes of Gravel and his bosses, I will make it for me."

"That's cool. Go on."

"I can run big projects, I can find the resources, engage them, make lots of money." Midas outlined his ideas and spoke fluently about his business plan. He continued for a few minutes.

Nestor listened intently. When Midas had finished, he responded: "Can I share something with you, and I know that it might sound like a contradiction….

"I started to make money when I realized that attracting money was not my priority. I didn't go out to *want* money, I didn't become obsessed by it."

"What's this got to do with my money?" interrupted Midas.

"Attracting money follows giving; if you are doing something for someone that they want, they will pay you. If you set out to solve problems, give of your talent and knowledge, people will buy; then you make money. But your initial focus must be on providing a service or a product that solves a problem, finding a need people have, and answering that need – in the best way possible, being the best in the market.

"Many people approach money, as though money is the end in itself. They may make some money in the short-term, but that is not sustainable.

"Money is, and was, simply a function of your mindset, Midas. Money always matches your mindset. If your mindset is positive, focusing on helping and performing in a fulfilling way, and you are comfortable with using wealth in a positive way, wealth is drawn to you. If your mindset is negative and contaminated by greed, in that you think only about yourself, do not be surprised if you cannot sustain any business."

Nestor looked at Midas. He was thinking that he looked intense.

Looking back at Nestor, Midas said, "So are you saying, your whole life is a reflection of what is going on in your head. Thoughts are things. What you think, you manifest? And I should not worry about money, because money will flow to me? 'Cause I will be honest, it sounds far-fetched to me."

"Yes, in one sentence you have the basic principles," replied Nestor. "If you think negative thoughts you'll be surrounded by negativity; if you think positive thoughts, you'll be surrounded by abundance."

Nestor continued, "You cannot afford the luxury of a negative thought, it's so true. If people understood how powerful thoughts are, they would be more careful about what they think. Your thoughts, what you allow to go on in your mind, affects everything you do: your health, your relationships, your reaction to situations, how you feel about people, how you relate to people."

"Whoa! This is getting heavy," said Midas. "What else do you know? So do you think the people I mix with are important too? That what happened in my past is important? In my distant past?"

"Absolutely," replied Nestor. "You ask the questions, I'll explain."

EIGHT

Midas looked around. The bar was still half-empty, but it was eerily quiet. People were eavesdropping; some had swung around on their stools as though they wanted to provide Nestor with an audience. Some people had begun to hang on to every word that Nestor uttered.

Midas continued, "What was I asking?"

"Oh yeah, I know, I was asking you about what is important, I asked if the people you mix with are important too? If what happened in my past is important, even in my distant past?"

"Yes, of course, to both," said Nestor. "Those are two big questions."

Nestor continued, "Let me try to explain. Let's think about people who we relate to. Sit tight, I will tell you something that might surprise you.

"Do you realize that our thoughts are vibrations of energy that we send out? In fact, the whole universe, everything around you is energy in a state of vibration. And your thoughts and what is going on in your mind is transmitted into the universe as energy and vibration. Others, who may or may not be on the same frequency as you, pick up that vibration."

Midas listened, though with some degree of skepticism.

Nestor looked at Midas, "Let me try an example. Imagine you are meeting someone; you may or may not know them. You make a judgment about them, or what they are saying, not just based on their words, or even how they are looking or gesturing, but also by your own intuition."

Midas nodded in acknowledgement, "Yes, true. It happens often."

"This thing you call 'intuition' is the feeling you have when you pick up the vibrations associated with their thoughts."

"Wow," exclaimed Midas

Nestor continued, he took a napkin from the glass on the table, and pulled out a black, elegant, Parker pen. He drew a simple ladder on the napkin.

"Let me give you another perspective. People's minds and thoughts operate at different levels, or simply at different vibration or amplitude. Some people are less fortunate, have a very restricted life, and are fighting for survival. Now, in that state, their vibrations are said to be on very low amplitude, and it's a fact that they will attract around them people who are in a similar position to them – because they too are vibrating at that level."

Nestor marked a lower rung.

"But then, on the other end of the scale, are those people that are successful, positive, open-minded, who exude a vibration at a much higher plane, a higher amplitude, and they attract similar people around them. Success attracts success. Poverty attracts poverty. That's just one of the universal laws that keeps people where they are – they don't know how to move up a level or two to change." Nestor drew two pairs of little stick men on his ladder, two near the bottom of the ladder and two near the top.

Tapping his pen on the ladder, he continued, "Often, it is not the lack of opportunity that keeps people where they are, it is their own mindset."

Midas looked at Nestor, his mouth open. He reflected for a moment.

"Can people change their mindset?"

Nestor leaned forward. He came close to Midas and in a low secretive tone, he said, "Yes, of course, if they really want to."

He then rocked back and forth slightly, and leaning forward once more, he continued in a slightly professorial tone, "Remember, knowledge is king. First understand, then seek how to change, maintain the will to change, and work on yourself ... but when you start, you will find it is a life's journey."

Nestor paused, sat up straight, and looked directly at Midas. He shook his head affirmatively, "A life's journey."

He repeated himself, "A Life's journey, but what an exciting journey, and Midas, you don't realize it, but you have already made the first step."

For a moment, Midas thought back to his father and how, over his lifetime he never changed his way of life, his type of friends, or his ambition; he wasn't being judgmental, but he thought that it was an interesting take on what Nestor was saying.

Midas wanted to take a drink, and realizing his glass was empty, called the waitress to refill their glasses. He was quiet, reflective.

He had a full glass again and he looked at Nestor, "You said something about laws. What you mean, laws?" asked Midas.

Nestor answered, "Yes, that's right. The universe operates on a set of 'natural laws'. Now I know there are people who disagree with me when I say that, but I can tell you that for centuries great writers, philosophers, scholars, have all identified the fact that the universe operates on a set of immutable laws. Many, if not all, of the most successful people know, apply, and use these laws. It has been a secret that is now understood and applied by many, and is being taught and absorbed in the lives of hundreds of thousands of people as we sit here. I am not talking about religion I might add. The 'natural law' that I refer to is beyond religion – which is more often than not a dogma preached to exert control over the masses of followers, rather than to liberate them.

"Oh and don't get hung up on terminology – some people refer to these laws as 'The Secret', some refer to the 'Law of Attraction', I have heard it referred to as the 'Abundance Factor' or the 'Attractor Factor'. Names do not matter, and to be honest, I use many of these terms interchangeably.

"If you understand the basic principles – and I will help you understand, if you are willing to learn – once you understand how, let's call it, the 'universal law' works, you can tap into it, and adopt it and apply it. Your life will never be the same.

"But it can be a challenging journey. There is a lot to learn as you move to achieve your life's purpose, your life's goal – just ask any Olympic athlete."

For a moment Midas looked into his glass, he was thinking,

If what Nestor is saying is true, even if only partly true, then it is sad that we deprive so many of our children of this knowledge; knowledge that can make them happier, more fulfilled adults. Instead we have an education system designed to push out workers for a twentieth century system that is obsolete, rather than creative and fulfilled people which we so desperately need.

Midas's reacted intuitively, "OK, teach me."

Midas then looked at Nestor, he felt puzzled by his immediate reaction. "So, do I need to understand all of this as I step forward into business and create my own company, and do my own thing?"

"Well," said Nestor, "it will be very useful to you. You must learn that all successful entrepreneurs have recognized that understanding the universal law is essential for sustained success. They have developed the right mindset based on the law.

"You want to be successful, and this doesn't just apply to you and your business Midas, it applies to everyone. Understand that having the right mindset comes before having the right skill set. My greatest regret is that the universal law, or whatever name we want to use, and the creation of a success mindset, is given such cursory attention when teaching the skills and knowledge around entrepreneurship."

He continued, "Do you think that the mindset of Michael Jordan, Tiger Woods, of the late great Muhammad Ali, Bill Gates, Steve Jobs, Richard Branson, Mark Zuckerberg, Jeff Bezos, Oprah Winfrey, J K Rowling, have something in common?"

"Well, I guess so," answered Midas, thinking that was a bit of an obvious question.

Nestor continued, "Their mindset enables them to achieve the successes that they aspired to because of the way they thought – their thoughts, their desires, their belief in themselves and their ability, were conductive to, and sustained positive and appropriate action. Their discipline and belief in their ability to succeed was the foundation of their 'winning' mindset.

"At the same time, they polished their skills in whatever field of endeavor they chose. Their achievements were the result of skills honed to perfection when others gave up. Success did not come by accident but came as a result of belief (that they will succeed) dedication, perseverance, and discipline. They had a mindset that drove the attainment of skill sets honed to perfection."

NINE

"Okay," said Midas, his mind already reeling from an onslaught of new information that he had never heard before.

"Let me ask a question. You say that we all exude energy and vibration – emanating from our thoughts. And energy attracts like energy. And that energy vibrates at a different level in different people."

"That's right," said Nestor.

"So, I need to find a way to be on the same energy level (or thought waves) of a person I want to relate to, to be successful in that relationship whether it is a coworker, customer, or even girlfriend?"

"Yes."

"So, if I walk into a gathering of people, let's say senior engineers, business leaders, or even into a party, and I feel uncomfortable, then this is a reflection of or feedback from my mind picking up that I am at a different level from the vibration in the room. And this explains the behavior of people who set themselves apart in gatherings and fail to take advantage of opportunities that are in front of them." '

"You are correct Midas, well done. You have grasped it. That is an example, and there are hundreds more which we could look at – all of which you will need to learn (or relearn) as you build your business."

"Ok," said Midas, *let's stay with this*. "Why is my vibration like it is, why is it that it sets me apart from others?"

"That's an interesting question," Nestor responded, "let me see if I can explain it this way. When you/we are born, our subconscious mind is an empty vessel, and it gets filled by our experiences and what we see around us. We accept as true and without question anything and everything our senses experience, whether it is what we see, hear, touch, feel or taste, and we also accept that behaviors that we experience are normal. If we are berated and told that we are stupid, if we see poverty around us (we don't recognize it as poverty because we do not know the term), if we are told to give up and not waste time when something doesn't work out the first time, if we are told we are weak, or by contrast, if we are told we are strong, in a few short years these experiences create our embedded belief system – this is our 'normal'.

To some people, success and attainment, or the ability to change our circumstances, is normal but, to others, giving up is normal, and to a further group, not believing things can be different, or that we have the ability to change, is normal. The experiences are reinforced as we grow through childhood and adolescence by a range of teachers, authority figures, and media which are around us. There are a huge disparity in people's own 'normal'. Achievement is 'normal', violence is 'normal', love is 'normal' and so on and so on…"

"That's programming!" exclaimed Midas.

"Yes, exactly," said Nestor. "Programming is all around us."

"Media is programming?"

"Yes," Nestor laughed, "the TV has programs. I say they are called programs because they 'program' us – program our thinking."

"Social Media is programming, advertisements are programming, all the time people with their own personal agendas – and they can be corporations, government, politicians, etc. – all want you to think and respond in a way that suits them, not in a manner that is good for you."

Midas looked at him, his mind was working overtime, "Am I programmed?"

"Yes, of course," answered Nestor, "to some extent we all are."

He continued,

"Our belief system determines how we behave and react as adults. How you will react in your business. If we have been empowered as children, brought up by nurturing parents, and been encouraged to excel and given permission to fail and learn from our mistakes, don't you think that is the behavior we will exhibit as adults and potential entrepreneurs?

"I get it," said Midas. "When I walk into someplace, the reason I feel uncomfortable is a function of the beliefs that were ingrained in my subconscious years ago. Yeah, I get it. So what happens is because someone's childhood was characterized by poverty, or lack of opportunity, or constraints and restrictions due to money, or - for example - religious beliefs, all of this 'rubbish' is going to be carried forward into adulthood."

"Yes," Nestor nodded.

"Whoa!" exclaimed Midas. "I never thought of it but I can understand where you are coming from. Was this why I felt uncomfortable in KPMG? Could this be why I turned the job down? Because I didn't think I was good enough and that came from all those years ago?"

"So, if I want to be successful what I need to do …."

"What is success?" interrupted Nestor.

"Okay, I'm not being specific," replied Midas. "Let's say success in business, success as an entrepreneur. Is my mindset going to impact that?"

"Of course, of course, without question," says Nestor, "it is fundamental. You will never be successful without a success mindset."

Midas started to think to himself about how growing up, his father was blue-collar and his mother worked in the shop. They were happy within their limitations, and they believed that everyone had their place and should stay in their place. Midas had fought against that as a child and as a teenager but was frequently and firmly rebuffed.

I wonder how that's going to affect me, he thought. He remembered again how he had broken away from his family, his friends, his neighborhood, and had gone to university – which his parents were both proud and aghast at. Proud because he made it to university but aghast because university was only for rich people!

There were a lot of things that were starting to make sense to Midas and he realized that, in the intensity of the conversation he and

Nestor had, they long since finished their drinks, had ignored the waitress, and had sat there with empty glasses.

He called the waitress over once more and ordered another round. This time he didn't feel as though this was a drink of desperation but rather a drink to celebrate a realization that though he had a lot to learn, the fog was beginning to clear – if ever so slightly.

Nestor declined. He got up to leave.

"Nice to meet you Midas. You've got great potential. Will see you around.

"And you don't need to worry," added Nestor, "the great universe will set up another meeting when we need to see each other. And if anything occurs to me, I will mail or message you."

In the next moment he was gone.

Midas looked at his drink; it was a Coke. He had never ordered Coke in a bar in living memory! He reflected on the evening.

Okay, so I am going to be an entrepreneur, I'm going to build my own business. It's time to change, time to get my act together, sort my head out, get off my butt and start to make a difference.

He got up and walked towards the door.

TEN

Since Pat had moved out and he had no job, he had thought it wise to economize. He had vacated his apartment on Du Page Road and moved out of Elgin. He had gone towards the city and had found a place he deemed adequate, in South Shore. He convinced himself it would be temporary.

Midas climbed eight steps to the tenement front door. It was ajar. It was always ajar. The tenants complained about security and the landlord didn't do anything – typical for this less prosperous part of town to which Midas had relocated. Midas pushed open the door and scrunched back the pile of flyers and catalogues that had accumulated behind the door and set off down the hall. The dim illumination, which passed for a light, hardly allowed him to see his way to the downward stairs to his basement apartment. He thumped the timer switch at the top of the stairs and an industrial looking light, fixed to the wall, illuminated the depths leading down. He felt this was what it must have been like to be led down to the dungeons in the past. He fumbled with the key in his lock, reminding himself that he must lubricate the lock or he will come home and never access his room. But then, Midas thought, *what does it matter? I'm going to be out of here.*

His door opened and he made his way in to his two-roomed version of shoebox living. It had the appearance and airs of a true geek's pad; untidy music equipment, TVs, computers, servers, peripherals, cables, and more wiring festooned to the wall, the floor, and almost every conceivable space except for the kitchen table that, by contrast, was littered with empty pizza boxes.

Midas grabbed his laptop and this phone and went through to his bedroom. He threw his jacket across the room, and propped himself up on the bed. He flipped open the machine and checked his mail.

There were two emails from Nestor. He ignored them while he trawled through the remainder of the new mails, scanned his Facebook, opened a couple of chat windows, and shared some banter with a couple of his friends.

He came back to read Nestor's mails. The first one had a subject heading "You have got an idea?"

Really... thought Midas, as he clicked the mail open and scanned it quickly. What Nestor was saying Midas realized was, "Okay, Midas, you have something, you have idea? Right? You just have to find it."

Midas scanned the clues that Nestor had given him. "Think about your, passion, your experience, resources you can get your hands on, possible customers." Midas thought was all this was a bit nebulous. The mail continued:. "Here's a list of questions to get you started,

- What are you now?
- What are you good at?
- What are you passionate about?
- Is there a market for it?
- Can you access the market?

Once you have answered those questions, think about this these:

- Knowledge - do you have knowledge enough to be credible?
- Market – can you access the market?
- Resources – can you get the resources to deliver a service or product?
- Investment – does your idea require small, medium, or large investment?"

So what do I know? I am a top-flight technical project director, implementing big systems, creating new business processes, transforming business, yeah that's what I was good at, I know a lot and a lot about that. I must have been good; KPMG wanted me to do just that for them. So why don't I do it to myself?

Is it something I can feel passionate about? *Certainly with Gravel out of the way.* Midas thought back to the way he would get a kick out of attending client meetings, leading client teams, negotiating the pitfalls of company politics as things began to change, and ideas were being implemented. He liked the idea of standing at the conductor's rostrum, in front of the orchestra. It was an appropriate metaphor.

He would listen and watch; the slightest nuance of someone being out of tune would not pass him, he would redirect, encourage, coach. His goal was the creation of harmony in a disparate team. He was good at that.

He could paint a vision, he could paint a large canvas of possibility, he could create almost impossible timescales, and get teams to buy into them, like they were by buying into a cause to change the world, when in fact they were they were changing their own world. Midas was good at creating results in this kind of game.

Was there a market? *Yes, of course businesses change every day, someone needs someone to help realign the business, implement new technology, change technical strategy. This is all bread-and-butter.*

The next question was interesting. What industry do I know well?

Okay, I know something about the airline business, I know a lot about aircraft maintenance technology, I know a lot about inflight services and airline catering technology, I know something about food production technology – all areas that are ripe for technology-driven change and disruption.

Midas thought to himself. *How little people actually know about what goes on behind the scenes to keep airlines operating, aircraft off the ground, and service in the air.*

He was visualizing it now. Airline operations he knew well. He could picture the minutest detail.

Some airlines still laid on a full service for the passengers on board and some of the European carriers, the Middle Eastern carriers and the Asian carriers have retained an exceptional level of service in the air. These require global logistics functions, and massive food factories to supply the tens if not hundreds of thousands of meals being consumed by passengers departing from any one of the major airports in these regions each week.

Aircraft Maintenance, and Airlines Services on board, were two niche businesses, but very big niches, both being multi-billion industries with a level of complexity which very few people understood. As a result of previous work, Midas had become quite an expert in the technology in both areas. Maybe there is something provable there and then smiled to himself at the plan that was in his mind.

Midas went back to Nestor's questions.

As he read them, Midas could see that it was an interesting framework, a framework to fit his idea, and for next hour he asked himself questions, teased answers out of his brain, and, at the end, came to a conclusion that a consulting business in the airline space could be a good bet. He enjoyed the sexiness of the airline industry, the complexity of everything that happened behind-the-scenes, the technology challenges at almost any and every level of everything.

Midas pictured in his mind three potential contracts that were becoming available. He recalled them from information that he picked up when he was with his previous company.

He tested his business idea against the second four questions

- Knowledge – was deep, current, and respected in specific sectors
- Market – he knew the market, had good contacts
- Resources – he had a great network of contractors and people who, ultimately, could become employees
- Investment – this was a tough one. He had some funds, he hoped it was enough.

Tomorrow morning, he would start to reach out to the various contacts he had made.

He lay back and watched the fan above his bed turn lazily, doing little to disturb cobwebs and even less to annoy the occasional insect that flew nearby; the downward draught would not cool anything, but the clicking and humming of this ancient piece of electrical equipment was a permanent source of meditation.

ELEVEN

The next morning, he moved the pizza boxes from the table to the floor, and started to sketch out a plan from the ideas from the night before. He realized that he had never stepped out into the big world by himself and this fact suddenly started filling Midas with apprehension.

He poured himself a coffee and opened his mail. Was anybody writing to him with anything of any importance these days? No. He reached the stage very recently when even spam mail made him feel mildly comfortable, knowing that somebody, somewhere knew he existed, even if he was just digital record amongst millions in an obscure database.

He recognized the name Nestor. The subject matter was "Who / what is an Entrepreneur?" He read it. Nestor had shared the characteristics of an entrepreneur. When he finished, he thought he had just read an inventory of the characteristics of Superman:

> From: Nestor
>
> To: Midas
>
> Subject: Who / what is an Entrepreneur?
>
> Hi Midas:
>
> I think we can categorize the attributes of an entrepreneur in four categories:
> - Personality
> - Ability
> - Experience
> - Resourcefulness

Let me share what I think is relevant in each area;

Personality: An entrepreneur is a well-grounded individual exuding positive energy, presence, and commitment. He/she is courageous and fearless, and confident to go where others have not gone before. They are explorers and creators, exuding a burning desire to leave a positive mark where they have been. The entrepreneur is resolute when facing difficulties; they are determined and willing to take risks. They are tenacious and driven, but they know when to show patience. The entrepreneur is curious, inquisitive and creative with a balance between right-brain and left-brain capabilities. They will be found to have a healthy disrespect for established rules. They are driven; driven to deliver innovative goods and services to people. They will champion and lead their business as though it is a cause, they do not see their role as occupying a job but changing the world. They recognize that their cause is the creation of services and products, jobs, and wealth. Their business will generate profits, but they see that generating profits is the (appropriate) by-product of delivering exemplary service. Alongside these powerful attributes, the successful entrepreneur will demonstrate a degree of humility too.

Ability: The entrepreneur is perceptive and creative person who can see a big picture but has a very effective zoom lens to focus on detail when it matters. They can be innovative and creative to carve a niche that has been invisible to others. They are strong visionaries. They are enthusiastic and articulate communicators, with speaking skills that project energy to complement and leverage their strong networking skills. They are great 'people persons', attuned (for example) to what their current generation of employees want and desire – they have their finger on the button. They are phenomenally hard workers, maintaining an unswerving laser-like focus to the exclusion of near-term gratification in return for long-term reward. The successful entrepreneur will marry these abilities with very high execution skills.

Experience: You will find that a successful entrepreneur has previously demonstrated achievement in any of a multitude of fields – academia, sport, business, or public service, for example. They will have a track record of success, albeit littered with some failures – demonstrating that they have tried and failed, got up, and tried again – learned and then succeeded. They will have been exposed to multiple functions to understand how business fits together. They will have spoken and presented and communicated to diverse, small, large, and very large audiences to hone this critical attribute. They will have used emerging technologies and understand how such technologies can be implemented to achieve transformation, innovation, and disruption.

Resourcefulness: Above all else, this is the key to success. The entrepreneur who has, or creates access to, or can gain access to resources, will win. Resources - a network that can provide: funds, advice, talent, engineering and design, marketing, logistics, lawyers, accountants, and other skills that the fledgling business requires. Leveraging a network can often yield all kinds of win-win deals that do not consume a lot of cash in the early stages of a business. And the successful entrepreneur will encourage this array of resources to follow the cause in the anticipation of future business and reward.

I am sure that you have many of these attributes, and you can develop and acquire the remainder.

Yours truly,

Nestor

Midas started to feel depressed, he didn't measure up to Nestor list. But then he thought, *What the hell! What I don't know, I can find. What I don't have, I'll acquire. And maybe, just maybe, I'll make it. Trying is better than sitting on my butt.*

He closed his laptop, dropped it in his backpack, and pulled on a sweater. He yanked the door of his prison open, and slammed it to close it. Another thump on the timer switch, the light came on and he stepped upstairs and out onto the road.

These days his morning running routine had been replaced by a stroll through a park to a coffee shop run by a crazy Australian who made the largest breakfast sandwiches you can imagine, and whose coffee tasted like black nectar.

Fifteen minutes later he walked into the coffee shop, and the guy behind the counter gave him a high-five.

"Usual, Midas?"

"Yeah, usual," and Midas headed to a large circular table tucked away at the back of the shop, around the corner of a dividing wall, which was relatively quiet and private except for busy lunchtime periods. Midas could command and use this space as his executive office; Wi-Fi was fast, the coffee was hot and free flowing, and the music was quiet and acceptable. He had just sat down and opened his laptop when a familiar voice broke into his thinking.

"Hi Midas."

Midas looked up at Nestor. "Argh," groaned Midas under his breath as he raised his hand to his forehead and looked down at the table momentarily. *Do I really want another session with Nestor now?*

Nestor smiled, held out his hand, and Midas shook his hand. Nestor pulled up a chair and sat down.

"You are you going to start your own business Midas?" asked Nestor, seeking to reaffirm Midas's brief comments in the bar.

"Okay, okay, I'll play along with this; I think you're annoying me but I've got nothing else to do but to sit here, listen while you talk about something that I don't want to know about, that will go in one ear and out the other. But if you feel you must, then okay, I'm not going to do anything else today."

"Thank you," said Nestor, smiling at Midas' response, and he continued. "What are you thinking? Starting a business is all about…"

Midas interrupted. "Well it's taking my idea, checking it out to see whether its viable, seeing if I can get some money, some resources, if I can build a profitable business out of it. If I'm very lucky, maybe I can scale, build into a really big business, and make a load of money. Before you came in, I was about to start sketching out my business plan."

"Classic," grunted Nestor, as he munched on some French toast that had just appeared on the table. "You want to begin but you are missing one thing Midas. A massively important building block."

"Many people who start off on the road to building a business get so far before they meet what suddenly become insurmountable barriers and problems. I fear that a high percentage of businesses that are started by young, and not so young, entrepreneurs, fail. Another serious percentage do not meet their real potential. Few, and really very few, make it to the big-time."

"Now, there are many reasons for this," continued Nestor. "Maybe the idea was not that good to start with, maybe it's bad timing, maybe it is this, maybe it is that."

"But I tell you from experience and that of many, many more people, that one of the factors that is critical in how you start building, creating, sustaining, growing, your business is the mindset we discussed in the bar. Can you remember?"

Midas looked blankly at Nestor. He remembered the meeting some days back. He had tried to make sense of it on a number of occasions since he left the bar. He didn't get it all. He felt that there were some enticing ideas, and the conversation had stimulated his mind, but not answered all the questions it had thrown up.

"Let me remind you, if you don't mind," said Nestor.

Midas interjected, "Look, yeah, OK, so, I'm positive, I'm optimistic."

Nestor responded, "That's good. But to be successful, you have to have the right mindset, and the right skillset. Mindset comes before skillset in EVERY CASE. Do you remember?"

Midas thought he remembered, and nodded.

"Good," said Nestor. "Can I remind you? Do you recall how many people, in their formative years - and remember we talked about how everything we learn in the beginning we carry with us for the rest of our lives - how many people are actually given permission to succeed and permission to fail? How many people are taught to be resourceful? How many people are taught that it's okay to have a great expectation of wealth and abundance?"

"Kind of," answered Midas, slightly agitated by the thought of going over all this again.

"How many people are taught that love rather than aggression will give you the opportunity for greater success in whatever you do? How many people are taught that discipline is a virtue, that seeking excellence is a higher calling, that you need to delay gratification – build to your rewards? How many people are taught that greed is a fear of lack of abundance? How many people are taught that giving and sharing your wealth is good – it makes space for greater abundance?

"So few, Midas, so few. But if you take the trouble to understand what many, many successful people before you, from all walks of life, have taken the trouble to understand, you will be successful."

"Okay, okay. So where do we go from here?" asked Midas.

TWELVE

Nestor was quiet; he was looking at Midas. He was willing Midas to answer his own question.

Midas looked blank, then he spoke,

"You want me to go talk to people who are successful."

"Yes, exactly," answered Nestor and he raised his coffee cup as a toast to Midas, "that's a perfect idea".

He continued, "Midas, are you a networker? No you're not, I know. You're not a natural networker.

"Ask yourself how many people you know among your peers who are successful business people?

"And, I think we both know the answer. Your peers are great guys, great people, but they are people stuck in jobs. And they will probably stay there. So you need a new group of people in your life, to learn a new mindset. You need to up your game, you need to learn from people, make mistakes. You want to take off and create your own business idea and that's terrific. I am not belittling that in any way. It's really great that you have got an idea; some people don't even have an idea. You know that Midas, some people do not even have an idea.

"You want to start your business, have one standard – and that is to become excellent. Excellent in all that you do in your chosen field. That is what the most successful people choose to do…

"Excellence in entrepreneurship demands that you must talk to and mix with a culture of excellence."

"I don't know anybody," said Midas.

"It might be a really good idea if you go and find some people. Find where they go, where they meet. There are all kinds of forums in this city and on line where there are people, good people who would be willing to talk to you.

"You are resourceful, Midas. Use that resourcefulness to access great people, and go and ask them why they thought they were successful. Take notes, take time, then consolidate. You will be surprised how few, if any, will tell you that their basic business skills like marketing, and selling and engineering and accounting, were the key to their success. Sure they are important, but they are not determinants of greatness. How they think, their mindset, is the key. Take that learning, along with this great idea that you've got, and then set off down the track to your greatness."

"How do you think I should start?" Midas asked

Nestor drained his coffee, stood up and shook Midas's hand, and as he left he said,

"Don't worry, the way will be shown to you, something will happen, it always does, there is nothing left to chance."

For a long time, Midas sat and thought. He had a bemused look on his face as he pondered what he had just heard. He went back to his laptop; he checked his mail and started to browse the web, searching for local forums for entrepreneurs. He felt rather uncomfortable.

The waitress topped up his coffee again. He had so much caffeine that he could have floated a meter off the floor.

He heard a voice, "Hi, can I use this seat?"

Midas looked up, thought to himself as he looked at his new table companion, *she is thirty-ish, casual but smart, smiling, polished but not aggressive, little bit Asian-looking, long black hair, and fashionable glasses. A black, clearly expensive but understated handbag exhibited confidence.* Midas was impressed and feeling shy at the same time.

"Yes, sure. Why not," stuttered Midas.

"My name is Lynn," she introduced herself as she held her hand out.

"Hi, I'm Midas."

"Nice. What you do Midas?" She smiled the question.

Midas hesitated. *Should I lie? Should I tell the truth that I am unemployed? Should I admit that I am an unemployed, wishful thinker, a dreamer, and very recently, an alcoholic? Now that will not impress her!*

"I'm between gigs, waiting to be an entrepreneur," he laughed.

Lynn repeated, "I'm waiting to be entrepreneur. Well that's different, but don't wait too long. Entrepreneurs are always in a hurry."

"What do you do?" Midas asked, expecting the answer to be 'I'm a headhunter' or 'I'm in PR', as though those roles would've fit her persona in Midas's mind.

"I'm a journalist, I write for the Wall Street Journal," answered Lynn, "I write a column on emerging tech and new business."

Midas sipped his coffee again to check whether there was anything that tasted unusual because either he was drinking something or smoking something, as he couldn't figure out why, at this particular time, someone who might just be incredibly valuable to him had appeared at his table. In all of the café, with empty chairs, and in a street of coffee shops, she was sitting on the chair in front of him!

"Tell me more," asked Midas.

"I have always been interested in business and entrepreneurs," said Lynn. "They are fascinating people. Are you fascinating Midas?"

Midas thought that he would miss that question but he started to sketch out some ideas about consulting in the airline industry, about technology, and soon realized that his thoughts were not sufficiently mature to be crystalized in a few sentences.

Lynn listened, nodding politely. "Have you done this before?" she asked. "Starting your own business?"

"Actually, no," admitted Midas.

"Well, maybe you could use some help."

Midas: "I'm okay, I'm okay"

Lynn replied, "You sure? I've got an invitation to an event tomorrow evening. I don't really want to go. It's a gathering of business people – a reception. If you'd like to come with me then we can have a drink, maybe something to eat and you can meet a few people. And you will be doing me a favor because I can see one friendly face in the room."

She laughed.

"What's the event?" asked Midas

"It's just a fairly low-key gathering of some people, some entrepreneurs and editors, people that I write for and write about," answered Lynn.

Midas hated these functions; he hated the party scene, the cocktail party scene, and any so-called networking event. He avoided them like the plague. But there were echoes of the conversation with Nestor earlier today about changing who he mixed with, and something about Lynn's level of gentle insistence made him think that he might just have to go to this one.

"Well I guess the worst case is that we will get a decent dinner and a glass of wine. OK, let's meet tomorrow – what time?" mumbled Midas.

Midas realized he was blushing and feeling very hot under the collar. Although this was not a 'date' as such, he had been out the dating scene for so long (he knew his ex Pat didn't count, she had just deposited herself on him and then departed) that he couldn't remember whether he should now suggest a place to eat or he should suggest a place to meet and shouldn't be drinks before or drinks after.

Lynn rescued him: "It's an early evening event, about 6:30, my office is nearby. I'll come in here, like about 6 o'clock, say? If we're not too overdosed on caffeine and hyper we can walk across the Common. Just an easy chat with a few people, okay? Oh, as I am officially there on business, WSJ is paying for dinner – see you!"

Midas smiled. Next moment Lynn had waved and had gone.

Midas now thought he should pinch himself or something. He was not sure if he was in control or not.... He felt decidedly odd.

THIRTEEN

A little over twenty-four hours later Midas was sitting at the same table. He had dug out some crumpled chinos and a business-like shirt – and even found shoes. He was certainly not comfortable – and he didn't expect it to get better. He was watching the news channel. He normally tried to avoid the TV because it was at best boring, at worst, terrifying. He felt that the vast majority of media was intent on scaring the American population to death on a daily basis. Thankfully, the main channel was not on and the local news anchor was announcing a business gathering of some of the top entrepreneurs in the region attending a summit on the following day.

So, I guess Nestor wants me network with those guys and get ideas from them. Well, I am not ready for that. Anyway, that's for another time. Lynn said tonight was low-key.

Lynn appeared promptly. She wore an attire similar to the previous day's but a different color scheme, and she looked like she had just stepped out of a business magazine

"Shall we go Midas?"

They walked out of the coffee shop and across the road. As they crossed the road, Lynn slipped her arm into Midas's. Midas was utterly thrown. He didn't know where to go, what to say, what to do, nobody had shown even the slightest bit of intimacy with him for months – if not years. And here he was, Lynn who he met only last night slipped her arm into his as they walked across the crosswalk. She dropped it at the other side but it was a pleasant feeling while it lasted.

They walked down the block to the Hyatt, walked inside to the conference suites where tomorrow's top summit was to be held. They turned off towards an anteroom.

They stepped into the room, waiters and waitresses, smartly dressed, with trays of drinks, and canapés, formed a semi-circle, which Midas and Lynn had to navigate to get into the room. Midas picked up a soft drink.

Oh, how I hate these things thought Midas, *I really don't like these but I'm told I have to do it so here goes.* He thought it better to keep a low profile; he was running away but failed to acknowledge it. He walked towards the window. He was retreating from the fray.

"Not so fast," a smartly dressed guy called out, "my name is Peter. Lynn has just told me your ideas Midas." The guy who had called out, with Lynn at his shoulder smiling at Midas, walked towards him. Peter held his hand out. Midas received a firm but friendly handshake. "You seem to have some good direction there. Tell me more." Lynn smiled encouragement from the sidelines, just in Midas's vision. For a few minutes Midas outlined some ideas and prayed he was not making a fool of himself.

"Here's my card." Pater handed Midas an expensive-looking embossed business card, "I have some time before the summit tomorrow, come and have coffee. There's a great coffee area tucked away at the back of the lobby. See you then, nine-o-clock."

Midas looked at the card; he recognized the name. Peter was a well-known, high-flying, tech entrepreneur who had just IPO's for a nine-figure sum. Midas's jaw dropped. This 'low-key' gathering was like the informal Ivy League of entrepreneurship.

During the next forty-five minutes Lynn shepherded Midas from one person to another. He was collecting business cards as though he was going to do a magician's show at the end of the evening.

"Midas, this is my editor," said Lynn, as she watched a bear of a man navigate towards them.

"This is George Harbinger. George, this is Midas – you remember? I mentioned him to you." George was overweight, rotund, greying, with round rimless glasses, and had a cynical look that seemed to beset most editors. He shook Midas's hand, grunted something indistinct, nodded, and without a further word, turned and wandered off.

Lynn grinned, "He's like that with everybody, he'll remember you. Time to go; the boss has seen me so I can leave now." It was as though George's wandering over to Lynn and Midas was an unspoken signal that her job was done for the evening.

The next hour and a half saw a wonderful Chinese meal of Beijing duck and the trimmings, a bottle of wine, lots of laughing and chatting – then it was over. Lynn called a cab, and Midas chose to walk back to his basement.

Lynn shouted as she left, "I want some feedback from your meetings tomorrow morning." Midas had five appointments with some of the top entrepreneurs in the region. And he didn't even plan it. *Who was conducting the orchestra now*, he thought?

FOURTEEN

The wind was light and the sea was as calm as the millpond. Midas was sailing, he had been on the last watch of the night, just monitoring the direction of the wind and the course he was following. It was a quiet time when he could reflect and think about life. The new day had yet to arrive. In the hours before this dawn, Midas had watched the dark night sky, filled with a million stars.

He had always enjoyed this time of the night, on his frequent voyages offshore, and today was no exception. He was on the deck to watch the dawn break, as it inevitably does - a fixed certainty. The sun had not yet crept up over the horizon, but the red dawn filled the sky in the far eastern end of the bay. Midas stood at the front point of the yacht, the bow, his hand lightly holding the forestay, the line that ran from the bow to the top of the mast some six yards behind him.

He had the sails raised, and the yacht was being steered on autopilot. He could hear the bow of the yacht beneath his feet cutting through the calm waters as the light breeze propelled the yacht at around six knots. He stood there and in his solitude he marveled at nature; powerful, beautiful, awe-inspiring. And at the universe – so predictable, so secure, so reliable.

Right now Midas was hypnotized by the growing light of a new day when he was blasted out of his trance-like state. A terrifying ship horn cut through Midas's world like the sound of an unexpected rocket explosion. He turned in panic, and saw it bearing down upon him, one hundred thousand tons of container ship that shouldn't be there, that had crept silently, and stealthily up to his yacht. It was just fifty meters from the stern now. The ship's bow was the height of a massive office building. The ship's horn blasted five incredibly loud blasts, and Midas rushed towards the stern to grab the tiller and to turn the yacht away from the steel behemoth, the bow of which was now approaching at seemingly breakneck speed. As he ran towards the stern, obviously shocked, he tripped. He fell and banged his head on a cleat and for moments he thought he passed out.

He pushed himself up on his right arm and, through his very hazy eyes and the feeling of a searing pain in his right temple, he saw a pizza box lodged under his hip and the duvet wrapped around his legs. His alarm had gone off and he had fallen out of bed. He shook his head. Unsteadily, he pulled himself up on the side of the bed, and rubbed his eyes. He grabbed a bottle of water from a bedside shelf and took a long gulp. The bottle was half-full. He poured the rest down his neck. He was awake now, but felt as though he was still trembling from the onslaught of thousands of tons of commercial cargo that had appeared above him as he slept.

Still bleary-eyed, he made his way to the shower and some many minutes later he emerged refreshed, shaved, and he sat in his boxer shorts at the table, watching the coffee machine dispense the life-giving caffeine-laden brown liquid which he studied in his hand before he drank it in a few short gulps. He was starting to feel relatively normal. It was then that he remembered the previous evening. He saw a small pile of business cards amongst the debris that littered his table. He picked them up. He felt nauseous; it was fear. He looked at the names, remembering them from the night before. They were all at the top of their game. They appeared in the business press as often as some celebs appeared in the trashy end of gossip media.

He walked over to his rail of clothes; his wardrobe was considerably less extensive these days. Minimal would be the right description. A couple of pairs of chinos, a few t-shirts, a sweater, and a pair of jeans and some running gear made up the bulk of his wearable clothes. He also had two shirts that were remotely acceptable at a business function, and one pair of shoes! He pulled on the black chinos and dragged a blue shirt from its hanger. Creatively creased would be a fitting description.

He was not happy; he was going where he did not want to go. *If it was not for Lynn, I would not go*, he thought to himself. His phone pinged. *If that is Nestor he is going to get blocked, deleted, removed*, thought Midas as he picked up the phone.

It was a message from Lynn. "Have a great day, Midas. Go and hit them. The day is yours. Enjoy. Cu". Midas looked, he felt terrified.

He climbed the stairs from his room, and stepped out of the front door. It was early, the traffic was heavy, and there were people around. He had plenty of time, but he waved a taxi down. It would be a twenty-minute walk, and although there was time, he felt that he could collect his thoughts while he was in the cab. The traffic was slow as they moved downtown towards the Hyatt. Midas propped his chin with his hand, his elbow placed on the worn armrest of the door. He leaned forward to peer outside. His stomach felt bad; the coffee he had drunk seemed to be churning as in the depths of some cavern beneath a mountain. He could feel the sweat running down from his armpits. I hope that doesn't show on my shirt! He thought.

Eventually, after a lot of stopping and starting, the taxi drew to a stop outside the hotel, and a liveried doorman opened Midas's door. Midas handed a ten-dollar note to the driver and stepped out of the taxi.

"Good morning, Sir. Welcome to the Hyatt." These words the doorman would repeat over a hundred times a day, but were delivered with the same sound of sincerity that had been practiced and honed to perfection. So much so that Midas felt that he was being welcomed personally.

What was it that Nestor had said about excellence? Midas asked himself, and then answered his own question. *I guess that excellence applies to every job including the doorman.* He smiled and head towards the hotel entrance.

Midas walked through the enormous glass doors and into the cavernous lobby of the downtown Hyatt. He had been here the night before but had not noticed the size. *This is so much larger than the KPMG office block, and that impressed and intimidated me*, he thought. The lobby was a magnificent, a vaulted atrium ceiling that soared to cathedral dimensions above him; strategically placed but unobtrusive desks for all manner of services were manned. Around ten or twelve uniformed staff discretely observed the patrons coming and going, ready to step forward to help a guest. He saw the sign for the coffee shop and walked towards the right hand back corner of the lobby where a dark oak rail marked the boundary between the public space and a comfortable looking coffee lounge.

As he stepped through the opening in the rail, a smartly uniformed young lady smiled at him.

"How many sir?"

"Two," Midas answered. "Have you somewhere quiet?"

"Yes sir, step this way." She led Midas to a dark wood paneled booth about fifteen meters from the entrance to the coffee lounge.

Midas could see who came and went, but it was far enough to be relatively private. He sat down, ordered himself a long black and waited. Peter was to be the first to arrive, and within a couple of minutes he presented himself at Midas's booth.

"Midas, Good Morning. Great to see you."

They shook hands, the waitress appeared and Peter ordered a macchiato.

Midas had checked Peter out the evening before when he had gotten home. Peter was described as a 'tech billionaire'. He was building his empire in cloud computing. His company had already taken on four increasing rounds of investment from Silicon Valley. He was one of the darlings of Wall Street, described as a visionary. His company had listed on NASDAQ three months ago.

Midas had now remembered reading about Peter some three years before when Peter had spoken at a select conference on the future of technology, held at Sundance. Peter had described his vision of the future of the technology environment, where almost everything, applications for every conceivable use, would be delivered from the cloud. Not only did he talk about it, he delivered on it.

Peter talked in a soft, quiet voice; a voice that was low in volume, but heavy in authority. Midas was trying to probe the reasons for Peter's success; he really wanted to hear about Peter's technological genius. But that was not forthcoming. What was said surprised Midas and made an immediate impact. He remembered Peter's words:

"Whatever you do, whatever your business, Midas you have to love what you are doing, you have to love your customers, you have to love your employees, you have to love your partners. You need to be perceptive and inclusive. Be aware of everyone around you. Anyone can be your ally or your enemy.

"As an entrepreneur, you are a creator, you are creating goodness and wealth, wealth for all of the stakeholders who are in some way or other associated with your business. In this way, love does not mean weakness. But it means strength, it means confidence, it means the passion, all of which comes from your heart. If you start from that position, Midas, no one will be able to do distract you from your path. The more you give out, the more you will receive back. When you give out, when you invest, you're making space for more goodness to come to you. The more you give, the more you receive.

"Some think this is a paradox and want to hold on to money until they have more and then they will give. But the Universe does not work like that Midas. You have faith."

Peter smiled and continued, "Some people think I'm really smart, a genius, very clever, a technology wizard, but actually I'm not. I surround myself with great people and never, never compromise.

"Midas, never compromise on the people that you work with and who are within your team, and the people that you recruit to your business. Never compromise."

Peter shook his head and looked intently at Midas, "Set one standard of excellence. I can assure you that if you compromise, it will come back and bite you – hard! And make sure that everyone in your business understands the philosophy of giving and creating wealth, in whatever form, for your customers, your employees, your suppliers, your partners, and the community that is around you. It will always stand you in great stead, it will be repaid."

"Let me add," continued Peter, "Midas, you will see that you will benefit and grow. As you do, embrace those that are around you, do not leave anybody out, communicate – particularly with your detractors, if they work for you. And if or when you cannot bring them onside, you cannot convince them of the goodness of your cause, to see the journey and the vision of greatness for your business, then, regrettably, they will need to leave. Do not carry passengers. Deadweight becomes heavier by the day.

"Midas, I hope you don't mind, I seem to be talking, like it's coming out in a flood – right?" And he laughed.

Midas responded, "I am all ears, just keep going."

"OK. Thanks. Allow me to tell you a short story: Margaret Thatcher, the British Prime Minister took on an immense task of transforming the British Economy when she came to power in the 1980's. She had to assemble a cabinet and a team, that were not only intellectual heavyweights, and politically astute, but also shared her dream, her vision, her passion. Her most damning criterion for selection to the core of her government was, 'Is he one of US?' She could not afford to have anyone who was a passenger on her team. Maybe you should keep the question in the back of your mind as you build your new team and your new business."

Midas was spellbound by Peter's oratory and sincerity, which seemed to permeate every word.

Peter went on. "Forgive me belaboring the point Midas, but demand of yourself excellence, commitment, tenacity, humor, and, remember, Midas, you and everybody around you human, show humility now and then.

"I must go, but I will leave you with another true story.

"I remember a meeting a real gentleman, the late Tan Sri Lim Goh Tong in Malaysia. He had created the Genting Group and at one time was the richest man in Malaysia, if not in South East Asia. In his very early life, as a teenager, he made his money collecting tin cans. From that humble beginning, over his lifetime he built a massive land, hospitality, and industrial conglomerate. But it is said that he never forgot his roots, nor the ordinary person he was. And often, while his guests would eat at a wonderful table at lunchtime meetings, he would content himself with a bowl of noodles.

"He once told one of his very senior executives, who frankly was being a bit of an arrogant son of a bitch, 'Humility is not a sign of weakness; it is a sign of respect. When you give respect, you may earn it back – but do not expect and demand it. If you demand respect, like the rain you need in a drought, it will never come.' And on that note Midas I will go and prepare my introductory remarks. I wish you well. You are on your journey. Feel free to contact me at any time. I want to know how you go on, how you go forward with this great idea of yours."

Peter stood up, shook Midas's hand and walked out into the airiness of the white marble-clad lobby area. Immediately, he was greeted by the delegates who were passing through on their way to registration for the summit.

Midas had just had his first lesson on the clear distinction between mindset and skillset – more were to follow.

FIFTEEN

After his session with Peter, Midas's meetings continued through the morning. Midas met Tom, Mary, Amos and Ole.

Tom was into shipping and logistics, with a global empire that stretched from New York to Norway and down to New Zealand – and all points between; Tom was confident and quiet, astute and open, clearly highly experienced. His takeaway was always being open to ideas; you never know where they come from. And trust your intuition. Business plans are for accountants, "But regrettably they get it wrong; they don't use their gut!"

Mary was a publisher, and by the time she was thirty had built a large online and hardcopy publishing house with over one hundred titles. Her takeaway was never give up on your vision. Stay away from your family, and your friends, they are inevitably 'dream stealers'. Surround yourself with like-minded people. In particular, look at the five people you most frequently interact with – that is how YOU are. They are the barometer of your mindset and attitude. And if you don't like what you see, move on; get yourself a different set of acquaintances, and associates, and friends.

Amos proved to be an amazing and unusual individual eschewing corporate business, and even a 'normal' route to entrepreneurship. He, along with his two brothers, had built themselves a trading empire that supplied thousands of different product lines, from egg timers, to Bluetooth earpieces, to air-conditioners, to clothing, to cutlery, to car parts – all branded (multiple brands) and sold on Amazon. Amazon was his sales channel for his multi-million-dollar empire, with sales last year 'in nine figures'. He was reputed to be one of the most knowledgeable and experienced 'Amazon sellers' – and those words was not even descriptive enough; there were few people who knew more about e-commerce, buying, product selection, logistics, copywriting, or marketing, than Amos and his team.

Midas remembered an Amos looking at him with an ardent look, his brow creasing, and his black Hasidic hat pushed back, "Midas, excellence and dedication must be part of your mantra. Every sportsman, every businessman, every inventor, every creator, every entrepreneur, believed in excellence, along with commitment, dedication, tenacity, and an unswerving desire to deliver his or her vision. It's the unseen hard work that delivers the outcome: in the gym, the nights in the practice room, the dedication of the swimmer rising at four am to have an empty pool for three hours' training, and the failure of a thousand tries to make the simple product that changes people's lives. Our public, our customers, see the end result. Only you, and your coach and colleagues, see the hard road to success."

As Amos left him, Midas struggled to comprehend that someone could build a business with a billion-dollar turnover on Amazon!

Before lunch, Midas's last meeting had been intriguing; it was with a Norwegian called Ole.

Ole had been a long-time corporate executive in Cisco who had flipped to being a tech entrepreneur. In Cisco he acquired companies, built them, integrated them, reshaped them, and folded them into the corporate inventory of technology innovation and delivery companies that was Cisco. Now Ole was in the trenches, for himself and his investors, as he described it. Ole covered some of the ground that Midas had heard through the morning. But his main takeaway for Midas was 'passion, agility and execution'.

Midas could picture Ole; tall, dark haired, casual, optimistic, positive, and intense. Towards the end of their chat, he had leaned forward over the table, as though he was going to share a secret that no one should hear. In almost hushed tones, he looked directly at Midas and said quietly and earnestly, "Whatever your idea, whatever resources you collect, whatever funds you can acquire, what other great ideas and passion you may have, I can tell you… It will all come to NOTHING, NOTHING, hear me, NOTHING, unless you excel at my troika – passion, agility, execution.

"You will need passion because you will have an insane workload and you will draw on all your personal resources, powered by your inner fire, passion.

" You will need agility, because whatever you start with you will need to change and adapt – fast.

"And you will need to execute relentlessly and with discipline."

On that note, as though a dramatic exit was called for, Ole stood up, shook Midas hand and smiled, "Until next time, Midas, until next time. See you." And then he too had left.

Midas was in a daze. He had been overwhelmed with the generosity of people who he saw as 'Entrepreneurial Gods'.

Sitting quietly and reflecting on everything that had been said, he felt like he had attended a remarkable day-long seminar in a Master's Program on Entrepreneurship in the highest School of Life and Business that he could possibly attend.

Being an entrepreneur was a calling for sure, but no one had implied that they were geniuses, no one had said, that it had not been hard work, and all agreed that you need unswerving passion and belief to see you through the difficult and challenging times. They all said that big goals are essential, and Midas should set himself a target of financial independence, not financial sufficiency. There was much more said and implied, but Midas thought he needed space to get his head straight now.

Midas walked out into the sunlight of the early afternoon; he felt overwhelmed and grateful for what he had learned.

Now it was up to him.

SIXTEEN

Midas pushed open the heavy wooden door; it was ornate, glass paneled, brass handled, and heavy. It had swung back and forth for tens of thousands of times since it was installed one hundred years ago. He thought of all the people who had passed through this entrance and walked the fifteen or twenty meters to the marble pillared archway that opened to the vast Reading Room of the City Library.

The Reading Room had changed little in its form during the past sixty or seventy years. The long rows of desks, tables, and wooden chairs that would now be rated as antiques, filled the center of the hall. Shelves of books radiated out to dark corridors housing glass-covered shelves containing historical and important literary works. At each end of this vast room, more shelves contained texts and books of ancient and modern vintage, and even though contemporary reading had shifted online, some recent publications could be found on the shelves, acquired and purchased from the city library's meager budget. Thankfully, the city had found ways to maintain the infrastructure of the Library and maintained it as a public service. Today, in the time of austerity, cuts in Federal budgets, cuts in welfare, cuts in city services, there was this island of quiet reflection to which Midas frequently escaped.

The weeks had passed since the networking event at the Hyatt and his morning of intense education about business and creating wealth from some of the top people in their field. He had had the time to think, and in recent days his mind was crystallizing the ideas Midas thought would propel him forward as a successful business entrepreneur.

Lynn and Midas met on a few occasions; she was travelling in and out of the city with increasing frequency but they still managed to get the odd coffee and meal. She seemed to be genuinely interested in his progress and was supportive and encouraging in her way. She exuded an unbounded optimism, and had promised him he would be a success. Midas was beginning to believe in the possibility.

Nestor had been quiet; he sent through a few short and interesting emails – short checklists of things that Midas should consider as he reflected on the direction he would go. Although Nestor had been notable for his absence, Midas thought that if he went to search for a book on any one of the three hundred shelves he would, likely or not, find Nestor peering through the book shelves when he withdrew two or three volumes. *He'll turn up, I guess; when they're ready, or maybe is it when I'm ready?*

He found himself a quiet table at the far left-hand corner of the hall, within a few paces of a water fountain and with the natural light of a tall stained-glass window. It was here that he would spend several hours each day; thinking, reading, writing, with headphones on watching videos – mainly of inspirational speeches from entrepreneurs and motivational experts. Some he dismissed as being nothing more than snake oil purveyors, wanting you to sign up for an expensive course. He had reached the point where he could sense the pitch within minutes of the start of the video, or within the first few lines of an email. He now habitually looked at something new with this finger hovering over the delete button.

The fact that phone calls were frowned upon in the library was a godsend; at least it was good to remove that level of interruption for a few hours. He alternated his library office with his table at the coffee shop. In the coffee shop he was in a semi-public space, but the ambient noise meant that phone calls could come, be taken or made without any irritation to other people.

He had started running, and each morning would take the first hour to jog through the park, get in touch with his ideas and prepare for another day at the office. He laughed at this statement. He dreamt of the time when he'd have an office; he could see his firm's name on the glass door. He had yet to decide on a name, but nevertheless, he saw the glass door to his corporate office in a trendy low-rise tech area on the outskirts the city. His name would be known, and whilst the prospect of success was frightening, he could live with a minimal dose of celebrity-factor status. But at this point in the evolution of

Midas's business empire, he was genuinely bootstrapping every conceivable aspect. After all, at this stage his employee count was ONE – himself!

He was resourceful; he reached out to many people – friends, acquaintances, and almost to people that he passed on the street – to gather some advice, some help. He hated networking receptions, but he was comfortable online with the relatively distant connection to people. In these days he had learned to become selective about the people he spoke to, realizing that the friends he had at this previous company - who were still languishing in their grey cubes - had nothing much to say. They were firmly entrenched in their jobs, which held no attraction for Midas; a job was the furthest thing from Midas's mind.

He formulated some ideas and thought that he could create a credible story about being able to provide consulting and technical services in the sectors that he knew something about. He had created his website. He had given himself a business name, Castel International Advisors, and had written some simple but quite compelling text on the challenges of executing large enterprise technology projects. Of course he recognized that when starting out, his personal credibility, and his businesses credibility was, to say the least, on small foundations in a shaky ground. He got over this by implying that his past experience, which was extensive and genuine, appeared as his company's endeavors. This was a challenge all entrepreneurs face – and there was an element of 'bluff' that was needed whether purists liked or not.

He laughed at himself a short while after creating his website and business cards, realizing that Castel International Advisors had the acronym 'CIA'. He decided to leave it and use the joke as a humorous talking point.

He reached out to a number of people who worked as contractors, some employees who had flexibility in their contracts, and Midas created a pool of talent and resource that, when the contracts materialized, would step forward. He would engage, motivate, manage, direct, and deliver; he was the conductor who today had an empty orchestra pit but had a hotline to the on-call members of Midas's future orchestra.

Financial resources were as strapped as his labor resources. So far, he got by on a day-to-day basis by raiding the savings he had hidden away at the time he was working. He secretly longed to buy an antique sports car. His mind had been set on Jaguar XK 150, but when he saw the price tag of $250,000 on an auctioneer's site, he figured it would take some years before he achieved his dream. The thought that the more he saved, the more the price of the car would inflate, didn't deter him from keeping some funds quietly stashed away. But now he was raiding those funds out of necessity. He had passed through a period of financial optimism after he had been fired; his lawyers had told him he had a case for compensation and had embarked on a no-fee-no-win claim. Midas had forgotten that and was now resigned to it being a windfall if it ever happened.

Midas opened his laptop and pulled up a prospect list. To be fair, it was an impressive list. He had already reached out to his friend Ming who was in Shenzhen China, who had a software house that was a general contractor for businesses in China and North America. He knew Ming's reputation. He was solid. Midas had already agreed that if he got any work in the SAP enterprise application space he would contract to his friend David Lim at Hand Consulting in Shanghai.

Midas had close relations with David Dunkley, the GM of one of the biggest Middle Eastern airlines, with Alan who was the CEO of a major Aircraft engineering company, and with Randall who was the senior Technology Innovation VP with a major food production facility in Dallas, Fort Worth. Any, or all of these people could provide Midas with sufficient work and revenue to lift his fledgling business off the runway.

He had posted his new company and his new position as President and CEO on LinkedIn and had received a flurry of congratulatory mails with the promise of introductions, but no work. It was now time to leverage those contacts and to be brave. He would have to rely on his own enviable reputation and his personal connection to gain access to some of the opportunities, but that did not deter him. He spent the next couple of days writing to a wide variety of contacts he had built up over his tenure as a Program Director.

As inevitably happens, as soon as his business appeared on the radar in the public domain, he was inundated with offers from headhunters, marketing agencies, PR agencies, search engine optimization companies, you name it. Everyone had a service to offer at a price, and again and again had him have his finger hovering over the delete button.

After three hours, he closed laptop and threw it in his backpack. He left the library, picked up a sandwich and a Snapple at the local deli, and walked across the road to a small downtown park. He sat down and his phone pinged. It was a message from David in Dubai. "Hi Midas, thanks for your mail, it is timely. I'd really like you talk to Angus, my operations manager. He's got some big problems and I remember you are a tech wizard of some kind, I think you can help."

SEVENTEEN

Was this for real? Midas had reached out, prospected, and then received a response in less than twenty-four hours. *What do I do now?* he thought. He had never been in this position before. An email popped up. It was from David. "Call me at seven am my time, my Skype ID is at the bottom the mail." Midas quickly figured out the time difference between the Central Time Zone, America and Dubai - nine hours. David will be going to bed. *Patience, I can wait until later, I must call him at ten pm my time.* Although waiting was a trial of major proportions, he kept looking at his watch, calculating the time David would arrive in his office. *I am to call him at seven am, that's going to be my ten pm.*

Time passed very slowly through the day, the evening was even longer.

Ten pm eventually arrived and Midas was excited and nervous. Midas gave David the necessary time to pour himself a coffee and then pinged a Skype message. "Hi David, I got your email. Great news, terrific! How can I help?"

Three minutes later Skype rang out, and with his earphone firmly jammed into his ears, Midas listened to an outline of the problems being experienced.

Food production was a complex industrial process; not only did the shop floor have the challenge of producing tens of thousands of dishes for the airlines that left Dubai every day, the timescale from production to consumption could be anything from up to twenty-four to thirty-six hours, and temperature control of the food product was paramount. The systems to collect and monitor temperature performance at different parts of the production process were antiquated at best and non-existent at worst. They needed a system by which the data could be collected, collated, transmitted, and in real-time presented to operations control. This was a substantial ask, considering they were in 2007, and sensor technology, communications, data analytics, and data analysis and accumulation were not as prevalent as they are today - in the middle of the second decade of the 21st-century.

David pulled Angus onto the call and Midas heard a Scottish voice. Angus greeted Midas in a friendly manner and started to outline the problem.

"Let's be honest, I've got my own IT department, but they are not up to the task. At best they're able to maintain current systems and even that is stretching their limits. We don't want to hire somebody permanently so maybe you can sort something out for us. Come on over and let's have a look at the problem."

"Sure," answered Midas.

"Ok, we will send you an itinerary. Leave the arrangements to us," David said, and with a couple of pleasantries, rang off.

It can't be so easy, Midas thought. *I'm a few weeks into creating my new company, and this has just dropped onto my lap. But good-bye. I have no money.* His mind was racing. Maybe his Jaguar XK150 funds would have sufficient money. Maybe he would figure that one out.

The following afternoon, in the back of the coffee shop he made some calls to Ming in Shenzhen, waking him in the middle of the night. Blasting Ming with a torrent of optimism, he quickly outlined David's problem. Ming's sleep-laden voice at the other end said a perfunctory "Yes, yes, Midas, sure. Call me when its daylight!"

Midas was buzzing. He was excited. He could hardly contain himself.

Over the next twenty-four hours, nothing happened; no calls, no mail, no communication from Dubai. Midas went through the day staring at his email account, willing an email from David or Angus to appear. But it did not.

To take his mind off Dubai, Midas focused and continued to write and prospect amongst the people he knew. Randall, his friend at Airshef, a major food factory at Fort Worth was promising in his reply. He knew that Midas was a whiz when it came to complex enterprise systems. Randall's business serviced airlines in over 200 airports around the world.

"I've been contemplating where to go next in our technology platform," Randall's email read.

Randall had the job of recommending to the company's Chief Information Officer (the 'CIO' – the most senior technology guy in the business) a suitable computer application, and a service provider who would design and rollout the next generation of Technology Applications, or 'Enterprise Systems' across multiple selected locations. Once established and proven, a trained internal Airshef team would take on board the implementation across the world, but there was a significant amount of work – which Midas calculated to be in the hundreds of thousands of dollars – to be done before that stage was reached.

Here were two big fish, which he might be able to land. Through the good fortune of timing and personal contact they were swimming into his net. *Can I do all of this without overstretching myself*, Midas pondered? Midas had a high level of confidence in his ability, his challenge was going to be resourcing, but that was down the line. He remembered Ole's comment at the Hyatt, "It's all about execution". *If I get either of these contracts Ole would be right, it's going to be a challenge to execute and deliver.* Midas put that at the back of his mind. He had to translate two emails into reality.

Midas laughed at the thought, he laughed at the absurdity of the whole thing. He, a one-man band, sat in a library, bidding for work with two major, very major organizations. Audacity - that was the word. He thought that his approach was truly AUDACIOUS. But he had read about dreaming big. Do not limit your horizons. Believe in the impossible.

There was so much that he had learned from the reading and studying and reflecting on his life in recent weeks that he was mindful to accept the premise that anything was possible.

EIGHTEEN

A mail dropped into Midas's inbox. It was from David.

Excitedly, Midas clicked on it. The message was short:

> From: David
>
> To: Midas
>
> Subject: Travel Arrangements
>
> Hi Midas:
>
> You are booked into the Airport Hotel; your flight tickets can be collected from New York JFK. We booked you on our non-stop flight on Friday, October 6. Leaves in the morning and you will arrive on the SEVENTH.
>
> Thank you for your offer to help.
>
> See you in Dubai.
>
> David.
>
> P.S – Relax on Saturday. A car will pick you up at 0700 on the 8th

A separate message came from Angus, "I enjoyed our conversation. You have a message from David. I think it is the least we can do to invite you to come to have some exploratory discussions." It continued with some logistics issue.

Midas leaned back, his mouth dry, his pulse racing, and his mind all over the place with chatter and noise. He was setting off on a journey across the world on his first major contractual discussion. He knew David well. He knew Angus from his reputation among other friends in the industry. He knew the company; they had a budget, they had a need. Midas believed, with Ming's help, that he had the ability to provide and supply what they wanted. This was a software job; Midas had done similar jobs. Nothing should go wrong, he just had to manage his way through it all. He had done it many times before.

Days later, Midas departed Chicago's O'Hare airport for JFK. He was flying to JFK a day early. He was leaving nothing to chance.

He overnighted at a cheap airport motel and checked in for his Dubai flight.

It was a long flight, reputed to be one of the longest commercial sectors flown – fourteen hours. He had not had been given the privilege of business class, nor did he expect it, tourist class was adequate – the seats were slightly larger than the norm, and the leg room generous for the back of the aircraft.

After the long flight, he checked into the Airport Hotel, Dubai. It was 10:00am.

The following morning, as scheduled, the car picked Midas up. Within fifteen minutes he was drinking coffee, renewing acquaintanceship with David, who he had known for a few years, having met him at conferences. Angus came in; he was tall, around six foot. He wore a long white work coat, as required in the workplace. In his Scottish lilt, he talked about the problems that they had faced, and the inadequacy of the internal IT department, the head of which reported to a different director and ultimately the board.

A tour around the production facility followed, with meetings with QC, food hygienists, and production personnel.

Midas got the general landscape; it was becoming clear they had already done a lot of work on the actual process. They knew the points where data needed to be collected, they knew how it needed to be accumulated, they knew how it needed to be presented, they knew the reports they needed, so this was really becoming the software development project.

Suspicious of designing new systems in well-established production environments, Midas asked if there were presently any available proprietary systems on the market. The answer surprised him, "No. The regulations that we have to adhere to have only been published in the last six months in draft form and they don't become mandatory for another one year so no one is caught up with the needs, never mind a solution," said Angus.

David added, "Midas, if you get it right here, there must be a massive market elsewhere."

Over the next six days, Midas wrote a business requirement definition and systems requirement specification and sent it over to Ming in Shenzhen. Midas received an affirmative reply that it was not difficult to build the software application for a relatively modest budget. A short timescale was needed to answer questions, and also for Ming's company to assemble the different technical components of hardware and software. Midas could create a viable commercial proposal with Ming's help.

He had been in Dubai for ten days now; the company had been generous in covering Midas's expenses locally so he had not needed to dig deep into his personal resources.

He had just put a commercial proposal on David's desk with copies to Angus and, out of courtesy, to Ismail, the IT manager, who would seldom be seen. The IT manager had been lukewarm to Midas's presence and quietly hostile to any proposals, as it showed his department's inadequacy in full view of the management team. The highlighting of that inadequacy was being felt along a chain of command that ran parallel from David's line to the Board, to Farood, the Arabic Administration and Finance Director on the main board.

Midas had met Farood on the third day of his visit. His meeting had been cordial and short. Farood asked what Midas was doing, which struck Midas as slightly strange as he had assumed that both David and Ismail had briefed him. When Midas outlined the brief he had been given, Farood was immediately dismissive and told Midas that he could see no justification for flying someone from America when he had a perfectly capable IT department in-house.

Midas knew that the IT department was not capable of doing the work and did not enjoy the confidence of David and the Operations team to deliver anything that was remotely acceptable in an urgent timeframe. He chose not to challenge Farood's view but he would mention it to David and let David deal with the internal politics.

On reading the proposal, David gave Midas a verbal acceptance and told him to go ahead to build proof of concept (a demonstration system that would behave like the final solution). Midas was taken aback at the speed of the decision and the immediacy of work. He calculated the cost of the prototype in his head. The prototype would have to resemble the final production system so he would have to do around eighty percent of the work that was necessary, just to build a proof of concept. It was a significant investment, which he should ask for payment for. He hesitated.

David sensed his hesitation and told Midas that on delivery, the cost could be incorporated into the quotation for the final system and the proof of concept money would be paid upon signing the substantive contract. Right now Midas must operate in a pre-sales mode and deliver the proof of concept as a demonstration that he could do the work.

At this point, Midas should've heard the alarm bells, but he was so excited by the ensuing work and potential global application that his project manager's mindset went into overdrive and within an hour, Ming in Shenzhen had received the papers and between them they were planning on how the solution should be delivered. Ming also raised the inevitable question about how he was going to be paid and Midas persuaded him that all was well and in just a few short weeks, with a proof of concept being accepted, the money was as much as in the bank.

To emphasize his optimism, Midas offered to fly to Shenzhen to meet the team before he went back to the United States – an offer that Ming accepted, and days later, Midas was negotiating a visa on arrival in Shenzhen's Skekou Ferry Port, having flown from Dubai to Hong Kong and transited on the ferry service to Mainland China.

NINETEEN

Ming's software company was located in Shenzhen's high-tech zone, in Nan Shan, to the west of downtown Shenzhen. Ming had assembled a small team, two of whom were English-speaking, and he assured Midas that the team could deliver against the written requirements in the space of about four weeks. He'd insisted on at least a token deposit and Midas promised he would transfer some money from the US, at the same time praying that his XK150 savings would be sufficient to keep Ming happy.

Midas was now torn between staying in Shenzhen, going back to Dubai, or making the long haul to Chicago – to return almost a month later. He chose to head back to Dubai en route to Chicago. He took photographs of Ming's team, the high-tech zone, and the office housing Ming's developers. He emailed them to David and Angus before heading back to Dubai via Hong Kong. He spent three days in Dubai with David, Angus and the operations team, refining specifications and getting answers to the stream of questions flowing from Shenzhen. Ismail was noticeable for his absence from any of the meetings; Midas did not pursue his absence but rather left Ismail and Farood to their own devices. He headed back to Chicago.

The next four weeks passed in a flurry of activity and emails, Skype calls, and deliberations in the middle of the night – because of the time zone differences – but the proof of concept had been created. The data would need to be entered manually at various points in the production process, but that was adequate for this stage.

In the meantime, Randall had reached out to Midas and invited him down to Dallas to discuss a proof of concept for their enterprise system. It seemed that Midas was becoming true to his ancient namesake and was indeed delivering gold from each contact that he touched.

Midas flew back to Dubai on the 4th November. Ming had previously mailed the software programs to Angus and Midas. Midas could operate them on a powerful PC that Angus would acquire, and the demo was scheduled for the 8th. The day of the demo arrived and with David, Angus and the Operations team in attendance, and also with Ismail present, Midas went into 'show' mode. He had done this many times, he was confident, accomplished and was working in familiar territory – as a Program Manager outlining a business transformation that would take place.

The software program, the intelligence in the data, the reports generated, proved to be the solution they had been looking for. Within the next twenty-four hours, a formal substantial proposal had been drafted and contracts sketched out. Midas was feeling positive and elated. In many ways, he felt like he used to when he was delivering top-class results on big programs that he managed; now the only difference was that the money would flow to him. He could already feel the crisp hundred dollar notes in his hand.

Friday, 9th was the Sabbath day in Dubai and Angus and Midas headed to the beach with Angus's family and some friends. Midas felt relaxed and confident. He was within hours of clinching his first major contract for Castel International Advisors.

Over the next two days, Angus's team worked with Midas, putting up with Ismail from the IT department, who now had to provide servers and technical help to execute the programs from China. All went well, Angus was happy, David was happy, Midas was happy. All that remained was the formal Board sign off. Angus was already pulling his team out of their normal day jobs and he had appointed a local project manager to lead the efforts across the business.

David met Midas on Wednesday afternoon. "The board meeting is tomorrow morning," said David, "so it's an early start. You don't need to be there. I'll come over to the hotel and bring you the news. Let's plan so that we can celebrate over the weekend."

Eighteen hours later Midas was sitting in the breakfast room at the hotel encouraging his laptop to send emails on a not-so-efficient Wi-Fi system, when David strode through the glass doors of the restaurant and quickly threaded his way between tables. David walked quickly to Midas's table and sat down. He declined coffee; the contract was in

David's hands. Midas had expected to be asked to sign the contract at breakfast but it remained closed.

David looked up, he was pale. His eyes glanced away and then down to the contract. He then lifted his head slightly and shook his head. "I'm sorry, I do not have good news."

"What do you mean?" asked Midas as he experienced a massive sinking feeling. He wanted the floor to swallow him up at this point.

"The Board threw the contract out."

Midas was quick to retort, "Why? It's got your signature; it's got Angus's signature. We have been over this many times in the last days, you know it works. It's within your budget, it's within your timescale, so what IS the problem?" Midas felt a level of aggression in his voice. He was trying to maintain his control, and fighting fears and an unfathomable anguish.

David leaned forward, "The problem is that when it got to the Board, the Chairman asked if everyone was in agreement. Farood voiced an objection, he told the Chairman he did not agree. He had not signed the contract."

Farood, the Administration Director, with responsibility for Finance and Administration, was a man very close to the owners, and to the President and the Chairman of the company to whom David reported.

"Simply put, Farood complained that you had not taken into account his requirements, you had not consulted with IT, and you had exceeded your brief. In short, you had frozen him and his department out of the process.

"At the same time as you were completing the proof of concept and doing the final demos, Farood and Ismail was negotiating another contract with the local office of international consultants, Ernest & Lee, and had it had been ratified and signed at the board meeting this morning. They will deliver something very similar to your solution, at three times the cost - but that doesn't matter. It would not surprise me if your specifications had been leaked."

"I am afraid you're out of here." David reached into the inside pocket of his jacket, "I have your tickets; they were booked and signed off by Farood and you are on the afternoon flight today.

"I'm sorry, there is nothing I can do. Believe me I feel bad, really bad."

And with that, David got up, held Midas's hand for a moment and shook his head. He walked out through the same glass doors that he had entered not five minutes before.

TWENTY

Midas slumped in his chair. He could not believe what he had just heard. He was in shock. He owed Ming money for the development; he had wasted three months of his time. His dreams of rolling out the solution to multiple companies across the world disappeared faster than the dream arrived. Without a client site, a proven system, a happy customer, no one else was going to listen. Where had he gone wrong? A technically solid solution, a competitively priced proposal, a rapid timescale… everything was aligned. Except ….?

It was a very long flight back to the US. Before he had left the airport in Dubai, he spoke to Angus who had attended the board meeting as an observer, as he always did, supporting David.

"You didn't do anything wrong. David supported your proposal; he supported you all the way. I was asked for my comments, I reaffirmed the work you had done and gave you the support of all of Operations. But Farood, whose signature was required, made it very clear that his department, and IT, would not support your solution, allegedly on technical grounds. He said he would not sign your contract under any circumstances, and had already found an alternative supplier, whom I suspect had been passed your documentation by the IT department. Sorry my friend, that's Dubai."

When he landed at JFK, the sky was grey. There was a cold wet rain and biting northeast wind. It was a very cold homecoming for Midas. It was his first taste of losing as an entrepreneur and he felt an acute level of frustration and disappointment. He would catch the Delta connecting flight home.

He wanted to call Lynn. He had been exchanging messages with her from Dubai and from China. His enthusiasm had been infectious and she was rooting for him. She had become his personal cheerleader. How could he let her down?

He picked up his phone, but embarrassment, guilt, shame, overtook him. He could not call. He already had felt that she was in a different league from him and his failure in Dubai would reaffirm that. No doubt she was waiting for the news of another great beach party.

He put off the call; he would see her this evening.

Flight 4087 arrived on time at 4:04 PM and taxied to the pier.

Midas walked through the arrivals gate and reached baggage reclaim; as he waited to pick up his luggage his phone pinged.

The message read "Hello big man! Welcome back; hope that contract is safe in your pocket. I know you are tired but take me for a drink, pleeeease. Love Lynn."

The last time that Midas had communicated with Lynn was a short, "I am on the way home, must run." He added his flight details from Dubai airport.

Prior to that, on the day before the fateful board meeting, he had emailed her and had briefly outlined his optimism and expectation that he had won his first contract. Now he had arrived home and he looked at Lynn's message and felt sick. The message was a reminder of his vulnerability as a nascent entrepreneur.

If he refused the date she would first enquire politely, and then verbally bludgeon him until he shared his excuse for turning her down. If he went he would have to explain and relate the whole depressing episode.

He sighed and thought he had to get it over with. But Lynn was always a beacon of optimism and she would listen to what he had to say, and Midas would try his best to sound nonchalant; then she would brush off the failure like wiping some crumbs from the table and she would smile, look into his eyes, and say "Okay, so what's next? There are still hundreds of opportunities waiting for someone like you, Midas."

Midas thought he needed such a dose of optimistic therapy. He sent a message back, "See you at Antonio's at eight, OK?" The affirmative "OK" came back in a few seconds.

Outside the exit doors from the arrivals area it was cold and windy, not much different from New York, he thought. The taxi line was long, mainly populated with the modern equivalent of road warriors, travelling executives. Each with their backpack, their heavy coat, their scarf, and their headgear. All shuffling forward. With only a little imagination, the scene looked like it could have been from a silent movie shot in some dark age where everything was monochrome; peoples' attires were in shades of black, grey, dark blue or sepia. The depressing color wash did nothing to lift Midas's spirits. It took ten minutes to get to the head of the queue. He threw his holdall into the trunk and climbed into the back of the taxi.

Midas gave his address and in the absence of even a nod of acknowledgment he didn't know whether the taxi driver heard or not. He repeated the address, this time a few decibels higher. "Yeah yeah yeah buddy, I've got you," was the response from the taxi driver and those five words were the only words there were exchanged during the journey. They passed through the outskirts of the city, navigating the evening traffic and buses carrying people back to their boxed existence in some outer suburb. Twenty minutes later Midas was home. He showered, changed, and was out again in twenty minutes heading to his date with Lynn.

It was eight o'clock. Midas was on time. The one thing he did was to pride himself on his punctuality. Whatever the circumstances, he was always on time. When he ran in the morning, his schedule was like clockwork. Despite his jet lag, this habit was one he could not break. The effects of the long flight did nothing to brighten his humor; he felt drained. The bags under his eyes had appeared and he thought he probably looked like he had aged a decade during the past three weeks. Midas was grateful for the physical support of the bar in Antonio's at this moment.

Lynn came in; she wore a big black winter coat, and a black fake fur hat. Underneath, she wore a simple, yet elegant, knee-length blue and white checkered dress, cut to emphasize her petite figure. It was slightly gathered around her waist by a narrow patent black belt and was complemented by her signature, simple Gucci earrings and neck chain. The whole outfit was a quiet statement of confidence and beauty. Her long black hair dropped to her shoulders and this evening she wore dark rimmed glasses. It made her studious, but her librarian-style glasses and slightly severe look was dissolved when she smiled. She walked towards Midas exuding happiness. She was pleased to see him and clearly anxious to hear his news. As she reached him, she gave him a light kiss on his cheek and turned so he could help her take off her big coat.

They ordered cocktails and sat on high stools alongside a long glass table that ran down the center of the floor. Other drinkers were scattered around the long table and the smaller, more intimate tables that circled where they sat. Spearing an olive with a practiced jab of her right hand, she lifted it from the glass and popped it into her mouth.

"Okay, big man. Tell me." She smiled and giggled. "Hey, you are going to be rich now? How fast will the empire grow?"

Inside Midas was crumbling. His stomach was knotted. His hands rested on his jeans beneath the table, so that Lynn could not see the sweat on his palms that would have smeared the glass top with the telltale marks. He stuttered something meaningless, as someone who was consumed with embarrassment might do as they tried to make rational sense of the words that were about to fall from their mouth.

He waited a few moments and then blurted out the latter part of the events in Dubai. He didn't dress it up, he didn't add how successful the proof of concept had been, he didn't add how Ming's team in Shenzhen had produced spectacular results in a short period of time, he didn't add how everyone in production was thrilled with the results. He simply stated the events of the Board meeting, the breakfast encounter with David and the details of the call from Angus.

Lynn's expression changed.

TWENTY ONE

Lynn looked serious; her seriousness turned to anger as the muscles in her face tensed, and even with dim light in the bar Midas could see her eyes narrowing. Both of her small hands were tightly clenched, fists with white knuckles protruding like small lumps of white marble. He was not quite sure what she was going to do next, whether she was going to slam her fists through the glass panel on the top of the table or, with a swipe of her arm, clear the glasses in front of them. She was clearly and visibly incensed. Midas wasn't sure whether she was incensed at him, the situation, or the events in Dubai.

At that moment Midas thought it was better to say nothing and looked down at his drink which, thankfully for him, had remained on the bar, and had not being scattered by Lynn's potentially swiping arms. He felt like a schoolboy sitting or standing in front of the headmaster, having been found guilty of some heinous crime – like that he had the temerity to break some archaic school rule about wearing hats in the classroom or something equally ludicrous.

The impasse felt like an age although, in reality, it was just seconds. He could see that Lynn's hands were slowly relaxing and color was returning to her fingers. Her shoulders had relaxed slightly and her face was recovering a degree of poise. She looked at Midas, and he felt a hint of compassion as she reached over and took his hand in both of hers. It was like a mother comforting a child.

"Bad things happen," she said. "This will be the first time, but it may not be the last time that somebody screws you. However, with your newfound experience, at least going forward let's hope that it is only going to be someone who *attempts* to screw you. You will be more perceptive, more aware, more circumspect, and you will be more grounded. In fact, you will reach a point where you will not even deal with such assholes! There was clearly something that was seriously dysfunctional; you might have seen it, but you chose to ignore it because you were greedy or needy, I am not sure which. But it's time to move on." She was smiling now and Midas felt her warmth.

She continued, "Remember, you are an entrepreneur, right? You're the captain on the bridge; you've got this great big ship of life and on a ship there are no rearview mirrors. What's behind is behind."

She took hold of Midas's hands, looked at him and leaned forward. He could smell the fragrance of her hair. Softly, she said, "Let me ask you a question. If you go to the stern of your ship, can you get hold of the wake of the ship and use it to control where you go, and how fast you sail?"

Her voice rose in volume slightly. "No. No more than the past can steer your future. The past is gone. Let it go. It's a lesson, put it in the memory bank. Say thank you for the lesson, forgive yourself, and move forward."

All this time she was looking intently into Midas's eyes; he felt the power of her sincerity and he visibly relaxed. He also marveled at her wisdom.

"Let's get out of here," he said and climbed off the stool.

Lynn gathered up her bag and slipped off the stool to the sound of her heels clicking on the wooden floor beneath the table. She took her coat, black hat and a big cashmere scarf from the doorman, slipped on the coat and wrapped the scarf around her neck. Popping her hat on her head, she smiled at Midas. Midas pulled on a heavy casual coat and they stepped outside.

They walked a block to the Chinese restaurant where they first had a meal together. Over dinner the mood was more relaxed, comfortable and enjoyable – and at times even humorous. Midas laughed as Lynn related stories of interviews that she had done, some serious, some hilarious.

She laughed out loud when she told Midas that her editor, George Harbinger, had enquired, quite inappropriately, on the status of her relationship with Midas. Lynn denied anything romantic and George grunted something about always losing his best female reporters and journalists to boyfriends who moved to different parts of the country.

She found this hilarious and Midas felt embarrassed at the very thought of a boyfriend status. His mind filled with horror and fear given the state of his bank balance. He could barely support himself never mind providing or contributing to the lifestyle of two upwardly mobile young professional people, with all their attendant expectations. Midas immediately pushed that thought to the back of his mind.

They talked and ate and drank a bottle of wine, and over the next two hours Midas felt tired but comfortable. However, he knew that he needed to get to bed as jetlag, and time zone shifts from a long journey were not creeping up but were approaching him at breakneck speed.

They left the restaurant and Lynn jumped into a taxi, waved a kiss to him, and was gone.

Midas waved down another cab. He pulled open the door. He was half in and half out of cab when he felt a mighty blow to the bottom of his back, which was accompanied by a resounding crash. The cab lurched forward three feet throwing Midas into the gutter and dragging him forward as his foot jammed between the door and the sill. Midas felt a searing pain in his leg and hip. He looked up to see headlights inches away from him. He blanked out.

A black sedan had crashed into the rear of the taxi. Two men got out and ran forward to the taxi. One ran down the passenger side and stepped heavily on Midas as he yanked open the front door. Midas felt nothing. The other was on the driver's side, screaming and yelling at the driver to get out. A gun had been pulled and the driver was in no mood to argue. He spilled out of his cab as the two guys took possession and with wheels screeching drove off, leaving Midas in the gutter and the driver on his knees in the roadway as the taxi sped away.

The restaurant had spilled out on the footpath. Hands quickly supported Midas's head. The driver was being helped from the road and into the restaurant lobby.

Midas was coming around. He opened his eyes and looked up. He could see eyes looking down at him and could not figure out what was happening. A searing pain in his hip brought him to full consciousness. He tried to stand, and helping hands hauled him onto his feet and supported him from both sides. The three hobbled towards the restaurant entrance.

TWENTY TWO

Midas slumped heavily into a chair near the door. Yi An, the proprietor's daughter, brought him a glass of water. Midas held it, his hands trembling. He sipped the water.

Welcome back to Chicago. He thought of the near tragedy of his homecoming.

Yi Song, the proprietor came forward and spoke to Yi An. Song spoke no English and relied on his daughter An to be in front of the house.

"My father has called an ambulance."

"No, No, Thank you. I will be ok. Just give me a few minutes and call me another taxi."

Midas was sufficiently conscious to realize that an ambulance ride and a night in Emergency was the last thing his budget needed. He had lost his medical insurance when Gravel dispatched him, his credit card was maxed out, and a few thousand bucks of hospital charges he did not need.

Reluctantly, Song relented, but the ambulance arrived anyway and took away the still shaken taxi driver.

Some forty-five minutes later, An helped Midas into another cab. He was home in fifteen minutes. He stepped inside his room, removed his torn jeans and shirt, and headed for the shower. He luxuriated in the hot water coursing all over his body, and stayed for a long fifteen minutes just reflecting on his welcome home and the life of contrasts in the last few weeks. When he stepped out of the shower and looked in the mirror, he saw the results of the confrontation with the taxi hijackers and thought that it was how he would look stepping out of a mixed martial arts session with an Alpha male gorilla.

The next morning, the alarm brought Midas back to life although he had been awake much earlier. On the one hand his body was still in a time zone that was hours different from his physical location, and on the other hand, he was stiff and sore from the last night's battle. He got up and phoned the rental car company, booked himself a car and headed back to the shower. He emerged more quickly than the night before and poured himself a second coffee; it would not be long before he was leaving the city.

The time the previous evening that he spent with Lynn had done a lot to restore Midas's balance. He was feeling philosophical; although the scars from Dubai were still there, he thought he would manage to get over things. His physical scars would heal.

He checked his bank balance and groaned inwardly. He was facing a dilemma. There was sufficient to pay Ming with a little left over, and somehow he had to get through the month, or months, he wasn't sure. Maybe, he might be able to negotiate with Ming an extended payment. He knew that there were prospects outside, and he would go back to his table at the library and to the coffee shop and start over.

He left his apartment and headed for the rental lot. He was going to spend the next forty-eight hours at the lakeside town of Door County, Wisconsin. It would take him about five hours to drive there. It would allow him time to recharge. He turned left out of the car park and threaded his way into the light traffic. It was 10:30 a.m.; the morning rush hour had finished and driving was easy. After about five hundred meters he slipped on to the I90 interstate, moved over to the center lane and drove at a constant speed towards the north. He flipped the radio to an oldies station and his hand beat the familiar tunes from his teen years. The miles started to pass beneath the car wheels and he been driving for about thirty minutes when he moved off the I90 and followed the I94 signposted Milwaukee. Two hours into his journey, now on the I43, he spotted a sign for a grill – Chili's Grill and Bar. A new name, a new experience, and worth checking out for food. He drove off the interstate down the filter lane and turned left.

A hundred meters ahead there was Chili's. He pulled into the car park. A van, a pickup and a couple bikes were all that occupied spaces in the large area of tarmac that had been divided into bays by fading white lines. He climbed the steps, pushed open the red door, and made his way to a booth. He picked up the menu as the waitress brought over a large black coffee. He ordered a stack of pancakes. He stared out of the window into the car park; there was no traffic in this part of the world. He leaned back against the red patent leather seat and closed his eyes. The next moment he heard footsteps, and within seconds, Nestor's smiling face appeared at the other side of the table.

"Hi Midas, how's it going?"

"Where did you come from? Okay, you've been following me from Chicago?"

"No. No. I was just passing. I thought I'd call in for a coffee, and – wow, a surprise - I saw you sitting here. You know, you remember, like the first time we met in the bar," said Nestor.

"Oh yeah," said Midas, "just a coincidence."

Nestor leaned forward; his eyes were smiling and friendly.

"Tell me your story Midas. What's been happening?"

His voice was gentle but authoritative. He sounded a bit like an elderly uncle who was incapable of judgment, but very capable of listening and counseling.

Midas thought to himself. *I guess I've got nothing to lose and I'm not going to get out of here unless I go through the recent events in some detail.*

He told Nestor everything; from the first arrival in Dubai to the visit to Shenzhen, to the applause from the operations team, to the clarity and professionalism of the contract that he put before David. He relived his feeling of confidence that there was a project that he could deliver. He sketched out the morning with David and the charade at the Board meeting. He stopped after about fifteen minutes; he had covered everything, including the challenges with Farood and Ismail.

"So what did we learn Midas?" asked Nestor, who continued to answer his own question. "Many times when we get a setback, when something doesn't turn out the way that we expected, then maybe we can use that as a sign that we could've done something different."

"What do you mean?" asked Midas

"Well. I listen to your story, there's such a lot there. There's so much; what an amazing experience. This is going to be an incredible investment for you Midas. If you allow me, I think I can suggest something for you to ponder.

"Remember the advice that you received on the morning of the Summit. Remember how Peter tried to explain about the feeling of love that you should have as you engaged your partners, your customers, other people you work with; how your service mindset is your guide to providing value. How you needed to be perceptive and inclusive. And how he told you that anyone could be an ally or an enemy.

"At the same time you will know, more than anyone Midas, that your mission now is to build a business, and you also know that your business is built on reputation and references from all of the people who come into contact with you. You have to keep an overview of the greater universe of everyone else who will be connected with you, of the people that you work with as a result of an opportunity.

"How do you think you could have done some things differently, Midas?"

Midas answered, "I am not sure, everything was so well done, it was impossible to fault it."

"Yet you didn't get the contract," said Nestor.

"That's right," said Midas who felt puzzled by the direction this conversation was going.

"Do you think it was possible," contemplated Nestor, "that you approached this business opportunity as a project manager, not as an entrepreneur, a creator.

"You were excited, you were elated, and you were fired up. This was a great opportunity. You knew what you needed to do at the technical level without anyone telling you. And, of course, in that realm you were absolutely second to none. But by slipping into the project manager persona, which was so comfortable for you that you did not realize you were doing it, you became the person that you were in your previous company. In your previous work your task was to implement, as a project manager. This was why you lost sight of some important dimensions.

"Of course this behavior was necessary, in your mind, to win the contract. And you did everything you knew how to do to get it. You needed this contract, you felt you deserved this contract, and this contract was necessary for the survival of your business and the growth of your business. Of course that's obvious. You singularly focused on delivery of the Proof of Concept and you pushed everyone aside to do it, and you delivered. You might not see it that way, but other did, and that's their reality.

"That focus on delivery is not wrong; it's admirable. But look what happened. The key player, who was in the outfield, was the guy that sabotaged the game. You met him, you didn't like him, you didn't relate to him; he was older and not on your wavelength. His IT manager seemed much less than competent in your mind, and you were dismissive of him.

"We communicate in all manner of ways, Midas. Much of our communication is at a subconscious level. The subconscious is much more powerful than words. Our thoughts are vibrations. Taking those interactions with Ismail and his IT guys, your words might have been polite, but your thoughts were negative and extreme to the point where you had written them off as being irrelevant. You were in a world of positive vibration with David and Angus and his team but not with all the people who mattered. When you put out negative energy, expect to receive negative energy in return. You hit somebody and they generally hit you back. Maybe they hit you then, maybe later.

"And that's what happened, Midas. The rejection of your proposal was nothing to do with its technical merit, or your capability. It was to do with the negative mindset that subconsciously you communicated to some people that really mattered in the decision process. Remember what we have discussed: to be a successful entrepreneur, mindset precedes skill set. In your case you relied on skill set and you ignored the mindset of yourself and some of the people around you. The really great entrepreneurs rely on their relations with all people and they are highly tuned to the vibrations of others. They may have good technical skills, but they have superb mindsets.

"Don't worry, it is recoverable. You can see this as an amazing lesson and I'm sure you'll go on to embrace many people within a customer's environment, within your industry environment, within your social environment, as you grow and change some individual aspects of yourself and re-focus.

"This lesson is worth more that the money you would have made. This is just the first step towards becoming a grounded, aware, non-judgmental, and connected human being. You will use your love and consideration and be in contact with the great universe. You might think that some of what I've said needs a lot of thinking about; yes, it does. But many have trod this path that you are on; they trod it, not yesterday, not last year, but through centuries past, and all great men have travelled your journey. You are a man with greatness inside you.

"I hope I did not disturb your coffee. Thank you for telling me your story Midas. I have to ask you to forgive me, I did launch into a monologue."

"No, no, it's ok. You have really got me thinking," answered Midas.

"OK, let me give you time to think, some space right now. We'll talk again. Reach out if you need me." Nestor got up and quietly slipped out of the restaurant.

Midas sat dazed, his mind had gone blank; his coffee was cold, his pancakes had been eaten although he didn't recall eating. He had a whole lot to think about in the days ahead.

He left Chili Grill and walked back to his car. He sat for a few minutes contemplating what happened in Dubai and setting it in the context that Nestor has described. There was much truth in what Nestor had said. They say that hindsight is an exact science – it is true. But now it was time to move forward again.

He pulled out of the car park and headed back to the I43 and turned towards the North and Door County.

It was going to be dark in a little under three hours. He planned to watch the setting sun overlooking the waters of Green Bay WI, an eighty-mile length of water that was parallel and joined to the northern reaches of Lake Michigan.

Ninety minutes later, he was driving in to Sturgeon Bay, which almost bisected the peninsular. He had to find his cabin that would be home for the next three days.

TWENTY THREE

He had rented a small cabin; it was out of season and inexpensive. The owners were happy to have someone in the one-roomed wooden building overlooking the expanse of Green Bay. He was on the edge of a wilderness that looked out at an expanse of water on one side, and hills, trees and an abundance of nature on the other side. He had chosen this place carefully; he wanted a degree of solitude, but also somewhere that was accessible.

He spent the day walking, and thinking. He was contemplative. He thought about how fragile life was. His brush with violence on the streets of Chicago on his return home could have been much worse.

He thought deeply about the many conversations that he had with Nestor.

He read. He was spending more time now trying to understand how the mind worked, and realized that the one part of his education that was missing was the education about himself and how his thoughts and his mind played such a dominant role in the relationships he attracted and the achievements he aspired to. His mind controlled the way he thought about others, and he realized that he was judgmental and critical. He should be more aware of the human frailties in other people. They were living their life, that was their Karma, and it was not his role to judge.

He thought a lot about the concept of love, not in the loving, romantic sense, but the feeling of love and appreciation, and the divine architecture of everything in the world around him. He struggled with the concept of the power of something greater than himself, and the environment in which we find ourselves. He had long ago rejected the concept of religion. While his parents found solace in their religion, it was not for him.

He was moving into the realms of spirituality and motivation. He had come across a book called 'The Secret' which intrigued him. He did not profess to understand it all; he kind of 'got' the Law of Attraction. He was beginning to understand the concept of abundance.

He could clearly distinguish spirituality from religion; he saw the latter as mind controlling and manipulative. He was enthralled by the fact that so many through the ages had been aware of the universal law and had used it to great benefit. They exhibited belief, dedication, perseverance, and discipline. It was clear that the 'law' did not work by itself in creating a person's success, some effort was required, and he smiled at this – effort was what he could supply.

He read great contemporary authors like Bob Proctor and Joe Vitale. He sought out the greats of motivation from the twentieth century, people like Earl Nightingale, Zig Ziglar, and Napoleon Hill.

He found the idea that thoughts are energy to be intriguing. It appealed to his logical mind. But then it became quite scary to think that his thoughts and those of others carry positive and negative vibrations and those vibrations are what attract similar vibrations.

He had listened to Nestor describe how people operate on different vibration levels, and he recalled Nestor's napkin presentation of the concept of a ladder, with low vibration at the bottom and higher vibration at the top, and the way people were stuck at their level, sometimes, from birth to death.

His parents were good people; they worked hard to provide food and shelter. But as they worked, they were clearly operating on a different level of vibration from those who had more creative ability and who had been motivated to run their own small business, and they were in a completely different world from those who created large companies and large enterprises that employed many people.

He could see how, without help and a very different form of education and a different mindset, they had neither the knowledge nor the ability to move from one level to another, and why, in keeping with so many of his people, they were stuck with nowhere to go. He recalled, someone had left copy of a book, 'Rich Dad, Poor Dad' by Robert Kiyosaki, on his table at the Library. He had glanced at the story of two boys, two fathers and a lesson in why the rich got richer and the poor remained where they are.

Now he realized that this was another mindset lesson.

Despite the recent challenges in Dubai, his diminished bank balance, and the fact that prospects of any real work for him was, at best, vague, he felt grateful for being fired from his job. The help that he had received, and the counseling and advice that appeared when he needed it, also overwhelmed him.

He felt optimistic that he could continue to work on his mindset. He felt that his skill set also needed some attention, but not so much as working on his thoughts, his beliefs, and how they motivated his actions and created outcomes.

He realized that while his network was extensive, it was horizontal, and not upward. He had many contacts on his LinkedIn network, but they were people that mirrored who he used to be when he was working in a job. It was clear that he would need to invest time to reach upwards into a new network. He had come to realize that there were certainly different levels at which people operate – that was not being judgmental, but factual.

He certainly needed to move up some rungs on Nestor's Ladder. *But how to do that?*

He had the contacts from in the morning of the Entrepreneurs Summit at the Hyatt, and Lynn kept offering to open doors and make some introductions. Midas thought that this would be a good idea, even if it was to listen to how people, who he perceived to be more successful, actually thought and how they organized and prioritized their life.

He realized that reaching out to people for advice or comment or counsel was the self-selecting process. Those who were too full of their self-importance, too arrogant, too judgmental, and always in a hurry to sprint along the treadmill of life, would not reply to him anyway. Those who were generous in their nature, confident in their self, balanced in their working schedule, would generally find time to help budding entrepreneurs on their road to greatness. These people he jokingly called his 'saints'. The saint-like quality of help and generosity fit them.

Each of his 'saints' helped in their own way; some made time to meet, others would be happy to take a call, some invested time to give tutorials and seminars on a pro bono basis. Someone wrote genuine learned pieces. Right now Midas was becoming blessed with a small but powerful group of influencers and entrepreneurs. Midas thought that he would be able to access quality time and quality advice. He listed networking as a priority when he returned to Chicago.

He emailed Lynn with his networking idea and a positive reply came back in minutes.

He was quietly grateful that Lynn had come into his life and found that he missed her company on this sojourn in Northern Wisconsin. He had not told her about his mishap after she left him at the restaurant. He did not want to bother her with an additional example of the trouble he had found himself in. She had been magnificent in her support on his return; he did not want to spoil that.

He pinged a message to her and got an immediate response. She said she envied his trip to nature and wanted to be with him. He felt shy and embarrassed.

In less than seventy-two hours his break was over. He felt refreshed and relaxed. He felt that he was making progress in learning more about himself. But he also saw that the more he knew, the more he realized he didn't know. Nestor was right; he had started on a personal journey of self-discovery that would occupy the rest of his life.

TWENTY FOUR

Midas had another situation that he had pushed to one side. His lawyers were pursuing his claim against Gravel and his former employers aggressively. It was something that Midas had mixed feelings about. It seemed that more reasonable minds than Gravel's had been brought to bear on the situation at his old company. There had been an acknowledgment that the manner in which one of their star employees had been removed was less than fair and Gravel had come under severe censure for his actions, not just in Midas's case but also in a number of other unfortunate instances.

Midas's lawyer had interrupted Midas's break with some encouraging news. It appeared that a settlement may be reached; it was certainly not headline grabbing but would help Midas during these early days in his new business, and he could pay Ming. They hoped to see a result and a settlement within the next 10 days. Although the figure was not confirmed, it ran well into six figures and, even after the lawyers' no-win no-fee contingency payment, would leave Midas with some working capital and a sensible amount to invest. He had watched the stock market move unrelentingly upwards and dreamed that he could play in that game and reap the benefits.

On his final day, as he was leaving Green Bay, he had lunched on smoked trout and salad at a small cafe just set back from the lake. *This is how my veranda will be when I get my house*, he laughed to himself. He felt comfortable with the thought; he was learning to believe that in the great universe anything was possible.

He headed back on the I-42 when his phone rang. He pulled off at the next truck stop and returned the call. It was Randall. He had been in touch with Randall earlier and there was some optimism that work may come from that direction.

"Hi, how's it going buddy," asked Randall.

"I have some great news. They've given me the green light to move forward on selecting a software platform and I think you can help me"

Randall reported directly to the CIO of global operations and he was speaking with this CIO's authority. Randall was the same age as Midas, and on the times they had met on the conference circuit, they got on well and created a rapport.

"Can you get down to Dallas at the beginning of next week?" asked Randall

"No problem," replied Midas.

"Great. I'll meet you at the airport. We can find someplace local where we can eat and talk. That way you can make it a day trip. Email me your flight"

Midas slipped the car back into gear and drove down the ramp to rejoin the interstate.

What was it that Nestor said? Midas asked himself. "When you open yourself up to receive, the Universe knows, and answers you."

While Midas still had a healthy degree of skepticism about Nestor's theories of the Universe, he was not dismissive. He smiled at receiving the call. Maybe there is something; there are things coming into my life when I need them. Just feels strange. He settled down to the steady interstate drive south, turned up some music and turned his mind off; it had been busy for three full days.

That evening Midas met with Lynn. It was clear that his mind was more relaxed than the last time they met. Over a bottle of chilled Chardonnay, he told her about the call from Randall. Lynn was happy for Midas; she could see that he was being proactive, he was reaching out, and he was getting results. But she worried. All this activity, more pre-sales, and more travelling, would consume money; which she suspected Midas did not have. When she raised the subject Midas brushed it aside with "No worries". It sounded like bravado to Lynn.

The following morning his lawyer confirmed the settlement figure. It was better than Midas had hoped for. Even after the twenty-five per cent commission-based fee, Midas believed he could deposit some funds into an investment portfolio and use the balance very judiciously to fund his business.

He made an appointment at a famous Wall Street banking group, GoldenburgNY to speak to an investment advisor. This was a whole new world for Midas. He gave banks a wide berth. His family never had money and had no use for banks. The little savings Midas had he kept in an interest-bearing checking account. So the meeting with GoldenburgNY was a new departure.

The following morning, he visited the downtown office of GoldenburgNY and met with a young, sharply suited, Brooks Brothers styled 'wealth advisor' – that was the title on his business card. Midas felt like challenging the absurdity of the title but thought better of it. He was probably three years younger than Midas but spoke with a level of confidence about the various products and opportunities and track record of the bank's investment arm. Midas listened and explained that he had a couple of hundred thousand dollars to invest. Midas was disappointed when he worked out the yield. It would represent a minimal contribution to his income each month.

The wealth adviser leaned forward and said, "There is a way that you could increase your earning substantially and in this market it is almost without risk."

Midas listened as the wealth adviser described how Midas could use his basic deposit as the first step in a leveraged portfolio where the bank would lend four times his deposit with minimal interest. That would give him a portfolio of one million dollars and, with the upward trend of the market that seemed to accelerate on a day-by-day basis, he would soon yield a capital gain and dividends far in excess of his initial deposit.

Midas would not need to worry because the money, all one million dollars, will be placed in a discretionary investment account which would be managed on a discretionary basis by the bank's investment arm. At any point Midas could cut his risk by disposing of any part or the entire portfolio and reduce his borrowings. Such action was only a phone call away.

Midas reflected on this and could do the math in his head; it seemed to make sense. Leveraging that initial deposit could make a substantial difference to him over the next two or three years. He allowed himself to smile; pretending to be a dollar millionaire appealed to his vanity.

Midas agreed in principle and promised to return in the next week, once the settlement had been finalized and the funds released.

He left the bank, looked up to the sky, and thought to himself, *The Universe is indeed real, abundance is flowing to me. Already I am a millionaire!*

He had yet to learn, that the great Universe also had some harsh lessons in store for him.

TWENTY FIVE

There are very few successful college dorm or teen rebel entrepreneurs. For every Bill Gates, Steve Jobs, Mark Zuckerberg, there are tens of thousands of aspiring 'wannabe entrepreneurs' on courses as established as those from the prestigious Stamford University to the lowly 'be your own boss' workshops at a local college. Can entrepreneurship be for anyone? Do you need to be rich, come from certain schools?

Research has shown that the average age when someone decides, categorically, that they want to be an entrepreneur, is twenty-seven. The same surveys show that they actually make the break from their employed life around twenty-nine or thirty. Success generally comes slowly, and those who do succeed would probably only consider themselves successful and financially independent a decade later. It appears to be a fallacy that money and family are the breeding grounds for a generation of entrepreneurs. In a UK survey, sixty-five per cent of successful entrepreneurs had no history of business in the family; less than half considered themselves as coming from wealthy backgrounds.

The profile of an entrepreneur has more to do with their personal attributes than their background. Making a break in the late twenties, either by choice, or corporate circumstances, allows the budding entrepreneur to have a bedrock of experience on which to build. Midas was no exception to this. He had been fortunate to lead big, exciting technology programs, and lead them successfully. He had sufficient knowledge of technology to be credible with CIOs, and detailed experience of certain sectors to be valuable. It was a good combination. It was this combination that Randall was interested in.

Randall's company, Airshef, was one of the biggest catering organizations and logistics businesses in the world, servicing aircraft on different continents. Their customer list read like a Who's Who of the aviation industry. Their production facilities were giant factories, not dissimilar to the one that Midas had worked in and advised on in Dubai. Randall's problem was different from that of the Middle Eastern operation. Airshef had grown through a series of strategic acquisitions. It had swallowed up large and small operations until it had gained representation at all the major US airports, US second-tier airports, and major hubs in other parts of the world. The consequence was that the seventy-five major production units that it owned used some thirty different technology applications to control their business operations. There was no commonality, so the economies of scale in buying, logistics, and production methods were difficult to obtain.

The CIO had recommended to the board that rationalization to create and install a single technology platform was essential. This recommendation had been accepted.

There were few enterprise-scale software applications that could manage the complexity and scale of all of the operations that Airshef owned worldwide. A preliminary assessment had ruled out the smaller software suppliers. The favored candidate was SAP, from Germany. While companies like Oracle and SAP supported operations in multiple sectors, and had industry-specific solutions, the Airshef business was, despite its size, a niche sector. It had the complexity of a massive production facility; producing thousands of meals, snacks and the myriad of items loaded for in-flight service, and at the same time it was a highly dynamic environment. Orders were based on an uncertain, ever-changing passenger count, which was being updated until the moment the aircraft closed its doors.

SAP had only once been implemented in this environment. Midas had been intimately involved in that program and, prior to which, he had managed the implementation of another system in one of the largest flight kitchens in the world.

Although he didn't realize it, Midas was a rare gem. He understood the production environment, he understood the airline industry, he understood big Enterprise applications, and had implemented a project using SAP Enterprise software. There were probably no more than 10 people in the world with his experience,

It was as though the stars were coming into alignment. He had left his previous company where he had gained the experience. He had set out on his own journey. He had met with one failure, but now there was an opportunity that seemed to be a perfect match.

Randall explained what was needed. They would take a version of SAP software and implement it in a flight kitchen at Manchester, England. Manchester was big enough to represent a full-service operation but small enough to be of manageable size. It had a willing and able team who were receptive to change and would work with Midas's team to gain experience.

Randall did not probe Midas on his young business; he did not ask how many employees, he did not ask what the balance sheet looked like, or how Midas was being funded. He wanted Midas's unique capability because Randall was charged with future strategy for Airshef. Randall would take a successful rollout of SAP at Manchester to ten more airports. SAP would then be rolled out globally.

Midas could be expected to deliver the first station (Manchester) and, if he could prove that he had the resources, he could deliver the next ten before handing over to a larger established global systems integrator. At that time, with success and team in place, Midas would have been ninety per cent certain that the business charged to execute globally would bid to buy his small consulting company. He would receive a significant multiple of their revenues as a basis for valuation and acquisition. This was what entrepreneur dreams are made of.

Randall asked Midas to assemble a team, give him a budget, and tell him how quickly he could deliver a pre-sales demo system. Airshef would provide access to SAP software and Midas would provide the expertise. They shook hands. Midas headed for his return flight.

Midas vowed that he would deliver this project. Taking his lessons from Dubai into account, he would make sure that he would embrace his relationship with this prospective client. He knew the resources they needed, he knew who they were, and he would have to attract them. He needed a team of four people. One for the complex ordering process and interface with the airline passenger systems, one on finance, one on production, and one for logistics.

TWENTY SIX

It was Saturday. Midas was at his table in the library. He typed out a two-page brief and emailed it to people that he had worked with before and prayed that they were in a position where they could support a pre-sales effort. He also wrote the delivery program and the project plan.

The first challenge was that the people he needed were not based in the UK, but were located in other parts of the world. So Midas would have to bring them together for a very intense period while the pre-sales proof of concept was completed.

See Yung was the first to reply. He was a Singaporean contractor and he was available. He was the guy who had the most complex part of the platform; he would also act as team lead. Angela Lin, based in the West Coast, who would deal with the financials, was the next on the list to answer affirmatively. Then Peter Brady and Alice Young said yes. Each had their questions, individual schedules, and workarounds were needed, but he had a team.

Midas drafted a note to Randall and hit the send button.

His next task was to complete the budget. He would admit afterwards his budgeting was cursory.

Over the next few days the emails went back and forth, and within certain constraints and timings, the team could be assembled to deliver around twelve days of consecutive days of work on the ground in Manchester, preceded by ad hoc days when they would build the core system, on a SAP template, remotely. On site, the team would include some staff from the Manchester base. Conference calls between Manchester, Randall and Midas crystalized the plan. Randall took it to the CIO and got the approval for this first preliminary stage.

Generally, in pre-sales environments, there is no budget; the vendor takes the risk. If Midas demonstrated competence and capability, he would be rewarded with the contract. In this particular case competition did not exist, so specialist was the area being dealt with.

Airshef used its influence with its airline customers to get low-cost or no cost tickets for the team to travel to Manchester, England. Airshef, Manchester, paid local accommodation. Out-of-pocket expenses and a day rate to the team members, had to be borne by Midas. His working capital from his legal settlement had arrived at the right time.

Randall promised that Midas would receive a significant deposit, including reimbursement for efforts during pre-sales, on the signing of the substantive contract. Midas trusted Randall and felt reassured that this was an investment which could not fail over the next weeks and months.

The pre-sales process stretched out longer than the original estimate and Midas had to twist Randall's arm to cover professional expenses. Given the progress that was being made, Randall willingly contributed to the team's costs in Manchester. The team was doing well; Midas was building great relationships, not only with the Manchester team, but with the UK senior management group. He was networking like he'd never networked before. He had learned his lesson and he was enjoying it. He was doing an excellent job in creating a coalition of top people who would support him once the major contract was signed.

It was now well into autumn and, in England, the nights were starting to become darker, the temperature was dropping.

By November, the final tests and demos had been done; the pre-sale system had been used on a number of flights, and had been proved solid, reliable, and accurate. Midas and his team had demonstrated their competence.

Midas and Randall regularly worked into the evening on the complex project and resource plan for the next two years. Success during that period would be well rewarded but in different ways for each of them. Midas would have established his consulting business; Randall would have rolled out a major platform under his initiative. The contract value came to three million dollars; the payment schedules generous to Midas. Randall understood Midas's position, and was prepared to help his friend who had delivered as promised.

It was the week of Thanksgiving in America when they reached the final agreed draft of the contract; Randall received the verbal agreement from his CIO.

Midas had won his first major contract.

Over dinner in the Grand Restaurant of the Midland Hotel in Manchester, they reflected on their respective journeys and how it had brought them together. They toasted the next two years of working partnership.

They were flying home to the USA for Thanksgiving. They were on different flights and the following morning they shook hands at the airport. Randall had the contract in his bag; he had already initialed it. On Monday he would go into the office and collect the CIO's signature. The deal would be done and Midas could start.

Over the Thanksgiving weekend, Lynn and Midas enjoyed a wonderful dinner at Antonio's. They walked in the park, and, for Midas, the world could not be better.

Monday arrived, and by lunchtime, Midas had picked up his phone and replaced it on the table a hundred times but there was no call. He rationalized that Randall had been away the previous two weeks, it was the first day after the long weekend, the CIO would be in meetings, and Randall would need to sit down with the CIO to brief him. He would then collect his signature. The afternoon ticked by; it was the longest afternoon Midas had ever known. Midas busied himself by reaching out to more potential prospects and resources. He was working on the logistics of the project. It would start at the beginning of January. There would be some preliminary work at Dallas Fort Worth and then the team would migrate to the United Kingdom.

It was six o'clock when the phone rang; it was Randall. Midas took the call, anticipating the good news that the contract was signed.

Randall said, "Midas I've not got a signature yet. You are not going to believe what I am telling you. On Friday, my CIO resigned. He came in this morning to collect his things and he was gone."

"He didn't sign before he left?" asked Midas, in hope, yet knowing the answer.

Randall continued, "No he could not, he was already out. There is an acting CIO being appointed this week, but he comes from Germany. He has no background to the work that we been doing. But don't worry, I will see him as soon as he arrives on Wednesday. You're the first item on my agenda. I'll call you on Wednesday afternoon."

TWENTY SEVEN

Midas's intuition had become more acute these days. He picked up the tone in Randall's voice, which did not suggest optimism; or, maybe, he picked up Randall's thoughts and vibrations through the Universe. Midas was not confident.

On Wednesday afternoon Midas received an email from Randall explaining that the new CIO from Germany had told Randall how the enterprise platform should be approached. He was going to use his German team. Randall been moved off the program and Midas's contract had been metaphorically and physically shredded!

Midas was angry. He could not comprehend how such a travesty could happen. He had just invested one hundred thousand dollars of his own money to build a system that demonstrated, without doubt, his team's capability and the efficacy of the software solution they had designed and built. He doubted that there were many people who could do the same.

An entrepreneur needs tenacity, and determination, and the ability to take failure. They need the ability to be knocked down, get up, start over, and win. But this was the second time in the last nine months that Midas had committed his personal resources to the roulette wheel of chance and lost. It was hard for him to comprehend. At least he had his portfolio behind him. He had the capacity to start over.

He realized that he been so consumed in his work, and had spent a long time in Manchester. He had taken no notice of the correspondence and the statements received from the bank, which had remained unopened during his absence.

There was no online banking system by which he could monitor the performance of his portfolio. He had read that the upward trend on the stock market had faltered, and there had been some casualties. But he hadn't worried too much as his portfolio was at the discretion of the experts inside the bank who would protect his downside. That was the deal. Whatever way the market had moved, his investment should be intact.

The following day, over lunch, he broke the news to Lynn. Her response was muted. Her natural optimism was absent. Midas went to lengths to explain that this was just bad luck and could not have been managed differently by anyone.

"Maybe you should get a job!" She sniped at him. She was dismissive. He was not sure whether she was being serious. But she did not smile. The lunch was one of the less pleasant encounters in the many months that they had known each other. That he was not at his best and preoccupied did not help. They skipped coffee and they parted – Lynn to a business conference, again at the Hyatt, and Midas went back to his apartment. He had not moved out of the basement dungeon; he promised himself that when he did move, it would be a move of significance. He pulled off the cap from a beer and gulped down the ice-cold liquid, momentarily allowing the cold alcohol to capture his attention.

The following morning Midas headed to GoldenburgNY. This time he met with a lady called Wendy, who was his new 'wealth advisor'. Smart and chic, she shook hands and smiled. Midas had not asked for a new wealth advisor, she had just been allocated to him she explained. The thought of wealth advisors building up personal and confidential trust and relationships with their clients over time seemed to be something that had passed by GoldenburgNY's attention.

He was shown into a small meeting room. Being a 'millionaire client', he had the privilege of access to the marbled ambiance of the investment bank on the second floor. He was served coffee in a china cup that was a marked difference from the machine-dispensed paper cup on the floor below.

Wendy brought in a folder that had Midas's statement inside. She passed it over the desk, already open for him to see. He looked at the balance, which had been netted by the eight hundred thousand loan that he had taken out. Midas looked and stared. He did not believe the net figure on the bottom of the page. His initial $200,000 had shrunk to $20,000. He turned the pages of the report to see if he could see a different number. This was so far from his expectation that he thought he was looking at the wrong page, no – at the wrong report.

Smiling, inappropriately, Wendy showed what had happened. The recent downturn had been savage in some sectors. These were the sectors in which the bank had invested Midas's money; the losses on the stock had been significant. Two stocks, in particular, had plunged. The net effect was that the value of his portfolio had reduced from the one million dollars, to eight hundred and twenty thousand dollars. Wendy explained that once the portfolio reached a certain level the bank had to liquidate to protect their position.

When the bank loan of eight hundred thousand was taken into account, it netted to twenty thousand to Midas. Wendy pointed out that because his portfolio was now less than one million, he was not entitled to enjoy the privileges and the services of the discretionary investment group. She added that he might think about taking the net balance and investing it in something much safer than stock.

Midas moved from shock to anger.

"You guys had discretion. You are the experts, how could you let this happen?" He was shouting.

"So what happens now if the stock goes up? This could be a blip? You are the investment geniuses; you have the information. You said there was minimal downside because you had experts monitoring it every minute of the day." Midas was grasping at straws.

This situation was so far from Midas's comprehension. How could a bank be so flippant with a result that all but bankrupted him? He sat there in silence, Wendy, having no doubt conveyed this message to other clients before. The bank had gouged out their share and threw the remains to their client. She waited patiently. She maintained her plastic smile.

After a few minutes Wendy said, "I'm sure that you will need a little time to consider, Midas. Maybe you could send me an email in the next couple of days."

And with that remark she stood up, moved to the door, and opened it. Midas's status as a valued investment client of the bank was over.

TWENTY EIGHT

He stepped out onto the footpath outside the bank. He declined the offer of a waiting taxi, and he walked in the general direction of the bar, where months ago, he had met Nestor.

I have been well and truly shafted, he thought. *Shafted in Dubai, shafted in Texas, and now shafted in Chicago. Where do I go from here?*

A little more that forty-eight hours later, Midas walked into a dimly lit bar. He had found this place the night before when he was wandering aimlessly on the outskirts of his neighborhood. The bar was cheap, the furniture was cheap, the booze was cheap, and the clothes that people wore were cheap; the whole place had a depressing air about it. This was a place where people found comfort in an alcohol-induced anesthesia.

Midas didn't care much. He'd moved on to hard liquor, with a very large shot of Bourbon in front of him. He surveyed the peeling wallpaper, smoke-stained ceiling, light bulbs that had not been cleaned for a decade, and the threadbare, worn carpet that ran from the door, stopping short of the linoleum floor that fronted the hardwood, stained bar. This was not Antonio's; this was far removed as you could get from the chic upscale cocktail bars he had frequented with Lynn and her rich friends. Patrons came to this bar with a purpose – to drink. This place was on other side of the tracks, both metaphorically and physically.

Midas sat down at a table, and put a large tumbler of Bourbon in front of him. He had not contacted Lynn since that grim lunchtime meeting, nor had she contacted him. He had seen from her Facebook posts that she was at some glitzy function out of town. She was mixing with the 'haves'; he was mixing with the 'have-nots'. The thought seemed to be very appropriate.

During the past two days he had swung from depression to determination, from anger to tears, and from fear to optimism. He was in a whirlpool of emotions. How could so much go so wrong, in such a short period of time?

He thought he wanted to get out of town, out of the city – just get away. He wanted to leave behind his dingy apartment, leave behind his growing rich, successful network. Forget he had met his mentor, with his sharp casual dress and easy authority. Leave behind the dreams of being a successful, wealthy, entrepreneur. Leave behind Lynn and her smart suits, expensive jewelry, engaging smile, and soft voice always brimming with optimism.

Midas was feeling sorry for himself. There was no way he could go back to Gravel, or to his previous company, or to his previous circle of friends and acquaintances. They were history.

The bar door creaked open; its hinges were already well worn and loose. Every time someone pushed against the door, the hinges all but promised to give way. Midas inwardly groaned. Walking across the wooden floor came Nestor. Midas had given up trying to figure out how he knew where he was. Midas shrugged his shoulders as Nestor sat down opposite him. Nestor ordered coffee. Such an order was blasphemy in this establishment, thought Midas. The waitress gave them a very strange look, turned on her heel and walked back to the bar.

Some minutes later she would appear with a cup of black liquid that looked as though it should be used for lubricating the bearings on the locomotives that clanked past the rear of the bar.

Nestor looked at Midas

"Why don't you leave?" said Midas. "You come with your great ideas, your great theories, and it's all garbage." Midas felt that the words came out of this mouth with a charge of acid. Midas was bitter. He was angry.

His voice rose, "So, do you know what happened? Do you know I was screwed? Screwed over by the bankers, and shafted by a CIO who got himself fired at the wrong time, right? From being a millionaire to a pauper in the blink of an eye. That's what happened."

Midas paused.

He then started to laugh, an executioner's laugh, "It's laughable isn't it, well it's laughable if it wasn't true. It's a disaster."

Midas stopped. They looked at each other. No one spoke.

Nestor broke the silence.

"You are right. And it appears to be a disaster. But when disasters happen you have a choice; you can rebuild or walk away. If you walk away, the debris of your life remains; it gets overgrown with weeds. Its once vibrant life is choked, and it remains that way until it eventually turns to dust. Is that what do you want, Midas? To be a decaying, overgrown derelict; one that had so much potential but is now just waiting to turn to dust. Or do you want to rebuild?

Midas looked at him. "How do you rebuild a city when the bank vault is empty?'

"Good question."

"Your bank vault, Midas – it is not completely empty of money. There are still a few banknotes on the floor, so maybe you pick those up to start with. Keep those safe. But your value, Midas, is not in your physical self. In the same way as the vibrancy of the city that was destroyed and is being rebuilt was not bricks and mortar but the soul of the city. That soul was not destroyed.

"Your body is only your vehicle through life, your mind is your strength, and your power is your motivation. Your motivation is driven by your thoughts. There is a saying, 'As you think, so shall you become'. It is a fundamental truth."

Midas was slowly turning his glass in his fingers, rotating it on the bare wooden table, staring at it. Maybe he was expecting it to turn into a crystal ball, showing him his new road to Nirvana.

Nestor looked at him and said, "The past months, though very difficult for you, will prove to be some of the most valuable months in your life, Midas. There are lessons to take from failure. Sometimes the lessons are related to mindset, sometimes they're related to skill set, and sometimes they are both.

"Without a complete dissection of the corpse and an extended autopsy, what are the obvious things that we can learn from the experience?" asked Nestor.

"I don't know," said Midas. "You are so clever, why don't you tell me?"

While there was a hint of sarcasm in his voice, inwardly he was begging Nestor to throw some light on what had gone so disastrously wrong.

TWENTY NINE

Nestor responded, "Okay, we talked about the Dubai experience before. There you stepped back into your comfort zone, as a project manager, and didn't behave like an entrepreneur building a business and being sensitive to all of the people around him. You drove hard and fast, with some contempt for those who could not stay with your pace, or could not fully understand what you were doing. The fact that they were being shown up to be less than competent by your actions did not occur to you, or if it did, it didn't matter to you.

"You were right, you were going to deliver, and you were on a mission. You relied on David and Angus, and their colleagues in their part of the business, to carry you forward. But you made the fundamental mistake of not understanding who the gatekeepers were, and who would influence the final decision, and you lost. That's history, but it's a great lesson. You showed a fantastic amount of initiative and creativity, the essential characteristics of an entrepreneur. But you demonstrated a lack of awareness, which you know, and which you can address.

"The Airshef project, you delivered perfectly. There was nothing that you did wrong. Or so it seemed. Technically, you did amazingly well, and so did your team. Randall was the apparent gatekeeper and influencer and he was on your side; he was cheering for you, and he wanted the contract go to you. You didn't know that another crisis, another political play, was being acted out between Germany and Dallas. The combatants were two CIOs – Randall's boss in Dallas and an emerging star, who had become darling of the board, based in Germany. Your CIO sponsor was actually fired on the Friday after Thanksgiving.

"What could you done differently? You could have checked out the politics of the business at the higher level, but that would've been very difficult. You're an outsider, and you were working for the US team. To gain insight into what was happening in Germany would have been almost impossible. At another time, in another place, you might be more circumspect, you might be more perceptive, you might look beyond what the seeming environment is, and see storm clouds gathering on the horizon, period, but who knows?"

Midas took some solace from Nestor's objective assessment of Dubai and Dallas, and accepted that they were lessons well learned. Under the circumstances and particularly where his immature mindset was still being developed, it could be no different. He nodded a thank you.

Nestor then continued, "The bank experience was very different. You hung yourself!"

"What do you mean?" asked Midas, his teeth gritted; even the mention of the bank affected his mental state. His voice and attitude became immediately agitated and aggressive.

"Let me explain," said Nestor. "First of all you need to understand what banks are. Banks are businesses; they exist to make profit. The days, if ever they existed, when the bank manager was a local, respected, individual to whom anyone could turn to for advice and where they could be assured of security and a responsibility for taking care of their funds have gone. Maybe that was always a fairy tale, but it has been the image that we liked to believe."

He continued, "Banks today have targets for revenue, for profit, for products sold. The title wealth advisor is a euphemism for a salesperson. You walked in with your settlement check like a lamb to the slaughter. The salesperson saw you coming. When he found that you wanted to invest, he saw a rich opportunity. It was an immediate win for the bank. It was all upside for them, and downside for you. You were cooked!"

'How do you mean? It seemed to be a great deal," retorted Midas

"I don't want this to become an economics lecture," said Nestor, "but the bank played your ego. They made you feel like a millionaire despite having only twenty per cent of that figure they loaned you. They charged you interest, and invested the funds. They would charge transaction costs and administrative costs on all they did. You gave them discretion, so they could make as many trades as they wished, charging you for every transaction; and if the portfolio continued upwards then they continued to collect interest and transaction fees and, admittedly, you would have seen a gain. But it would have had to climb a long way for that gain to be material after you netted off your interest and loan.

"On the slightest downturn, they ditched your stock to protect their loan, charging you more transaction fees, by the way, on the disposal. They watched until the balance of your account approached the amount of the loan and then closed your trading account. They handed you the difference, the meager sum that was left.

"When you heard that they had discretion to manage your funds, you assumed they would manage your portfolio in your favor; discretion meant the discretion to protect their position is not yours.

"You failed yourself, Midas; you let ego drive the decision. Then you allowed distraction and procrastination to stop you monitoring the performance of a very high-risk plan.

"Maybe there were other subconscious limiting beliefs that were at play. Limiting beliefs such as not good enough, not deserving, not worthy, fear of success. There are so many limiting beliefs we carry forward in our subconscious. The investment was likely to fail from the outset."

Nestor paused and looked at Midas. Midas was bowed, looking into his drink.

Nestor added, "I don't think we should deal with it now, not today, you've had enough feedback right now, but you should understand more about the limiting beliefs that we all carry with us from childhood and how we can address that and then remove them. If we do not remove them they will always be an impediment to our success."

Midas could now see his foray into the investment world and his transient status as a millionaire for what it was. He had not understood, nor chosen to understand, the risks involved. He was carried on the fantasy and glitz that the bank had woven into his tapestry, and it was all an illusion.

He smiled to himself. With the perspective of his recent adventures painted the way that Nestor had painted them, with colors of objectivity and love, he felt grateful for the experience.

He had to figure out when next. He was still broke. He had no job. The winter was cold outside. And while he dwelt well on these questions, Nestor quietly left.

Midas took his phone from his pocket. There was a message. He opened it, wishing that it was from Lynn. It was not.

It was a message that would take him on a new stage in his adventure of life.

It read

"Midas, can you swim?"

THIRTY

Midas slipped his arms into his coat, dragged his scarf around his neck and put on his baseball cap. He was ready to step out into the cold night chill. Unusually, he was sober. The last few nights had been spent in the bar, and had seen him leaving at closing time, zigzagging his way along with the icy footpath in a manner that only a man in a semi-drunken stupor can achieve. Tonight, he was clearheaded; the earlier conversation with Nestor had gone a long way to putting things in perspective, but – at the same time - did nothing to relieve his anxiety about the next weeks and months.

"Midas, can you swim?"

The message was enigmatic, but that was typical of the sender. It had come from George, a friend of his father's who, Midas would guess, was now sixty-something. George was a man's man. He was a larger-than-life character whose vocabulary had been polished with expletives from every oil rig, oil field, and the bars that accompanied them, spread across the southern United States, Mexico, Philippines, and the North Sea. There were a few places that were associated with oil that George had not visited. He had started as a roughneck and had worked his way to a tool setter and then to a rig operations manager. He was as hard as nails, but Midas had seen the other side of him. Beneath that exterior, he was man with a big heart. He made a lot of money; he drank a good proportion of it, and spent a decent percentage on women of various nationalities, yet he had given much to charity.

When Midas was much younger he remembered George's occasional visits to his father. George would walk to the park in the warmer months of the year and buy ice cream for the children who were playing there. He didn't care how many came, the more the merrier.

Midas could remember on the one occasion he had gone with his father George had bought thirty-five ice creams for the kids in the park. He would lend a helping hand to anyone, whether they were crossing the street, or when they were fitting shingle to the wall of their house. He had an incredibly generous nature.

His life had been a cauldron of happenings. There had been adventure, travel, and sadness. George had lost his sweetheart in a road accident. The driver who had run into George's girl was lucky to escape from George's insane anger – only the cops had saved him. There were times, in the summer, when he would sit on the steps at Midas parents' house clutching a bottle of beer, looking melancholy, and his blank eyes and mind occupying some faraway place.

The message "Midas can you swim?" was typical. George would not to use four words if two would suffice. He made the assumption that he could communicate in the briefest form.

Midas decided that he would wait until the morning to respond.

It was 10 o'clock when Midas, with his third coffee of the morning in his left-hand, tapped out a reply to George. With George's sense of humor, it was necessary to be equally obtuse in a reply.

Midas wrote the message "I swim like a water-logged sponge in an Atlantic gale."

"Good, you're just the man! Will call, George," was the reply.

Midas was no wiser. Knowing George, the call would come within the next hour

Midas busied himself answering emails. He had been prolific in his dispatch of mails in recent months, when he was prospecting for work, but he had set the follow-up of many of these to one side while he was in Manchester. Even today, there was still a trickle of replies, comments, and notes of encouragement. There was no indication of any work on the horizon. Midas's vision of an international consulting organization was far over the distant horizon as it could ever be, yet for some reason, he retained a feeling of optimism that something, from somewhere, would appear. He didn't realize that George held the key.

His phone rang, it was George.

"Midas, what are you up to? Have you got some time to help Uncle George?"

"Tell me more George," asked Midas. "As it happens I have time, at least some time. What can I do?"

"Well it's like this," said George, "I bought an old yacht, I know it sounds strange. I haven't sailed for fifteen years but I was kinda thinking that it would be nice to have somewhere to escape to and live aboard for a while. She is down in Florida. "

He continued, "Now here's the deal, I have to leave for Caracas in a couple of weeks, but there's quite a bit at work that I'm having done on her. I can't be there myself. I have been scratching my head thinking who might want to spend a few weeks, maybe two or three months, living on-board a yacht in the glorious Florida sunshine, and keep an eye on the contractors as they come and go. I thought that you might be the man."

The thought of an escape from the northern winter and the memories in Chicago suddenly appealed to Midas. He thought of Lynn but then dispatched that thought from his mind. Midas was sure that Lynn had given up on him.

George continued, "She's forty-two feet long. She has everything on board that you need, and I think everything works. She's in a marina where you got all facilities that you need, including Wi-Fi for that goddamn computer of yours. And I can give you some beer money and cover your expenses if you can do this for me Midas."

As Midas listened to George his escape plan materialized in his mind. He could get out of this dingy apartment, away from the cold weather and head south. He would join the snowbirds; he laughed to himself.

He rationalized that with access to the Internet he could continue with a partially credible pretense that he was researching and building his business.

"Sounds like a plan, George. When do you want me there and where do I go? You know that I don't know one end of the yacht from another and the last time I was floating on water it on was an inflated inner tube and I was seasick."

"I'll send you a ticket," said George. "I know it's a long journey, but you'll be able to get off and stretch your legs every so often."

Midas groaned inwardly. He remembered that George hated flying; he loathed it with a passion and tolerated air travel only to get to his work outside mainland North America. Internally, he used Greyhound. As a child, George had marveled at the coming and going of the Greyhound bus at the depot near his home. He watched destinations of cities and places far away. George was captivated by long-distance bus travel. And now he wanted or expected Midas to travel the length of the country in the same manner that George would. Midas guessed that the journey would take around 30 hours and cringed.

They chatted for a few more minutes and George signed off saying, "I'll organize everything and I'll see you in Florida."

Where in Florida? Midas had no idea.

THIRTY ONE

Midas thought to himself that maybe he should tell Lynn about his plans but he was hesitant to pick the phone or send her a text. He didn't feel worthy; he had moved off into a completely different place than the one that she inhabited.

The next day he gave notice to his landlord, who accepted his leaving without comment except to say "Pay to the end of the month and don't forget the electric".

Midas bagged his accumulated detritus of bachelor living, and donated some clothes for the charity shop. He thought that it was a good idea to limit his wardrobe to the Florida climate. He would keep one warm jacket for the journey because it would remain cold until he got south of Nashville.

True to his word George was on the phone the following day "Everything is fixed, pick your ticket at Greyhound, you'll get down here in around five days' time and I leave for Caracas a couple of days later. Once you get to Tampa you will need to get out to Palmetto and find Regatta Bay Marina. Call me when you arrive; better still, call me on your journey down then we can make sure you don't get lost. Make a note of the boat's name, she's called Bolero – 'cos she will lead you a dance." He laughed at this own joke. "You will find her at berth Z20 but I'll be there at the marina to meet you."

Midas's finger hovered over the SEND button; he was hesitating. He had written a short note to Lynn to say that he was leaving for some months and he had a new project. He didn't expand on the last statement.

"What the hell?" he said to himself and pressed SEND. He wasn't expecting the reply, which came back almost immediately,

"OMG let's meet before you go. You can't leave; I can't let you leave without seeing me."

Midas was surprised but felt pleased. He had heard what Nestor had said about childhood scripting, and of programming the mind, and he tried to suppress and delete his feelings and emotions. He was only partially successful. He was feeling apprehensive, would she come to meet him – really?

He didn't want to go to Antonio's so he chose a small coffee shop off the common. Midas suggested they meet the following day.

"Perfect," was Lynn's reply.

Midas stayed in during the evening, he slept well. It wasn't the sleep of a condemned man; it was the sleep of a potential escapee! It was probably the best sleep he had had for many weeks.

He got up early, slipped on a tracksuit and outer pants, a top and some gloves and went out for a jog. This was willpower over physical capability; he had not run for weeks or months, he couldn't remember. He was reduced to jogging very slowly, far removed from the graceful running style that he perfected and enjoyed daily until the middle of last year, when he allowed his work, his 10 to 12-hour day, and single-minded focus on delivery to push any other form of activity out of his schedule.

He stayed out for 45 minutes; it was long enough for him to feel that he accomplished something and to remind his stiffening muscles that to enjoy exercise it was something that you did regularly.

He was sitting in the corner of the coffee shop looking at the menu cover that described the establishment as 'shabbily chic'. This was a triumph of marketing speak over reality. The place was shabby; tables and chairs had long since seen a coat of paint or varnish, paint chipped pillars supporting the wooded beamed roof sat on a wooden floor. It was untidy and uncared for, but the atmosphere was amazingly warm, comforting and friendly.

Lynn appeared; she wore black tight jeans with knee length boots and a big chunky red sweater, a sweater that seemed to be fashionably three sizes too big. Given the temperature outside Midas could only guess how many layers it covered. Her sweater and jeans were topped off with her black mock fur hat, under which she had tucked her hair.

As always, she looked a picture of elegance. Midas stood up, unsure whether to put out his hand as a greeting, when she leaned over put her hands on his shoulder and lightly kissed his cheek.

"I've missed you," she said. "You disappeared. You were ignoring me; I think you must have left me for some other woman that you met on your travels"

She laughed.

Midas stuttered, "N…no, n…nothing like that."

Beyond those words, Midas couldn't reply; his mind could not articulate any words that he felt might be suitable. He didn't know whether he was embarrassed, flattered, pleased or simply dumbstruck at her comment.

They ordered. Lynn had a skinny latte and Midas an Americano.

Lynn leaned forward and looked at Midas. There was a torrent of questions all delivered in Lynn's normal, excited manner, "Come on, and tell me what's this all about. Where are you going? What are you doing? Who are you going with? When can I visit?" she was leaning forward looking at him intently and he was unsure how much of the truth he should tell her.

He was moving from a dingy basement apartment to live on the water, in some Marina on the coast of Florida. He could make the story sound a romantic, idealized, nautical adventure, with a casual freedom that was yearned for by many. Or he could tell the truth, that in reality he was dossing on a friend's boat, supervising the coming and going of workers, after which he would have to leave and start over once again. Diplomatically, he chose a middle ground

"A friend from a long time ago has acquired a yacht. He is travelling. He wants a lot of work to be done on it and it wants me to supervise. He wants me to control the contractors and make sure everything is delivered on time and to budget. It's a 42-foot ketch (Midas wasn't quite sure what that meant) with everything, all mod cons on-board and it sounds as though it can be great adventure in the sunshine."

Lynn clapped hands, "Wow, that's so amazing. What a fabulous adventure. Once you are down there and you've got yourself established you must invite me to visit. I've always wanted to go sailing." Midas groaned inwardly; all he knew was that yachts generally had a sharp end and a blunt end, had lots of pieces of rope attached to various things, and two very large poles which were generally referred to as masts." Beyond that, his nautical knowledge ended. The thoughts of Lynn flying down from Chicago to Florida with the expectation of sailing in the blue ocean, standing on the bow with a hair blowing in the breeze and her whole body being kissed by the sun, save small areas that were covered in a minuscule bikini, was regrettably something of a fantasy. But he didn't want to burst that bubble and he nodded with false enthusiasm.

They chatted for an hour. Lynn regaling more stories from the business world, Midas occasionally interjected. Ever so quickly, their meeting was over.

They stood up, Lynn smiled "Remember, I want to know you have arrived safely, and I want to know all about your yacht, and where you go sailing. And stay away from all of those young ladies in bikinis."

She laughed as she gave Midas a hug before turning on her heel and walking quickly out of the coffee shop. Midas picked up the bill and groaned inwardly, the place may be shabby, but the prices weren't. *Never worry*, he thought to himself, he paid the waitress including a tip that was the least he thought was respectable and he left.

The following day with his bags outside the door, he slammed it with a finality that felt good. Setting off, he climbed the stairs for the last time, and left by the front door. He hailed a cab to take him downtown to the Greyhound bus station. He threw the bags into the trunk, climbed in, and told the driver where to go. He settled back.

Midas was not ungrateful to his father's buddy for helping to escape his predicament, but could hear the question going around in his head, *what have you planned, George? What have you really done?*

Unknown to Midas, George had unlocked a new door, a door that one day, would lead Midas along a road that even in his wildest dreams he could not have seen.

But first, Midas had to put up with over thirty hours on a bus. That experience was about to start

THIRTY TWO

It was a long torturous journey. The cities rolled by as in a slow motion film: Indianapolis, Louisville, Nashville; Midas changed buses in Nashville. Birmingham, Montgomery, Tallahassee and eventually Tampa.

At each city, and at times in between, there was an obligatory stop. At major depots there was a thirty to forty-minute break.

Midas had hit Birmingham, AL, and Montgomery, AL in the early hours of the morning. Greyhound depots are far from salubrious; they are the haunt of the flotsam and jetsam of life – watching or passing travelers, students travelling on tight budgets, less well-off families, and old seniors trying to relive the glory days of the Greyhound before air travel dominated the continent.

Each depot was like its own movie set, with resident characters and a transient cast that come on stage, played their part in an imaginary ritual, and moved on. Some stages were desolate, some intimidating, and some dark and foreboding where staying on the bus would be the lesser of two evils.

Midas concluded that the bus took the best exit from the depot – as it left.

At Louisville a tall bearded guy, dressed in a long great coat with a black scarf around his head, boarded the bus, dropped into the seat next to Midas and immediately starting shouting that he had been robbed outside the bus depot. After the initial outburst, he slumped in the seat, wrapped a headset over his scarf and pressed the earpieces to his head, and spent the duration of the trip playing a PlayStation Portable that he claimed to have found in a trashcan.

While waiting in Nashville, Midas sat on a cold concrete bench when a guy lunged over him. He was sporting a ponytail and Hell's Angels leathers; he was bumming a cigarette. His jacket bore his name – Winston. Winston deposited his substantial body on the concrete slab next to Midas and started to narrate his life's story. Midas was trying to imagine the adventure that was going to unfold. He did not need to think too hard; Winston began his practiced monologue. Winston hailed from Alaska, where he lived in a remote cabin with no electricity, and was on the Greyhound because his Harley had broken down. Winston's fantasy took him to New York (ex-gang leader), Canada, Europe (seaman), Washington (bored), and now he was in Nashville to celebrate 'his' music. After ten minutes Winston took off to regale another passer-by and try to bum another smoke.

Midas's seatmate from Nashville was a 38-year-old homeless mother who had ears pierced with whalebones (or so she claimed) 'to ward off spirits'. She was heading south to visit her daughter.

They were all part of life's rich tapestry.

From Tampa, Midas switched to Amtrak trains for a couple of hours and was finally deposited at the 8th Ave / Riverside Drive Station, Palmetto, just minutes' walk from the Regatta Point Marina on the Manatee River. He arrived at the Marina gates, and the clubhouse, devoid of spirit and humor, just to be grabbed in a big bear hug by George.

"How was the journey? Great, yeah? I love those Greyhounds. Do you know I've done over two hundred thousand miles on Greyhound? Got a Silver Badge to prove it." Midas could not spirit up the energy to have an argument.

"It was fine George. Can only be bettered by a cold beer."

"No problem – AND the good news is I have you a real bed for tonight, pointing to the nearby motel. You can move onto the yacht tomorrow."

Midas hauled back the curtain and looked out of the window of his motel room. It was on the third-floor and it overlooked the marina. The bed had been a welcome respite from the Greyhound seat: he had slept solidly for twelve hours, he felt refreshed. He stretched and gazed out at what seemed to be the forest of masts, sails, and lines pointing skyward; he guessed he could see a hundred or more yachts. They stretched into the distance.

This was the first time he had visited a marina and did not appreciate the size of some of these facilities. He knew from the marina's website that they had berths for three hundred yachts. Most seemed to be of the thirty to fifty-foot range, just like George's – that was forty-two feet. Some, particularly those nearest to him were at least seventy or eighty-foot long. There was a lot of money tied up in the water.

He moved from the window, he had already showered dressed and had his coffee. He picked up his bag and his backpack and headed down to the lobby.

George was sitting in an armchair reading the newspaper when Midas appeared. He jumped up, shook hands, and put his arm over my Midas's shoulder. "Let's go man, it's going to be a great, great day."

Outside, they jumped into a big, red Ford pickup that George had rented, then drove to the entrance to the marina. He pulled into a vacant space near the gate to the jetty. They got out. Midas grabbed his bag from the back and George picked up a tool bag and an icebox. They headed down to the jetty gate.

A security guard, dressed in whites - white shorts, white shirt - opened the gate. He smiled and nodded at George. "Still working on her, I see," he said.

"Yeah, but my friend here is taking over. Midas meet Kurt, Kurt meet Midas." Kurt nodded and they shook hands.

"Any time you need something, let me know," said Kurt, and with that he opened the gate and George and Midas walked down the slope to the wooden jetty.

The walkways formed a giant herringbone pattern. The main jetty was the backbone and the fingers were the rib bones. The jetty led to 'fingers' or 'slips against which the yachts were tied, or 'berthed'.

It was a hundred-meter walk along the jetty to the 'Z' finger, which was at ninety degrees to the jetty. It was another fifty-meter walk, along the finger, to Z20 where Bolero was berthed.

Midas thought to himself; he had no idea what he was doing in Florida and even less idea what he was going to do sitting on a yacht for the next few months (or longer?).

THIRTY THREE

Midas was amazed at the variety: different sizes, shapes and colors. The age of yachts clearly varied. There didn't seem to be one that was the same as another. Some had single masts, some had two masts, some had the steering wheel ('helm') at the rear of the yacht in what are called 'stern' (rear) cockpits, and some helms were in the center of the yacht in a raised cabin called a pilothouse. The variety was endless.

They arrived at George's yacht. Midas saw the name on the stern; it read 'Bolero'. She was moored with her stern (the rear) pointing onto the finger and Midas thought, even with a non-nautical eye, that she looked a very beautiful yacht.

"She's a Hawaiian ketch," said George. "Ketch because she has two masts, the rear one being smaller than the forward one. There have been hundreds of them made; they're roomy, and solid. They don't sail too quickly but they're sturdy and they will get you home."

"This is your new home," said George as he slapped Midas on the back. Midas winced.

Bolero had a white hull and cream topside; at the stern she had a big wooden rudder, which was topped by a long, wooden, varnished, and highly polished handle, known as a tiller, which dropped into aft cockpit. There was a fixed canopy over the entrance to steps leading below decks. George pointed to what was known as the 'pulpit', a long narrow platform which protruded forward from the front of the yacht. "Great place to watch dolphins," laughed George.

Leaving their shoes on the finger, they climbed aboard. This was the first time that Midas had been on the yacht and he immediately felt the movement. Even when tied up, a yacht is always moving. A yacht in the water is never stable.

"Don't worry, you'll have your sea legs in no time and then you won't notice the movement," pronounced George, with the authority of an old sea dog.

Down below was compact, and cozy. The walls were teak paneled and gloss varnished, everything gleamed. The round windows, known as portals were brass. Ahead of them Midas could see a curtain which was open to reveal a large double bed. Coming towards him from the bedroom, the toilet, or 'heads' as it was known on a boat, was to the right hand side. A closet was on the left. In the middle of the cabin was the dark blue cushioned sofa to the left hand, and a dining table and seating to the right. Alongside him, to his left, at the bottom of the stairs, was the galley - a sink, freezer, cooker, a hob, and storage. To his right was a bank of instruments, switches, radios, and gauges - all of which were meaningless to Midas. The total living area was about thirty-five square meters. This was Midas's home for the foreseeable future.

On the table were sheets of paper with lists of what Midas assumed to be the jobs that he was supposed to supervise. He had some learning to do.

There was a knock on the cabin top. "Hello George. George, are you there? Can I come aboard?" George answered, "Hang on, will be right up."

George led the way up the cabin steps into the rear cockpit. Midas followed. Waiting to come on board was a bald, tanned Asian-looking guy, who was dressed in cut-offs and a T-shirt. He weighed no more than about 140lbs. The Asian held out his hand to Midas, and Midas shook it; George patted the Asian on the back and said, "Midas, meet David. David's your man. He's the guy who's got the workers that will do that list of jobs that you see below. After a few minutes of nautical chitchat, which was meaningless to Midas, David jumped off onto the jetty, "See you tomorrow, Midas," he waved and was gone.

The following day Midas saw George off at the airport. George's company insisted that he would leave the Greyhound bus to somebody else and he would catch a connecting flight to Miami and then on to Caracas.

David, with two of his workers, came down to Bolero and busied themselves for a few hours each day, lifting floorboards, opening cupboards, putting their heads into small holes, with a lot of grunting and swearing. They emerged with grubby hands and parts that clearly needed to be replaced. They would repeat the cycle over and over, during the following days and weeks.

Midas had found that the clubhouse had excellent Wi-Fi; the lounge was quiet except on the weekends. He had charmed Claire, the office lady, to allow him into use a small anteroom, and from there he continued to reach out to people. But more often than not he would be reading.

He wrote himself a reminder to contact Lynn.

Nestor had emailed him a reading list of books and a list of websites that he advised him to subscribe to. These covered a wide range: Entrepreneurship and Personal Development, and what Midas called Emotional Skills that Nestor had suggested were essential for him to progress to his full potential.

He was beginning to understand the concept of Energy, the Law of Attraction, and how his subconscious was the driver of his behavior. He also read about reprogramming the subconscious and he wished he had more help on this. He was becoming excited by what he read and could understand what Nestor had told him at their first meeting – that we all have infinite potential, and we can achieve great things. We all have undiscovered talents and greatness.

THIRTY FOUR

Midas made friends with a number of the yachties (sailors) who were nearby to Bolero, and he met others who frequented the restaurant and the bar. They were all incredibly generous with their knowledge and experience, and some came down to Bolero to explain to Midas what the job list really meant. Midas felt that he was on a steep learning curve. He enjoyed every minute of it; this environment was completely different from anything that he had experienced in his life before, and far removed from Chicago.

Midas had friendly neighbors. His nearest regular 'live aboard', as yacht-borne residents were called, was Mike. Mike was a Canadian, medium build, and tanned; Midas guessed he was around 45. Mike was on board a Beneteau 45 Catamaran called 'Mystique', at Z14, just four berths away from Midas.

About a week after Midas had moved onto Bolero, Mike asked him over to Mystique for a beer. It was early evening. The evening was cool and comfortable after the intense daytime sun. Mike and Midas were sitting on the afterdeck below a hard canopy. The table in front of them was stocked with beer, ice, and delicious salads, breads, and burgers, all sent from the Marina's restaurant.

Mike worked part-time; he had built up an e-commerce business, importing products from Asia and reselling in the United States. It was a successful business and was managed by a small staff in Fort Lauderdale. Midas had guessed that Mike was financially in a much better shape than himself (which, with Midas's recent track record, was not difficult). The fact that he was sitting on an almost new catamaran with a list price approaching a million bucks was testament to Mike's success.

They talked about life, the universe, and yacht stories – the latter left

Midas at a disadvantage, but he covered himself by asking lots of questions, which Mike was more than pleased to elaborate on. They talked about where they had been, where they hoped to go. Midas was being circumspect about his life story and was more intent on listening.

Mike's exploits, and his e-commerce business, had been a roller coaster, thankfully with more ups than down. Midas covered his story by saying that he was on track to become a successful entrepreneur and his time in the marina was planning time for his next venture. Mike toasted him on that score. He had told Mike that he had a couple of 'near misses', and that he was confident that next time he would make it. Midas felt that his comments to Mike might sound like bravado, but it was really a deep feeling of success awaits.

Mike listened to Midas. He was looking at this cell phone. "I am just checking dates," he apologized, and then added, "you need to meet a good friend of mine, Alisa, she's going to be here in a couple of days. She's a business wiz. She has some great advice; she's 'been there and done it'. And she is a really nice person too. Come over and join us for lunch."

Midas looked forward to the lunch date.

Two days later, just after noon, he appeared at the stern of Mystique. Casual attire was the dress of choice in the Marina, khaki shorts and a t-shirt was acceptable and comfortable. Mike and a lady, who Midas guessed was Alisa, were already on the upper deck of the yacht, looking over the marina. Mike called down.

"Come aboard, grab a beer and come up."

Midas climbed the stairs to the bridge, an ice-cold beer in hand.

"Midas meet Alisa. Alisa meet Midas. I was just telling Alisa about my new neighbor from Chicago. She said she was looking forward to meeting you."

Alisa stood up and reached out to shake Midas's hand. She was graceful. Early 30's, long blond hair and slim silhouette – she looked like she had stepped off a page in Vogue. She wore fashionable beige shorts, and a Fendi-styled white blouse with an upturned collar, and a necklace of large multi-colored glass charms. Her Hermes Birkin bag matched her green shoes (that had been left on the deck below). A beige scarf around her waist completed the fashionista ensemble.

Her accent was not Southern, and Midas was trying to place it when she said, "I am from your neck of the woods; well, nearly. I hail from Wisconsin. I admit I left a long time ago, but I am still proud of my home."

"Now you are here, we can eat," said Mike as he stood up. "Lunch is in the salon today; we can have the luxury of aircon for a while." He led the way to the main deck and the salon.

Once again, the Marina's restaurant had done Mike proud. An extensive cold spread graced the table with a couple of bottles of excellent Chardonnay to accompany the food.

Soon they were deep into the challenges of creating a business and of being an entrepreneur. Alisa was very articulate; she was on her third venture, and her first business had petered out. It was an online venture and, as she admitted, not thought-out, and unappealing. Her second business had promise – a great promise – but her investor had, as she said, screwed her by legal means, and stolen her idea. She had started again and was now on her way to her first $million.

Midas listened intently. Alisa was clearly a very intelligent and accomplished lady. Before she had embarked on her entrepreneurial ventures she had worked on Wall Street. She had a portfolio of Ultra-High Net-Worth clients, and had also worked around government circles. She had been involved in major negotiations in Asia and had spent time in Myanmar, as it was opening up. She had, briefly, been a partner in a business in China.

Midas asked, "Alisa, if you were advising someone starting out, someone who wanted to be an entrepreneur, what would you advise them to do? You have clearly been in the frontline, what are the big lessons?"

"Umm. That's a big question, you know? Stanford could fill a whole undergrad course with that," she laughed. "Ok, let me try – and this is for real, I will give you my one-hand version. That's five points, all my fingers," she held up her hand and she leaned forward, elbows on the edge of the table;

"First, and I know this sounds perverse, don't be surprised if you fail. Too many young entrepreneurs start out on their dream business and never, for one moment, believe it will fail. Don't get me wrong, I am not saying that they do not have confidence in their idea, and I am not saying their idea is necessarily a flop. But statistically, most start-ups fail. And many young entrepreneurs reach the point of failure and then give up. They go and find a job and spend the rest of their life being frustrated. They end their careers as entrepreneurs just as it was starting. Mind you, if that was their mindset, they should never have started out in the first place.

"Second, work damned hard. And I mean hard. That means, no parties, no clubbing, no weekends, no holidays, and sometimes no sleep. You are going to be working on your business before others are awake, and you are still going to be working on it when they are sleeping. You are giving birth to an idea, you are creating something that will change people's lives – there is no time to wait. Do it, and do it now. In creating your business, you will have to take your idea from a vision that has no substance to a business that has form and function, and that journey is a long one, believe me.

"Third, you have to be a risk-taker. You cannot play it safe. There will come a moment when you may have to bet your life savings, and if you are not prepared to step forward and put your money where your mouth is, then do not expect anyone else to.

"You are going to burn your bridges – leave whatever job you have behind. You will leave friends behind too; they will not understand you, they will be in their jobs, and in their 'normal' life. You have to tread your path. And it can be lonely at times. That's when you will draw on your inner strength, your faith, your passion – but I will come to that in a moment.

"Next, don't trust anyone. You are in business; it's a shark tank."

THIRTY FIVE

Alisa was now animated and intense. She was looking at the two men with a force of conviction.

"Look at me. I was naïve. I took my idea from just that, an idea, to a product, and marketing and business plan, provisional contracts, and I was ready to launch. I needed funds. I took the first investor that came forward. He promised me all the money I needed; he did not want other investors involved. I was seduced by the idea that now my baby had life, and I could launch and expand."

She paused, her voice softened and her eyes dropped. Did Midas see a tear in the corner of her eye? "I gave away fifty percent of my business."

She looked up and her voice rose, "Can you believe, I gave away fifty percent of my business AND I did that without a Shareholder's Agreement? The next thing I know, he's not come forward with the money, he's stolen the formulas, he has taken the business plan, and he has set up his brother in competition."

She had a wry smile, "But, but he failed too. I had some specialist suppliers who refused to supply him.

"But, at that time, I had lost all my life savings, and three years' work." She took her wine glass, paused and then sipped the cold Chardonnay. She said "Sorry, I do get carried away."

Mike gave her a reassuring nod, "You are doing fine, we are all right here with you. More, more, carry on …"

Alisa continued in a measured tone "Today, I check out anyone I do business with. I have legal contracts for every stage of engagement – yes, it costs money, but it is worth it for peace of mind."

Mike poured some more wine. He said, "Alisa, this is fantastic, carry one, you still have five fingers left."

She laughed. "OK, let me see, there are a few more very important points."

Alisa stood up. She was holding court, and she was again speaking with intensity and commitment. Midas and Mike both moved to the edge of their seats in unison. Mike was nodding and agreeing, Midas wanted to take notes but had nothing to write on and was hoping it was all being committed to the depths of his memory vault.

"Now let's move to the exciting stuff. Passion.

"People talk about passion. Find your destiny. I think that is a bit clichéd. Yes, you must do something you love and love what you do. To me, what is important about passion is that it is a manifestation of your commitment and belief. Passion is that intangible that becomes palpable when you start to talk to people. That's when they know you are for real."

Alisa was becoming interestingly intense again.

"I think, you definitely need an insane determination and lots of stamina – maybe driven by passion – that carries you through the long nights and dark days when you have to keep going.

"There are also mundane jobs that you have to do – even simple things like recording your expenses, and putting the trash out. You are bootstrapped (or should be). Sometimes it is boring – you have to do everything, not just that which you think is 'sexy' and fun."

She paused, and her voice dropped just slightly but noticeably, and she had her hands clenched.

"You know, I guess it's like when you are in the pits of despair and think that you are crazy, something picks you up and drives you forward. It comes from deep inside. It's like a white heat. Passion, destiny, determination – whatever you want to call it – carries you through these times."

She paused again, she looked thoughtful, "Yeah, I think for me, my greatest driver is my vision. I see my product changing how people live, what they consume, healthy food and drink, that's my gig, as I told you; I see it on the shelf in the store, I see it sold online, I see the website, I see it manifesting in all kinds of ways.

"You have to be able to visualize whatever you are doing, see your customer, see how you are giving them value. Value, value, value. It's value for your customers – that's what it is all about at the end of the day. We have to learn to think with our hearts, and then let our brains do the calculations," she said. "In business, giving value translates to making decisions based on humanistic values, as well as purely economic ones.

"If you do not see this in your mind, and know all the building blocks to deliver that vision, then you cannot convince anyone to follow you. And... OK, my final point, I promise,

"You cannot do this alone. You have to have people who help you – employees, a board, and mentors. You must do your best to get the best. If you compromise, it will bite you. I know it is a dilemma. Look at me; I am an itsy bitsy startup that failed before. Who wants to work for me? Well, I can tell you someone does, and someone very good does, and someone who will make a difference to my business does. I just have to find them. And, if you believe in the Law of Attraction and the power of something out there that we do not understand, they will also find me."

Alisa sat down and reached for the Chardonnay. "And on that note, I am having some more wine." She smiled and laughed.

"Wow!" exclaimed Midas, "That was amazing, I thought you were never going to stop, you were in full flight."

Mike raised his glass, "Alisa, that was one of the best descriptions I have heard, of this crazy world we inhabit as entrepreneurs.

"Do you mind if I add just one point? Although you have really covered a lot of ground."

"Go ahead."

"I think there is one more attribute that sets entrepreneurs apart from other people. When I think about entrepreneurs that I have met, including you both," Midas was flattered to be included, "entrepreneurs have the ability to connect the dots, they see opportunities where others do not see them, they take 'A' and they take a seemingly unrelated 'B' and add them together and they have something new, innovative, and a potential product or service.

"Or they look at something, which to them is obvious, but no one is doing anything about it. So they look a bit deeper and find that the only reason no one is taking the opportunity is that, even if 'they' had seen it, they cannot be bothered to get off their fat butts to take action. Entrepreneurs take action – they don't sit around to wait for someone to tell them, they do. They live by JDI. Just Do It. And then, in no time, there is a new business."

Alisa clapped her hands. "Mike, of course, you are right. Ummm… Now why did I not say that?" she asked jokingly.

"Because you forget how talented you are, and how that attribute comes naturally to you," Mike replied.

They high-fived each other. Midas raised his glass.

Midas stepped off Mystique an hour or so later, waving good night to Mike and Alisa. His head was spinning and it was not from the chardonnay. He had just been through an intensive course on entrepreneurship from two experts. He did not expect a marina in Florida to be one of the places where he would step up and change his knowledge.

He lay on top of the main cabin on Bolero and looked up to the stars. He thought of Chicago, he thought of Lynn, he would call her in the morning.

He started to count the stars, and in moments he was asleep.

THIRTY SIX

Midas ran into the coffee lounge on the second floor of the Marina Building. He had just had a long chat with Mike as he walked along the dock, and now he was in a hurry to get his morning caffeine fix.

The Marina Building was an imposing block with a red-tiled pitched roof and white walls; all of the windows had blue wooden shutters fastened open.

Midas's favorite location, when he was not in the small ante room he had begged from Claire, was a corner table in the coffee lounge that allowed him to see the comings and goings in the casual eatery and, at the same time, look out on the panorama of masts and sails. He was learning to distinguish between different types of yachts just by viewing the masts from his vantage point.

He had been in the marina for three months and he enjoyed the relaxed atmosphere. The ability to communicate with the outside world via email and the web allowed him to maintain a low level of momentum in forming his next business idea and, at the same time commit an hour or two a day to reading.

Nestor had been excellent in sending through recommendations both for books and videos. Midas had also built up a list of websites and channels that he subscribed to. These channels provided him with a regular dose of video, voice, articles, and ideas that were directed specifically at the would-be entrepreneur, or upwardly mobile corporate highflyer.

He realized that he had lost the discipline of reading; at college he tolerated books but preferred the hands-on activity in the development labs. He realized that he had not opened a book of any note for some ten years. He was certain that the result of social media, Twitter, instant newsfeeds, sound bites, and the like, had been to remove from most people's daily habits, the pleasure of reading. It was a significant loss.

He also noted that most of the well-known and highly successful entrepreneurs and corporate leaders acknowledged that reading books and informed articles on a regular basis was necessary to keep the mind sharp, to stay abreast of latest trends, and to challenge conventional thinking. Midas had read that Warren Buffet, one of the world's wealthiest men, was reputed to read for a minimum of five hours each day.

Earlier this morning Midas had read a small book, no more than twenty-two pages long, called 'As Man Thinketh' by James Allen, which had been first published in 1903, and described by Allen as showing "… how, in his own thought world, each man holds the key to every condition, good or bad, that enters into his life, and that, by working patiently and intelligently upon his thoughts, he may remake his life, and transform his circumstances. The price of the book is only one shilling, and it can be carried in the pocket." Midas wondered how many copies of this wonderful little guide had been printed since 1903. Midas conjectured it would be hundreds of thousands.

One passage from the book particularly struck Midas:

> "A man sooner or later discovers that he is the master-gardener of his soul, the director of his life. He also reveals, within himself, the flaws of thought, and understands, with ever-increasing accuracy, how thought forces and mind elements operate in the shaping of character, circumstance, and destiny."

Midas thought of his own character, circumstance, and destiny; he had some work to do!

As he finished his Americano, he looked across the room as he heard the doors swing open. Crossing the room, in his now familiar style, came Nestor.

Midas stood up and shook hands. "What brings you to this part of the world, I didn't know you were a sailor."

"I thought it was time to get some sunshine," answered Nestor, "it isn't too far to travel."

"The way you appear out of nowhere makes me think you live down the street, wherever I am," laughed Midas.

Nestor had become Midas's mentor, at least in the realm of Midas's personal development and growth. Nestor sometimes strayed into the world of business, but he was primarily initiating Midas in behavioral ideas and concepts: his mindset, attitudes, and understanding of who he was, and what he could become. This suited Midas. He had managed to build a good network of advisors and friends since he attended the networking event with Lynn eighteen months before; however, they were very business-oriented and he did not feel comfortable exploring the labyrinth of his personal fears, doubts, and aspirations with them.

"How have you been with the reading and video material?" asked Nestor.

"Good," answered Midas. "However, the one thing that I am still trying to think through is how do I ensure success of my next venture. Any ideas?"

Nestor responded, "As you know by now, Midas, asking that question is opening a Pandora's Box. But let's think about a few things that we have not discussed before. There are all kinds of answers to the question – a lot, of course, business-related: what market, what sector, what services, location, and so on and so on. But do you remember when we met in Wisconsin, that I told you mindset precedes skill set? So in answer to your question, what do you think you need to give attention to?"

Midas responded thoughtfully, "Mindset?"

"Yes, of course Midas – right on."

Midas continued, "Ok, but we have discussed all kinds of things before – how our thoughts manifest themselves, how like people attract like people, the universal law, abundance, programming... You gave me a lot of reading – I am working my way through it."

Then he added, "Slowly."

"That's ok Midas," answered Nestor. "All in good time.

"Now, let's get back to your question. How can you ensure success?

"Well, I don't think there are any guarantees as in 'ensure', but we can work on a lot of things that may inhibit your success … and get them out of the way. How about that?"

Midas nodded.

Nestor continued, "Let me give you some headlines and you can follow some of this up by yourself.

"First, I want to remind you about 'limiting beliefs'. These are beliefs that will inhibit success. They are what Joe Vitale calls 'Thieves in the night'. As a sidebar note, Midas, you should read Joe's books. He is a prolific writer; some of his books are ideal for you to understand how to be a success. Have a look at 'Attractor Factor'."

"What are the Limiting Beliefs – the 'thieves'?" quizzed Midas.

Nestor replied. "Ok, I will explain. First, you need to align your mind with where you want to go and what you want to be. And, of course, I will assume you want to be wealthy in all aspects of the word – health, money, friends, experiences, and relationships. Right?"

"Of course," acknowledged Midas.

"Then you must align your mind with where you want to go and what you want to be, long before you get there."

"OK," nodded Midas.

"I think we can both say that if we do not have the mindset of a champion we will never be one. Agreed?"

"Agreed."

"And if you want to be wealthy, you have to have a wealth mindset, before you achieve wealth."

Midas looked puzzled. "What do you mean 'wealth mindset'?"

"A wealth mindset is a mindset which says it is ok. No, let me correct myself. Not ok, it is GOOD to be wealthy – and GOOD that your success is evident in every dimension: money, relationships, health, experiences, and relationships.

"Do you realize how often people are taught that wealth is bad, wealth is not for them …. I could talk about that myth all afternoon," sighed Nestor.

"So, Midas you need to develop a wealth mindset NOW."

Midas looked across the table and said, "But, if as a child, or in formative years, I was never allowed to think that wealth is good and wealth is my or our entitlement, then are there ways in which my subconscious will sabotage me?"

Midas groaned inwardly, a light had been switched on. *My family thought money was evil, wealth was not for them, and that poverty was purity, a spiritual blessing; they accepted scarcity as a result of their position in life, and an immutable fact. What mindset have I inherited?*

Nestor acknowledged, "That's very probable Midas. We just have to work on getting those old beliefs – or childhood scripts that we carry around, as I sometimes call them – out of the way, and replaced with good stuff, good beliefs."

"How do I do that?" questioned Midas.

"We are not going to have a therapy session this morning," joked Nestor, "but I will give you something to think about".

He continued, "The three thieves that Joe Vitale mentions are:

- I don't love myself
- I don't deserve to succeed
- Wealth is not good

"When the thieves live in your mind they will stop you – forever – from being a success in whatever you do."

"Wow!" Midas pushed pack in his chair, "How can anyone think that?"

Nestor looked at him, "These are the three negative core beliefs that most people carry with them through their life."

"You said 'most'?"

"Yes, I said most," answered Nestor. "So, you need to be on your guard. You do need to be introspective, and examine what is going on in your mind."

Midas answered, "So, I need to build that success mindset – which is, surprise, the exact opposite, right? The ability to say honestly and with conviction, I love myself, and I deserve to succeed, it is good for me to be wealthy. I know it sounds trite, but is it as simple as that?"

"Yes and No," answered Nestor. "The answer is yes – because you have observed the simple dichotomy – the opposite conditions. However, sometimes, when we think quietly about the statement, 'I love myself' or 'I deserve to succeed', we find ourselves scraping up a lot of inherited and implanted beliefs we don't really want."

"Tell me what you mean." Midas was puzzled.

"Well, think about 'I deserve to succeed.' What is success? Do you find yourself putting artificial limits on what success means to you? Where do those limits come from? There is no reason for you to put limits on your success. If you do – and you think about those limits – I suspect you will find they belong to someone else, some authority figure, some societal norm, some programmed limitation. Or somewhere deep in your subconscious, you are saying 'I do not deserve' to be so wealthy. Understand what I mean?"

"Wow, yes, I can see that," Midas said loudly.

Nestor continued, "Midas, I guess that sometime soon you are going to map out what your next venture will be. The actual business does not really matter. What matters is how you approach it, and your mindset. Approach it with confidence in yourself, and an admiration for your own greatness. That's not an ego trip. You can always retain humility.

"Approach your new business from a sense of love for yourself, and for whoever and whatever you are going to embrace, a sense that you deserve success, and when you make your fortune, then use that money for good purposes – first create your own financial independence so you can choose to do whatever you want to contribute back to society."

"Nestor, I have to admit, you always challenge me, but that's not a complaint. I am learning. Now it's my turn, let me share with you some of my newfound knowledge about sailing – I will give you a tour of the marina."

The two men headed to the marina and Midas's first 'expert tour'.

THIRTY SEVEN

Midas was becoming frustrated with David. He guessed that David had a diary that he overfilled with meetings and appointments. He frequently did not show when agreed. Midas asked for quotations for each piece of work. Although the quotations may not mean much to him at this stage, they were an important part of the process. He could get advice from any one of the number of friends he had made. When a batch of work was completed, Midas asked David for invoices. Some invoices appeared but they were meaningless. They were a few lines and a single total figure in dollars, which could not be substantiated by parts, and labor costs.

The work that David's team delivered on board was of an excellent quality. It was not backed up by David's administration. And David's promises of delivery by a particular date were generally in the realm of fiction.

Midas had been in the marina for around sixteen weeks. He had chatted with a number of the owners, some of who lived on board, some of who visited over the weekend. There seemed to be one constant complaint – yacht maintenance.

The Marina facilities were acknowledged as being excellent – the restaurant, bar, the convenience store, the gym and the spa were first class and the staff were all outstanding. The marina was not expensive. BUT, apart from David and his small team, who came and then disappeared, there were no maintenance facilities based at the marina, and this was an issue. This meant that work that had to be done was often delayed while owners struggled to find the necessary expertise and labor. It was difficult to find labor that was prepared to come to the marina to work on yachts. When they did come, the callout fee was normally astronomical.

It was the first weekend in August. Midas had driven with Mike to see some of Mike's friends at the next marina along the coast. At the other marina, with two-thirds the number of yachts, Midas heard similar stories. Once again the topic of conversation was the challenge of getting maintenance work done.

Midas's entrepreneurial instincts were much sharper today than they were a year ago. He could spot an opportunity and there seemed to be one staring him in the face. Why was there an absence of maintenance on-site, or on-call, at affordable rates at both of these marinas?

The more he asked around, the more he realized that there was a demand waiting to be filled.

Midas contemplated the idea of creating a marine services business, first in their own marina and then expanding. Mike and Midas talked about the idea on the drive back, and then well into the night and after several beers decided that the venture would be a slam-dunk success.

The idea was obviously worthy of far more sober analysis, which Midas started to do over the next couple of weeks. He looked at the number of yachts, typical maintenance cycles, work that yachties would do, work that owners would do, and work they would prefer to subcontract. He chatted with David and with David's foreman; there were skills available. A major yacht manufacturer that had been based in Palmetto had recently closed, transferring their production to South America. There was a reservoir of skilled talent looking for work.

Midas and Mike sketched out the plan. They would need David to cooperate. While he only did a fraction of the potential work available, he knew all the people in the marina and in the marinas nearby. He was acknowledged for his expertise, and his ability to understand problems and work out solutions, but his administration was awful. They suspected that fifty percent of the work that David's team delivered went un-invoiced or badly invoiced, to the point that it couldn't be collected. His credit control was non-existent, and as a consequence he was barely making a living despite having a team of six tradesmen working flat out five or six days a week.

They did some rough calculations; they guesstimated what the revenue could be. They knew the labor rates and they knew what trade discounts were available on parts and supplies. A very simple business plan showed them there was money to be made.

Midas floated the idea privately with the Marina's GM. She was overjoyed; she sought assurances on insurance, licenses and formalities, but otherwise guaranteed the Marina would be supportive.

Midas tried to rationalize the idea of the business idea based on the many talks he had with Nestor. Money was not the objective, providing service to the large population of owners and yachties was. He liked the people around him, and as a potential supplier in their midst, he had to make sure it was a successful business with outstanding service.

Midas was feeling motivated – broke, but motivated! He still didn't know how long he would stay on Bolero, George had become very vague about when he was going to return and in his last message he said he was about to leave Caracas and he was en route to Abu Dhabi.

With Mike's help, Midas planned to get the idea off the ground and then adapt their ideas as they moved forward; there were lots of other opportunities in the marine services field.

Midas and Mike had mapped out an idea. They would join forces in a new business. David would be the Sales VP, and they would bring in a new foreman who would report to Midas and be responsible for delivery. Midas would be responsible for quotations, billings and collections. Mike's knowledge was far more extensive than Midas's, and between them they could put a credible face to the business. Mike was well known and trusted and the idea had some merit. Whether it went ahead was, in reality, David's call.

Would David agree?

THIRTY EIGHT

Two nights later they met with David on board Bolero.

David listened intently; his head was bowed slightly, as though he was being admonished, his shoulders slumped, and his hands down between his knees. He stayed like that for some time. And then he looked up; he pulled himself upright and looked at Mike and Midas.

"There's nothing wrong in your analysis; what you guys say is spot-on," said David. "I make no money but I enjoy the job. We live because my wife works. If you guys think that we can make this into business, then I'm right behind you."

Midas was touched by the honesty of the guy. It was as though David had been waiting for someone to come and rescue him.

Over the next month agreements were drawn up, the foreman was recruited, a website created. Mike put some money in the bank account in the company's name - First Integrated Marine Services Inc.

For a long time, Midas had not spoken with Lynn. He had felt he had failed her and let her down. She had been supportive. He pinged her a message. "How's Chicago? Where are you? How are you? I am starting a new business here."

Almost immediately the phone rang; it was Lynn. Midas answered.

"I thought you had drowned. I thought you had gone sailing and fallen overboard. I have been soooo worried. And now you just pop up on my phone as though nothing had happened." Her voice rose, she sounded angry.

"You are impossible Mr. Midas. Impossible! Well, what's your excuse? And what is this business you are starting? In Florida? And, just so you know, I have missed you! But I don't think you have missed me."

It was a ra-ta-ta-tat of a call; Lynn had barely stopped to breathe.

There was a pause; Midas was unsure what to say. Before he could open his mouth, Lynn continued

"Ok Midas my dear entrepreneur, what are you doing? Tell me. And what's the weather like? I think I should visit you." Her voice now was the more familiar Lynn; there were bright lights in her voice and her trace of accent was back.

They talked for ages, with Midas relating stories about yachts – and he actually mentioned Nestor, but was very guarded in what he said. Lynn had been to Europe and told Midas of her expeditions to Paris and London. It was familiar and warm; as though now they were connected and there had been no gap.

Midas held his breath; he was about to tell her of the formal opening of First Integrated Marine Services next month. Would she come? She was a high flyer. Would she want to come to see him and Mike and David, in what was slightly larger than a mom and pop business?

He thought that it might be better if he sent a mail later; he could tell her more.

As they rang off, Lynn repeated her desire to visit and Midas said that it would be great. They would arrange something. She signed off with a cheerful, "Miss you. Hope to see you very soon."

At the beginning of October, the new business was formally launched at the Marina's Annual Regatta. The response was overwhelmingly positive. Midas was alone; his mail to Lynn was still in his Drafts folder.

Mike and Midas did a tour of the two adjacent marinas and spoke to owners. Their initiative was applauded. Even when they made it clear that no work would be started without a substantial deposit, owners started to send them lists of what jobs they required to be completed.

Another three guys on casual contracts had supplemented David's team of tradesmen. These were older, excellent tradesmen who had been laid off from the yacht builder that closed. They were happy to work on an on-call basis to supplement the family income.

One challenge that faced them was itinerant yachts that would call in to the marina for emergency repairs. This was a true 'on-demand' service with no pre-planning. It took some nimble footwork with tradesmen and suppliers to turn around the visitors. But it paid dividends. News of the marine services company travelled quickly amongst the yachting community and soon brokers and even fishermen were calling on their time.

Time and tide wait for no man, as the old saying goes. And in the marina the seasons changed and some of the summer yachts moved out to be replaced by winter visitors. Some customers moved on, new customers arrived.

Midas spent a lot of time with the tradesmen, often in the bowels and bilges of yachts. He was learning the various systems – what they did, where they were vulnerable, what equipment was good, what equipment was bad, which suppliers were reputable, which suppliers were reliable, and who to avoid. Soon he would have been in the marina for almost a year. In that time, he continued on an almost vertical learning curve.

Midas was running a business, he was an entrepreneur, a business owner, and his dream was far away from the ideas he had sketched out two years before. Mike was a part-time partner but a solid one. He ensured that the working capital to continually expand the business was available.

They were expanding their workforce; Midas was dealing with suppliers, insurance companies, and agencies, and enjoying every moment. Jobs were getting bigger. The average revenue per job was increasing, and Andy, their foreman of Malaysian descent proved to be a godsend. He was detail-oriented and he recorded accurately, every component, every part, screw, washer, and bolt used on every job. His timesheets were inscrutable. If there was any challenge to an invoice Andy could provide sufficient evidence to satisfy even the most critical customer. Fast Integrated had built a reputation for quality work, and honest pricing – factors on which a service business lives or dies.

It was late afternoon and Mike and Midas was sitting on the bridge of Mike's yacht, looking out to the Manatee River. Another couple of hours and it would be dark. As they looked towards the west they could see the estuary opening in to the Gulf of Mexico beyond De Soto Point some four miles distant. It was busy with sailing yachts but there was something unusual. On the horizon there was a yacht –

a massive yacht – bigger than anything they normally saw. It dwarfed everything around. It was heading up the River.

"Hey, here's our next job," joked Mike. There is a saying about being careful what you wish for.

After about thirty minutes it was clear that she was a giant two-hulled Catamaran, and from her course she was heading for the Marina. The radio crackled in the cabin below. "Brave New Horizon, Brave New Horizon this is Marina Office, Marina Office, Over." The yacht's skipper acknowledged, the Marina Office continued "…Brave New Horizon, Brave New Horizon, head to the North Channel and to B Dock, there are open berths and a crew will assist you. Copy?"

"Copy, B Dock. ETA twenty minutes," came the response.

B Dock was the same jetty that Midas saw from the motel window many months before, on his first morning at the marina, the one with very large yachts tied up.

Mike and Midas watched the giant, all-white craft, as it approached. It was immense. Mike recognized it.

"Whoa, that's the new Beneteau Lagoon 62. She was only launched this year. It's a giant; she's sixty-two feet long, and thirty-two feet wide. That giant mast is one hundred feet high. Sleeps up to fourteen guests. Geez! She's something. Minutes later, Brave New Horizon elegantly glided through the entrance to the marina, and past Mike's yacht, which paled into insignificance alongside the giant white lady.

"I think a visit to Brave New Horizon is called for first thing in the morning," said Mike, raising a beer. Midas agreed.

What they would find would surprise even an experienced sailor like Mike.

THIRTY NINE

In the corner suite of the offices on the forty-second floor of the Chrysler Building in New York all was not well; the atmosphere was so intense it could be cut with a knife.

Faxed pictures were strewn across the large oak desk and a substantial Norwegian gentleman was shouting at his secretary. "I don't care where he is, find him, and tell him he is looking for another job when I have finished with him!"

Known as 'the Viking', the Norwegian was the head of a considerable international group of companies with interests in shipping, logistics, mining, marine biology, and renewable energy. His geographic influence spread across the globe. He was regarded as a corporate titan in Scandinavia and was one of a small group of Norwegians at the pinnacle of the country's commercial, political and social life. His wealth was unknown, but deemed to be considerable. These days, out of choice, he operated from New York. Both his sons attended Universities on the East Coast.

He was normally affable and he was well liked by his friends, and respected by his foes. When he was upset he could be a formidable character and was not afraid to speak his mind. Depending on who was the subject of his onslaught, his language could be abrasive as the grit from one of his deep mines. He could swear in five languages. Yet, his normal demeanor was charming and gentlemanly.

Today his 'victim' was his yacht captain. The Viking had come into the office earlier than usual, only to receive news that his pride and joy – his brand new yacht – had been in collision with not one, but two fishing boats in the Gulf of Mexico and was now in a small marina near Palmetto. It was supposed to be en route for Houston. The pictures had been sent from the yachts communication console.

The Viking was the owner of Brave New Horizon!

The speakerphone on the desk rang. Vanessa, the Viking's secretary had put her head through the door, "It's Joe". Joe was the now unfortunate, and maybe soon-to-be ex-captain of the Brave New Horizon.

Given the pictures on his desk, the Viking was remarkably restrained. He spoke in a measured but definite tone.

"Joe. Now tell me; there's over six hundred thousand square miles of water in the Gulf, and you occupy two hundred square yards of that, how the heck can you hit something?"

"I didn't, boss. They hit me."

"What! What hit you? You're big, white, and with your sails up, the size of a small office building, and they could not see you? What happened?"

"You are not going to believe this, boss." Joe did not sound confident.

The Viking's voice raised a few decibels. "You're right, I am probably not. And by the way, I hope you have another job to go to!" He was not yet shouting, and whether he would enter the sound level where he didn't need a phone to penetrate the airwaves all the way to Florida would depend on Joe's next answer.

"Honest boss, it was not my fault; there was nothing that anyone on board could do."

"Go on..."

"We had come around Key West and we were to head North West to Houston, but there was bad weather in the Gulf so I decided to go North along the coast until we were beyond Tampa and then head West. If the weather came to us, we could shelter anywhere on the coast."

"I know all that, I have seen the navigation logs," shouted the Viking, "get on with it."

"Ok, Ok..." Joe was sounding hesitant. "We were off Longboat Key, west of Sarasota, heading North and doing around eight knots. The conditions were good, but the wind was light. There was a Boston

Whaler (an open fishing boat with small outboard engine), around fifteen-foot-long coming up behind us on the port side (left hand side). Just one guy in it. He was towing another Whaler, about the same size, behind him. That boat was empty and had no engine, as far as we could see. He was moving fast, too fast in my opinion. There were waves and he was bouncing around a lot. He was about sixty feet behind us, and maybe twenty feet away from us, when he realized that he was probably going too fast. He cut his throttle and slowed down but the boat behind didn't slow so quickly, and the line between the two boats went slack. That's when the problem happened. The slack line caught his outboard engine and jammed something. The guy tried to push his engine sideways, and before he knew what had happened he had turned his boat hard onto us. He yanked on his rudder again and pulled off the collision course, but not fast enough. He scraped down our hull on the port side and gouged out the fiberglass for about fifteen feet before pulling off."

"Idiot," exclaimed the Viking.

"Did he stop? Don't tell me, I know the answer."

"He just kept going and accelerated away, those Whalers can move."

"I know, did you get a number, any registration, any ID?"

"Not at the time. We checked the ship's video cameras immediately after and radioed the coast guard. There were no identifying marks that we could see. By the time the coast guard was mobilized he had disappeared."

"OK Joe. That's bad. What's the damage?"

"At this time, it looks superficial, no structural damage. We berthed last night and this morning I will take a detailed look, measurements, depth of the damage, some photos and a video."

"Thanks Joe." The Viking had calmed down, it seemed that Joe's job was safe, for now.

"Get me a full report, and I will get on to Beneteau. Tell me where you are; I will fly down in the next couple of weeks. I guess you are going to be there a while."

The Viking's visit would yield more than an inspection of his yacht.

FOURTY

Midas and Mike walked along B dock, and approached Brave New Horizons. It was late morning. They had the courtesy to let the crew get settled on their new berth before visiting.

Whichever way you looked at her, she was a giant of a yacht. Magnificent and elegant. A cruiser, and private resort on the water. Her two white decks raised her upper canopy to twenty feet from the water. Her vast rear deck was laid out with an open dining area to the left side, and a suite of sun loungers to the opposite side. This layout still left ample space to walk towards the double sliding doors that accessed the giant main cabin, the salon.

Mike and Midas stood on the dock and Mike called to the deckhand. "Is your skipper on board?"

"Sure, he's down below. I'll call him."

Moments later, a guy dressed in a white uniform shirt with four bars on his shoulder came on to the aft deck of the yacht. He was mid-thirties, short, well built and had a smiling face. As Midas would see over the following weeks, the smile was almost permanently etched. He was 'Navy', pressed shorts, clean shirt, trimmed hair. He suited the yacht.

"Come aboard."

Mike and Midas walked up the boarding ramp. Joe, the skipper, shook hands with the two entrepreneurs. He introduced himself and two of the crew who stood nearby. Midas handed over a business card 'First Integrated Marine Services Inc.'.

Joe looked at the card, he started to shake his head, "Do I need you guys, I have some serious problems. Step this way."

Midas and Mike looked at each other. This was too good to be true. A courtesy call, turning into work, on the biggest yacht seen in the marina in years?

"But first, do you want me to show you around?" Joe smiled.

He led the way into the salon.

In the next twenty minutes, Joe led the two guys through the yacht – into every corner, every floor, and every deck. Crew quarters, master's stateroom, kitchen – galley, engine rooms, up onto the bridge, across to the sun deck at the front of the yacht – a massive expanse, the size of a small tennis court, and around the sides of the yacht on broad walk ways. In every dimension she was big, and luxurious. She smelled NEW and EXPENSIVE.

They sat at the large dining table on the rear deck. Annie, a young female crewmember dressed in whites, brought a French Press of coffee and three mugs. Joe had brought a file of drawings and photos.

Midas looked at Joe, smiling like a boy who had just been given a tour of an aircraft hangar or locomotive shed. "Thanks for the tour, Joe, she's amazing. Who owns her? Where are you heading? Where did you come in from?

Joe held his hand up. "All in good time, coffee first. Annie, can you bring some cream for our guests, please."

Annie slipped back into the galley and returned with a jug of cream and a jug of milk.

She stood close to Midas as she leaned over to reach for the French Press. She began to pour. Midas detected a hint of perfume, a feminine scent; it was pleasant. He smiled to himself, and thought, *style, elegance … in keeping with the yacht; maybe I have to visit again.*

At that moment a picture of Lynn flipped across his mind's eye, *Maybe not.* He realized that he missed his friend from Chicago.

Joe sipped his coffee and placed it back on the table.

"Ok, here's the story. The yacht's owned by a Norwegian guy, he's presently based in New York. This is his fourth yacht; he has one in Singapore, two in Oslo, and this. He took delivery about four months back. He's big in shipping and logistics and a lot of other things; not for me to know. But he has enough! He's a decent boss as far as bosses go. Fair, firm, you know where you are with him. Doesn't ask for anything outrageous."

Another sip of coffee.

"We were on a 'bedding down' cruise from New York to Houston. Ya' know, checking all the systems, getting the sails and the rigging set, see how she sails, see how she handles weather, and so on… you guys know the score. And then his happened…"

Joe pulled out some photographs from the folder on the table – it showed a long gouge on the side of a yacht, photographed by someone hanging over the rail that ran along the side of the yacht.

"That happened yesterday, off Sarasota. That's why we came in here. I wanted to be away from the weather in the Gulf and have somewhere where I can figure out what to do next. Spoke to the boss this morning. At first he was going to fire me, but then he calmed down when I told him what had happened. Come, let me show you."

Joe stood up and walked towards the giant control panel and helm beyond the saloon. Midas and Mike followed. Joe switched on one of the screens and tapped a keyboard.

"These are the onboard visuals. There are twelve video cameras, for security and monitoring. There are four on the mast that cover both sides of the yacht looking forward and aft. One in each of the engine rooms, two in the passage ways below, and the remainder are on deck."

Joe played back the incident. It was clear what had happened, exactly as Joe described it to the Viking earlier in the morning.

Midas realized they had not seen the damage when they walked towards the yacht; it was on the other side from the direction they came.

"How will you get this repaired?" asked Midas.

"The boss is already on to France where she was built. But that will take a long time, I have dealt with manufacturers before," answered Joe.

"Can we look?" Midas was curious.

"Sure," replied Joe. "Let's get into the tender and we can sail around to the side to take a close look. Annie, can you ask Max to lower the tender into the water?"

Five minutes later the three guys were sitting in a small motorized tender sailing around the massive hull. *From this low in the water she looks even more impressive* thought Midas as Brave New Horizons towered above them.

They came to the side where the hull was hit by the Boston whaler. "You can see the scrape; it has gouged out just the surface of the fiberglass. Along this wall of the hull the thickness varies from a quarter to three eights of an inch, upwards where the strengtheners are. The damage is really cosmetic. I hate the thought of bringing people from France just to fix this. But I know what the Boss is like."

Midas had a thought – a crazy thought; he couldn't wait to get off the dock and up to his tiny office.

Midas and Mike said good-bye to Joe and set off down the dock.

Midas was thumping the air, "Yes, Yes, Yes…"

FOURTY ONE

It took Midas a day to research the construction of Brave New World, contact the Beneteau dealer in Sarasota and speak with their engineer, drag David into his office and interrogate him about the feasibility of repairing Captain Joe's yacht. He went to Mike's yacht in the evening and he was buzzing.

"We can do it!" were his first words as he stepped on board Mystique.

"Do what?" Mike was not on the same page as Midas. Not yet.

"Brave New Horizon."

"Are you mad?" Responded Mike.

"No, no, no. Listen to me. The repair is technically easy – I have talked to David. I talked to a fiberglass guy who used to work on Beneteau yachts, and – you don't know – but we have access to the best fiberglass finisher in Florida."

"Midas, this is a yacht not a car! Who is this finisher?"

"Remember the yacht company that closed down here? He used to do all the final repairs before the yachts left the yard. In production they got scuffed and damaged and he had to send them out looking like new."

"And how much is this going to cost?"

"No idea, but I think we should do it, if we can. The kudos alone is worth a lot. I am not too worried about the costs on this, I just want to do the best job we can."

Midas was recalling all the lessons from all the entrepreneurs he had met – *have big ideas, be brave, have big goals, go where others would fear to go, give outstanding service, be excellent in what you do … the list went on. We might be just a bit bigger than a mom and pop shop, but that doesn't stop me from thinking the way of a real entrepreneur*, thought Midas.

The following morning, Midas was on board Brave New World with David. He sketched out how they could do the repair and have it completed in less than a week – long before the Viking was due to arrive, and weeks before anyone from the factory would even dream of visiting.

Joe was skeptical. He said he would speak to the Viking, which he did; the Viking was skeptical too.

Midas responded, "I will guarantee the work. If there is any trace of the repair, if it is not a perfect and invisible repair, and if she is not looking as new, I will personally pay for you to fly a finisher from France." It was a brave statement.

Two weeks later, the Viking's limo drew up outside the marina gates as the marina was waking up.

Joe, resplendent in clean and pressed uniform, was there to greet him. They headed to the yacht.

On the walk to the yacht the Viking quizzed Joe on the condition of the yacht and whether he had finally got the finisher from the Beneteau's factory in France. Joe's sidestepped the question, "You'll see boss – I tell you, you've not seen anything at all." As they approached the yacht, the crew were on deck; lined up, clean and pressed uniforms, ready to greet the Viking. But he didn't board, he went straight to the tender. "Come on Joe, I want to look."

Joe jumped into the tender, the Viking followed. They motored around the hull. The Viking said, "Take her close Joe, close as possible. I want to see. Closer, closer, I can't see anything."

For ten minutes the Viking moved slowly up the side of the hull, peering from this direction and that direction, running his hand on the surface, standing back, squinting at the surface at different angles.

"Where the heck is it Joe?"

Joe smiled to himself. "It's done boss, done – great job, yeah?"

"Those Beneteau guys did a great job!" exclaimed the Viking, beaming all over his face.

"It wasn't the Beneteau guys boss. It was that local guy I told you about."

"What? Who's that – I want to see him. It's good, very good."

Later that morning, Midas arrived at Brave New Horizon. He walked up the boarding ramp and Joe was waiting wearing a massive smile.

"You have a new fan – it couldn't be better."

Midas stepped into the main cabin. The Viking rose and walked over and grabbed Midas's hand. "I have heard so much about you since I arrived this morning. Sit down. You have made me a happy man. How did you do it?"

For the next twenty minutes, Midas explained how he had researched the production methods for the yacht, he spoke to fiberglass suppliers, and to the paint and coating manufacturers; and how David, the guy who started the little business a long time ago, had been a fount of knowledge. He had also managed to get a couple of fiberglass layup experts and, in particular, he found a 'matcher'.

A matcher is a fiberglass finisher who has a special knack of making sure the repair color and the original color are a perfect match – it takes an experienced eye and, it seems, almost a color blindness in certain ranges of the spectrum. Very few people have the talent, but there had been a lady at the closed down yacht builder who worked with the finisher to match the Viking's hull.

"Amazing. Please come and have dinner with me tonight. And bring your partner." Midas accepted the invitation but had to apologize for Mike who was out of town.

"No worries, I am sure I will meet him another time. See you this evening."

The dinner was simple but delicious; poached salmon and leeks vinaigrette salad, preceded by a classic vichyssoise. The Viking was partial to Chablis and a chilled bottle graced the table. Joe had joined them, but the conversation was a Midas and Viking affair. Joe didn't seem to mind; he was as interested as the Viking in Midas's stories, background and ideas.

"Midas, you strike me as an interesting young man. I want to know more about you. How did you get into this marine business, where are you going with it, what's your turnover?" The questions from the Viking came tumbling out. They didn't stop. No matter how and when Midas had answered one question, another was soon on the table. It was not an aggressive encounter; it was friendly, and the Viking was genuinely interested in Midas's take on technology as well as the marine business. They talked about entrepreneurship, and the Viking's responses reminded him of the morning at the Hyatt, on the day of the Entrepreneurs' Summit, two years earlier.

As the night closed the Viking walked Midas down the boarding ramp, shook his hand and said, "I am sincerely grateful Midas. Not just for the repair, but for the fact that a young man stuck his neck out and went for it. You took a risk, and you delivered – that's what business is about. Whenever you are in New York, I insist that you visit me – and by then, as I have decided Brave New Horizon will head back to New York and make it her home, we can go sailing. Thank you and good luck in whatever you do."

The Viking turned and walked back up the boarding ramp. He turned and waved to Midas, and then was gone.

Midas set off back to Bolero not realizing how important this mission had been.

FOURTY TWO

Brave New Horizon had come and gone, and so had many more yachts. First Integrated Marine Services' reputation had spread further and faster after the job for the Viking, and they had taken on more staff.

Lynn had finally managed to tie Midas down to a visit and she came for a week's holiday during the latter part of winter – a great change from Chicago. They had sailed on Mike's yacht and with a couple of other yacht owners. Despite Midas's insecurity and concern, Lynn did not seem to be the least concerned that their business was not a big corporation; she was really interested in everything they did and she loved sailing with Midas, who, at this time, had become a competent crewmember on the yachts they sailed. Lynn called Midas 'Her Captain.'

They were now in the third quarter of the second year of operation. Revenues continued to climb, demand continued unabated, sixty per cent of the work delivered was for repeat customers and the business had expanded to having representation in three marinas. Midas and Mike had brought in middle management resources to support Midas on accounting and to support David on estimation and quotation. David had survived this incredible transformation of his small business and admitted that Mike and Midas had delivered his dream.

Midas and Mike were sitting on the stern of Mike's catamaran when someone who they assumed to be a new customer approached them.

He introduced himself, "Hi, my name's Jeff, I am looking for Mike or Midas."

"You have found us both," said Mike. "Come aboard."

Jeff climbed aboard Mystique. Jeff said he was thinking about shipping boats from China and wondered if First Integrated could refurbish them when they arrived in the USA. He probed Midas and Mike on the First Integrated business.

Jeff came back again the following day and the day after and the day after. When he was not talking to Mike or Midas, he was seen around the marina talking to owners and climbing on and off yachts.

He walked up and down the marina counting the berths and measuring the sizes of the yachts in each of the fingers. Statistically, he probably knew far more than either Mike or Midas about what was in the marina. Not that it mattered.

The following week James, First Integrated's external accountant rang Midas:

"We've had a call from an interested party."

"What do you mean an interested party?" asked Midas.

"Someone is interested in acquiring First Integrated. You and Mike should come to see me this afternoon," said James.

Mike and Midas appeared at James's office at two o'clock. They were shown into a conference room.

"Sit down, and I'll tell you the story," said James.

"I was contacted by a gentleman called Jeff, he's an ex-corporate type from GE. He was let go with a very big settlement; it seems that he was very senior in the organization. He wants to, and I use his words, 'have a lifestyle change'. He claims that he has a long-time interest in sailing yachts and in the marine sector. I believe you met him, and his visit to the marina was not coincidental. It seems that he has done his research up and down the coast of Florida and First Integrated is the company that fits what is looking for. He believes he can expand it further and there is whole lot of untapped potential."

Midas looked at Mike and raised his eyebrows; Mike returned the look.

James continued, "This year you're on track to do eight hundred thousand dollars in revenue and two hundred and fifty thousand on the bottom line. He is prepared to pay two times revenue or at least that's his starting point. That's not bad at two years' work gentlemen, and if you want my opinion you should make a gentle play at negotiating, but then capitulate quickly, sign and get the money in the bank".

James carried on talking, "We all know that there is untapped demand, but the next stage of growth is going to be challenging from the point of view of resources and capital. I would let Jeff take on that responsibility."

The shareholding of First Integrated was Midas forty-five percent, Mike thirty-five percent, and David fifteen percent; five per cent had been set aside for staff and had been registered in a third-party's name.

Out of the sale proceeds, Mike would pick up loan repayments related to working capital funding of three hundred thousand dollars. They would divide the rest, which left Midas with net proceeds, before tax, all of almost six hundred thousand dollars. Along with salary that he had saved, or forgone, during the early days, which would be paid as part of the settlement, he would bank three quarters of a million dollars.

Four weeks later, First Integrated had a new owner. George had returned from Caracas to the news that his friend had transformed services on the marina, and had now sold out for a substantial sum.

David was ecstatic; from a failing business he now had money in the bank, and a contract with the new owner. Mike decided that he would at last do some serious sailing.

When Midas sent news to Lynn that said he was now leaving the Marina, she said that she was anxious to visit. He told her briefly about the deal and she was overjoyed for Midas. She flew down the following week and she took a room at the motel. Once again, they sailed in Tampa Bay and out into the ocean on Mike's catamaran for the three days. George was on Bolero; he was ecstatic about the work that had been completed and was going to sail down through the Caribbean.

Midas contacted Nestor, and told him of the developments. Nestor was pleased for Midas. Within a day Nestor had appeared at the marina. Together, over lunch, they discussed what had happened since Midas had arrived in the marina, almost two years earlier.

"I remember that you arrived with nothing, and no expectations; you were down and your friend George asked a favor. In fact, he threw you a lifeline – you have somewhere to go and rebuild your life, right? You had to make your own way," said Nestor. "The way I see it, the universe was opening a door for you, but you did not - at the time - see the door; you saw an escape hatch. But, you went through and made the best of what you could on the other side."

He continued, "In no time, you were active and searching for opening. You behaved like a classic entrepreneur; you saw an opportunity – one, to be fair, that had been staring other people in the face for years – and you took action. I like the way that you recognized that there was an asset you could use to help you – David – and at the same time, you helped David, a classic win-win. Your partnership with Mike was a great idea, again – you were being resourceful and creating another win-win."

"Yes," answered Midas. "And I realize I had to do something I hated – I was constantly networking. I was talking to people about their yachts and their problems and finding ways to help them. But this built up so much goodwill. And I think that the combination of resources – David, Mike and myself – was an excellent team. We also were very careful about who we hired; we got the best tradesmen and we controlled all the work meticulously."

"Midas, let me ask you a question. At what point did you think about money, about how much you could make?"

"I didn't. That's interesting. While I knew there was an opportunity and Mike and I did some ballpark numbers, I was really very interested in what David's team was doing, and the fact that there were lots of yacht owners who needed help. I became very passionate about building the business. Which, I guess I needed to be, given I stayed on the yacht for two years, in the marina, and people would wake me in the middle of the night; it was like being a doctor permanently on call, twenty-four - seven. I think the only time when 'money' really came up was when we got the offer to buy us out."

Nestor looked reflective, "So, passion was driving you forward, even in those unsocial hours. What else does that tell you? Do you remember the time that we discussed money? And the fact that those that chase it, never get enough, and those that see money as a good by-product of providing something that someone wants to the best of their ability and to the highest standard in the market, receive money. How does that fit your behavior?"

"Well, I guess it does," answered Midas.

"And now I want to add something else. You did not just think outside the box, you lived outside the box. You were in a new area of expertise, something you never did before. You were the CEO of a growing business. Then you did something that was truly inspirational, very entrepreneurial," said Nestor.

"That was your work on Brave New Horizon. You stuck your neck out, you took a big risk. Had it gone wrong, I would hate to think what would have happened. But you and your team did an amazing job, and it paid off."

"I never thought that it would go wrong," said Midas.

"Whoa! See the universe at work there," exclaimed Nestor.

"Remember what I told you? 'You will see it when you believe it'. You believed absolutely that you could do it, there was never a doubt, failure wasn't in the vocabulary, and you delivered. You have got yourself a big fan and a new networking buddy in the Viking." Nestor high-fived Midas.

Nestor continued, "I think there is one more thing? You learned and demonstrated humility. You knew that you knew nothing, and instead of trying to pretend, as some would do, you got in there with everyone, from the engine fitter and the mechanic to the captain of one of the biggest yachts to sail into here. And you didn't BS, you were straight, and honest, and fair. You demonstrated a great attribute – YOU ASKED QUESTIONS AND YOU LISTENED.

"You also were clever and focused: you didn't spend on unnecessary stuff, no fancy offices, you made a basic functional web site, you got down into the trenches, and you made marketing about your customer, not about the company. You were always selling, selling, selling."

Midas and his mentor finished lunch, shook hands and parted – until next time.

Midas checked his mail, he had received a wedding invitation from a friend in Zürich who was getting married and it took Midas only minutes to book a business class seat on Swissair to Europe.

The wedding would mark a new future for the newlyweds, and Midas, the new successful entrepreneur, would spend days in a hospital.

FOURTY THREE

Midas looked out of the window from his business class seat on Swiss Flight 65, as it was completing the nine-hour flight from Miami. The runway got closer and a slight bump announced his arrival at Zurich. It was eleven o'clock in the morning on 7 May 2011. As the aircraft taxied towards the gate, Midas stretched his legs in front of him in the spacious foot well; he smiled as he looked around the cabin. This was a far cry from the Greyhound bus he took from Chicago to Florida some thirty months before.

Midas was visiting a good friend Hans, and his family. They had met five years earlier when they worked on a large contract at an aircraft maintenance company. Hans was an unusually talented project manager, dealing with the digitization of a vast inventory of manuals, instructions, documents, and specifications that aircraft maintenance engineers had to access. Midas and Hans had maintained contact since the project. Midas had not told Hans of his trials over the recent years and he was sure that, over a few beers, war stories from both sides would be shared and toasted.

Hans had invited Midas to his son's matrimonial celebration, which was to take place on the following day. Hans' son, Darren, was to be married in the splendor of St Peter's Church in Zurich's Lindenhof. The seven-hundred-year old church was a splendid example of Gothic architecture and, in 1706, it was consecrated as the first protestant church in Zurich,

The airport was laid out with typical Swiss efficiency; Midas effortlessly navigated the corners and the passageways beneath the airport to reach immigration. Twenty meters beyond immigration was baggage claim. He did not have long to wait for his bags. Leaving Terminal 2, he joined the short taxi queue to go downtown.

Midas had chosen to stay at the Hotel Storchen, which was on the banks of the Linden River and two minutes' walk from St. Peter's Church. Tomorrow, some two hundred guests would attend the church ceremony, and the private wedding breakfast would be held in Storchen for close friends and family. Midas was flattered that he had been included in the select gathering.

The wedding day passed without a hitch; the groom was handsome, the bride looked splendid; the bridesmaids and the groomsmen, in matching dresses and formal wear completed the beautiful tableau. To Midas, there was something of a very quiet elegance about the wedding, the reception, and the whole event that was very Swiss, very European.

Midas had decided that a flight across the Atlantic warranted more exposure to Europe than a weekend devoted to a wedding and planned to stay the following week. Hans had taken advantage of Midas's plans and said that he had arranged an interesting visit to Lausanne on Monday.

Midas was going to the Lausanne General Hospital but he was not sure why. Enigmatically, Hans hinted that he had an innovative project that he wanted to share with Midas.

Sunday morning saw Midas running through the cold streets in the old city and along the banks of the river. It was a clear dawn; cloudless and cold. He had left the hotel at seven o'clock, and the temperature of four degrees Celsius reminded him of when he used to run the Fox River Trail in the wintertime.

After his run and a sumptuous breakfast, Midas strolled around the city in the morning and marveled at how the plethora of modern shops and offices in the Old City were hidden behind the five hundred or six hundred-year old buildings' facades. In the evening, he dined at the Lindenhokeller, a small restaurant located in an alley between the Lindenhof Garden and St Peter's Church. Midas decided on a mouth-watering lobster and scampi soup and, for the main course, the high mountain beef cooked in a slow oven. For an American, Midas had become adventurous in his eating habits.

It was Monday, at nine am sharp, when Hans pulled up outside the hotel's Storchen-Gasse Entrance in his VW Passat. After a friendly greeting, they set off on the three-hour drive to Lausanne. As they headed west on Highway 1 via Bern, Hans explained that he and his son, a computer science major, had been working on a video conferencing facility inside the hospital.

Midas and Hans were to visit the University's Institute of Pathology, where the head of department Dr. Prof. Jorge Berger-Muller would meet with them. Professor Berger-Muller was an enthusiastic supporter of Hans' project.

At noon they parked in the University car park and headed to the Department of Pathology. The Professor welcomed Midas, and after some friendly talk between Hans and Jorge, he went to his desk and started to show Midas a simple videoconferencing system. He was holding a three-way conference between his pathology lab, some five kilometers away, and a cancer specialist in another part of Lausanne. Images of cell samples appeared on one of the three, twenty-one inch, monitors on the professor's desk. The other monitors featured a Laboratory Analyst and a Consultant. An image of the professor was located in the top right corner of the center monitor.

To Midas it was interesting but not spectacular; he had seen videoconferences before. He had used them extensively when he was in Elgin. However, the application of choice then was Skype for simple one-on-one calls (unreliable), or a big complex telepresence system from Polycom when talking with clients' senior teams (expensive and cumbersome).

The image quality on the Professor's system was commensurate with any good quality videoconference system and the sound was clear and undistorted.

So...? Why am I here? thought Midas.

It was only when Hans pointed out that the system was using a consumer-standard webcam fixed to the top of the Professor's monitor, consumer-standard speakers, and a Dell computer, to which all three monitors were connected beneath the Professor's desk, that Midas started to understand the importance of what he was looking at. Enterprise, Business, and Hospital-Standard Videoconferencing were normally provided on specialist equipment over heavyweight networks, at costs that were generally prohibitive for wide adoption.

It was known that corporate and government CIOs considered that the consumer end of the spectrum – Skype, MSN Messenger, Yahoo

– featured limited security and was inefficient and unreliable for business or enterprise use. Equally, CIOs considered systems from the likes of Polycom, Cisco, and Lifesize, at the other end of the spectrum, to be expensive to acquire and service, and would be limited to few installations.

Midas's mind was racing: *Am I looking at a viable alternative for in-house use, a potential disruptor to the business and market held by the big players?*

Hans went on to explain that he created a simple network within the hospital, comprising a couple of servers which linked normal computer workstations in the Pathology Department and in the Professor's and Consultant's offices. The incremental cost of equipment was limited to a decent webcam and speakers. Hans charged the hospital a small monthly license fee to cover the cost of the servers and provide a modest profit.

Midas's mind had already changed gear. He could see a much larger, almost global application. He was visualizing a global cloud-based visual communication service. He needed to get his hands on the software that was installed on the servers to run his own test.

Over lunch, the Professor told Midas that he had, for the last six months, been running the small video conferencing communication network without any mishap. He was utilizing secure connections to the Internet between himself, his laboratory, and ten consultants. At the beginning, he had been concerned about security of images, and of the call itself. However, in all aspects, the installation, running on ordinary computers, without expensive specialist equipment, exceeded any security and imaging standards laid down by the University Hospital's CIO.

Midas's mind was active!

The next week passed with Midas doing cool, relaxing, tourist activities. He would stroll around the old city. He drove to Bern and to Geneva. He headed up into the mountains for a day's hiking, feeling the stresses of altitude.

Whatever he was doing, he could not get the demonstration he saw on Monday out of his head. He had fired off questions to some of his techie friends in the US. He had downloaded report after report from the web on video conferencing and communications. He had met

Hans and his son a couple of times and quizzed both Hans and Darren about the system.

He knew it would not be long before he would want to be active again. He had already been away from the marina for four weeks, and he was hankering to work on something new.

Had Hans introduced him to a potential new business?

It was the 16th of May – just one week after landing in Europe, and Midas could feel his world turning upside down again. He was heading back to Florida, in a window seat, 10A, on Swiss Flight 64. His eyes were closed. He was deep in thought and had already formed a vision of a new business. He was thinking of the pieces of a new puzzle. He felt a gentle touch on his shoulder.

FOURTY FOUR

A stewardess was trying to attract Midas's attention. She had a menu and drinks list in hand. Midas looked up. He looked past the stewardess, to the man standing behind her.

Midas raised himself from the deep cushions of the business class seat and smiled. He was looking into the eyes of an old friend.

"Nestor! I could have guessed you would be up here in the clouds," he laughed. "You just stepped in I assume?"

"Nestor replied, "Kind of, I was about ten rows behind you. I saw you come on board."

"Courtesy of the universe, I expect."

"Yes, I guess." Nestor was smiling.

The stewardess was looking at the two men, not sure whether she should interrupt.

Then Midas turned to her, and with the best charming smile he could manage, asked the stewardess, "Two beers please. Yes, I know he has just walked up from the back of the aircraft, and I know he should be in his seat, and I know you are doing your job, but I have not seen this guy for an age. And I promise I will not tell your boss."

She looked at him. "I am the boss."

She then smiled, and nodded to the vacant seat next to Midas, "I think you should both sit down and catch up with what's been happening, don't you?"

She turned to Nestor, her tone was friendly but firm, "And you sir, I didn't see. I don't want to see, and I only have two beers. Got it?"

"Got it."

Nestor was first to ask, "How have you been?"

"Great," replied Midas, "I have had a fantastic trip to Zurich. I can see another new business."

"Wow, that's fantastic. Now, as you reflect on your plans, be observant. See if there is anything the universe is offering you that's not obvious."

Midas retorted, "If it's not obvious, how do I see it?"

Nestor laughed, "Well done. You have a lot of personal knowledge now, and you know much more about yourself. You have been learning all the time you were in the marina. You know how, when you are open to possibilities, they appear. If you are closed, you cannot see."

"Yes, I know,"

"However, Midas, let me say one thing more. Be forever vigilant. Your greatest ally or your greatest foe is your subconscious mind. Over the past twenty-four months you have rolled back the tide of programming and negative beliefs that were deep in the recesses of your subconscious for decades. You have emerged a new man. You have had a mental awakening. You have addressed and countered the past with good positive thinking, new knowledge, and a love of yourself. In time you completely remove the effects and you will live a wonderful positive life, full of abundance.

"But your efforts on your journey require discipline. Think of an athlete who not only stops training, he/she stops exercising, and before long they are unhealthy, overweight, and their athletic abilities have been submerged by a sea of indolence. I urge you to continue to work on yourself, as well as your business. Remember…"

"Mindset before skill set…," Midas laughed. "I know, but I appreciate you reminding me. When we get back home, I would like your help to understand much more."

"Sure," answered Nestor. "Oh, and a question, where is home?"

"I don't know; I will tell you. Oh, but I don't need to, do I?

"No," said Nestor, as he got up to leave. "Thanks for the beer."

Nestor disappeared through the business class curtain, and was gone.

The thought of where to live had preoccupied Midas over the past couple of weeks. He left Chicago a couple of years before, and Florida had been a refuge and oasis and, as it transpired, a new world of possibility and reward. He was tempted to move to the West Coast. Now he was on the way back to the marina. Mike had asked him to 'house sit' for a couple of months, while Mike and his grown-up family headed to Asia.

Midas settled back into marina living, but without the stress of being on call for all manner of repairs. Jeff and David were working well, and Midas was not called. Regaining his small 'office' in the Marina building, Midas set to work.

Over the next eight weeks Midas researched the visual communications marketplace thoroughly. He understood the strengths and weaknesses all the various players. He was approaching the possibility of this new venture with a degree of thoroughness. He understood the infrastructure, the costs, and the charging rates that would be needed in a cloud-based visual communications service, which would be a new concept.

He believed that he had a price advantage over the traditional incumbents in the market, and a quality and security edge over the popular vendors. He concluded that, while the big players had a very large installed base, which they would protect, they had no product or service which could compete with price points and flexibility that Midas's solution would offer.

Midas had designed an infrastructure that required the couple of servers that he had seen in Zürich to be replicated in the West Coast, in the East Coast, in Europe, and in Hong Kong, to allow for true global collectivity. Midas had tracked down the vendor of the software that Hans was using to direct and control communications traffic, and had negotiated a license deal that, while expensive, would be easily amortized over the thousands of users he expected.

Midas quietly shared his vision with a number of people, but the size of the opportunity was lost on them. He thought, *most of them think the idea is ambitious and that I am crazy, that means I must be on to a good thing.* He laughed. He had reached out to Peter the tech entrepreneur who he had met at the Hyatt two years previously. It was not a completely unexpected contact as Midas had kept in touch, and every couple of months Peter would ask of Midas's progress. He had been overjoyed at the news of the sale of the business. Peter was good counsel. He saw Midas's vision. He counseled that because Midas could access a sound and functioning software, creating a cloud was no big deal. Midas would not be facing a technology challenge but rather a market penetration Everest?

Mike returned and Midas made his move.

He had decided to base himself in Manhattan, New York – possibly on the Upper East Side; it was an up and coming trendy compromise. He thought that it got him close to the hot bed of commerce, tech and art, at a price he could afford.

He had told Lynn he was heading to the North East. A day later she emailed him with details of temporary accommodation. A girlfriend of hers was going to Europe for six months – could Midas house sit.

The universe was supporting his moves, and Midas was becoming adept at house sitting.

A week later, Midas was stepping into a trendy apartment on 74th Street between Park and Lexington.

It was now time to start work. He had funding, he had an idea, and he had researched the market. He had spoken to experts in the field. He needed to get a small team – someone who could be the technical support guru and keep the infrastructure working, and someone who, with Midas, could hustle for contracts. He felt he needed a good, solid-sounding board. Not a techie, but a businessman who would, if Midas was successful, have companies who would use what Midas was calling a Visual Cloud Platform – Video Conferencing in the Cloud. It would be a while before Midas realized how far ahead of the market he was. He was a trailblazer, a pioneer.

Midas pulled out his wallet; he took out a business card and dropped it on his table, and picked up his phone.

He called a number; the worst that could happen was a "No".

FOURTY FIVE

Vanessa, the PA, pushed open the door and pushed her head through the crack. "There's a gentleman called Midas asking for you."

"What, he's here?"

"No, on the phone,"

"Put him through, put him through,'" exclaimed the Viking as he pressed the button on his lavish speakerphone.

"Midas, my friend, how are you, where are you?" The Viking's voice boomed across the expanse of his Chrysler Building Suite.

"I'm in New York," answered Midas, and before he could say anything else the Viking answered.

"That's fantastic; we must meet. You must come to see me. I have been telling everyone about your work. What are you doing in New York?"

Midas felt encouraged by the Viking's reaction to his call.

"We sold the business some months ago; we did well. I'm looking at another venture. I thought I might base myself here."

From the other side of his suite, the Viking aimed his considerable voice at the speakerphone, "You sold out, good for you. Is the new guy as good as you, if that's possible? I hope you made a killing. You deserve it."

"We did ok, thanks. The new team is working well," Midas responded, slightly understating the deal.

"Are you going to do the same business? There's a shortage of people like you in New York. I can't get any decent work done on the yacht. It's a disgrace. You would do well here."

"No, I am going back into tech."

The Viking cut him short, "Good, good, OK, enough of this chitchat, tell me more next week. Can we meet next week – Tuesday? Come to the office, you know where it is. Come before lunch, say eleven o'clock, we can then go to eat at my favorite steak house. Let Vanessa, my PA, know if it is a problem. Otherwise I expect to see you. Must go, thanks for the call Midas – thank you, it's great to hear from you."

There was a click. The Viking was off the line.

It was ten forty-five, on Tuesday morning when Midas arrived at the intersection of 42nd Street and Lexicon, the location of one of New York's iconic skyscrapers; built and funded by Walter P Chrysler, the Chrysler Building, an Art Deco masterpiece, had opened in 1930.

Midas pushed open one of the magnificent ground floor doors on Lexicon Avenue, a door that was clad in stainless steel with an inverted irregular pentagon of heavy stained glass in the center, and entered the lobby that had been the film set in innumerable movies. He went to the elevators and proceeded to the thirty-fifth floor where the Viking had his office.

He arrived, to be welcomed by Vanessa, the Viking's attractive and smart PA, and he was immediately ushered into the corner suite where he was greeted by his one-time customer with a firm handshake.

"Midas, come and sit here." The Viking led Midas towards a pair of exquisite sofas, finished in dark mahogany leather, positioned in front of an art deco coffee table of immense proportions, but which befitted the interior of the office. Midas was struck by how small the windows were, but then realized that the complexity of the exterior architecture would not allow for contemporary full floor to ceiling glazing.

"Tell me what you have been doing. How long is it since we met?"

The Viking interrupted the answer to his own question, "You did an amazing job on Brave New Horizons, I still cannot see any trace of a repair. I actually wrote to Beneteau and sent the photos; I told them in the time they were thinking about answering my request for help, a team of good American craftsmen – and a lady – had solved the problem, and they could stay in France and continue their lunch. It was a bit cheeky, but I enjoyed writing that bit." He laughed.

"Ok Midas, I will be quiet now."

Midas gave the Viking a summary of the buildup of the marina business – how they had expanded and then were bought out by Jeff, the ex-GE Exec. The Viking wanted to know the deal, and when Midas gave him the outline, the Viking slapped the arm of the sofa hard, "Excellent – great timing, great deal. I doubt I could have done any better."

Midas told him about Lausanne and what he had seen. He explained why it was significant. The Viking listened intently. Midas then went on to explain the concept of a Visual Communications Cloud that anyone could tap into – accessible but secure. He talked about how companies today spent hundreds of thousands of dollars on a video conference facility that might serve jut eight locations, and how at the other end of the scale, Skype and Skype look-alikes failed the Enterprise business test on the grounds of quality, reliability, and security. He articulated why his cloud solution satisfied an untapped market in business, and which could easily be extended to leisure applications.

"Midas, you have got something I have been looking for. You know I am into shipping; I want to communicate with my ships, I want to see what's going on, and I think you are saying that I can use your system to achieve ship to shore video. And I can use it for all my offices around the world?

"Think that if I had it on Brave New Horizons those bastards would not have got away – we would have had the video transferred to my office and to shore and recorded as it happened – which is one step forward. Piracy, think about piracy, we can have the skipper send live video in a pirate situation."

The Viking was racing through use cases, and how Midas's idea could change how he communicated with his businesses.

Midas did not want to stop the flow although he recognized that some of these use cases were a long step from the high-quality, multi-party business conferencing service that he was planning to start with.

"Time for lunch." The Viking rose from the opulent seating and escorted Midas towards the door.

They descended the elevator and the Viking guided Midas to the Lexington Ave exit. They crossed the street and entered Grand Central Market. Still heading forward, the Viking led Midas into the Grand Central Station and to Michael Jordan's Steak House set in the North corner of the great Beaux Arts concourse, with a view of the famous clock, and the constellation blue ceiling.

Enjoying one of the best steaks he had ever tasted, Midas answered the probing questions from the Viking. *While skills of the Viking were far from being technology-centric, he was very well-versed in what technology can do,* thought Midas. The Viking moved on to money, and investment and returns. He asked Midas if he had a business plan, Midas confirmed it was in good shape, not yet finished, but could be ready for review in a couple of days.

"I would like to see it. Can you send it to me? Send it to me then we can have a chat again. I have a couple of ideas."

They talked of sailing, and a little bit about the Viking's background; he was not a person to sit and talk about his many exploits as though he was trying to impress. But he did have a habit of dropping the odd snippet into a story that begged another question. Somehow the conversation had got on to gold, and the Viking sounded very knowledgeable about the gold mining industry. Midas asked him how he knew so much. The Viking casually mentioned that he once acquired a gold mine 'by accident' and ran it for five years before selling it on. Midas wanted elaboration of the 'by accident' comment but the Viking brushed it aside, "It's a long story, 'another time."

And by this time, the coffee had been brought and consumed. The Viking had paid the bill, and he rose from the table.

They descended onto the concourse. As they strode towards the famous clock in the center, the Viking said, "I will look forward to seeing you in a few days," and on that note he strode towards the Central Market and Midas headed for the subway.

What ideas the Viking had were anyone's guess, and it was taxing Midas's mind as he walked down the subway steps. He was so engrossed that he missed his footing and he slipped three steps to land on his backside at the foot of the stairs.

A hand reached down to help him get up. He looked up, and saw a lined white face, unshaven, and wrapped in a waterproof over jacket.

Midas did not care who helped him. He took one hand and pulled himself up; so strong was the other guy that they bumped into each other.

Midas nodded and thanked the guy, but the other man just acknowledged with a wave of the hand and set off up the stairs.

Midas limped forward. He put his hand in his pocket to retrieve his wallet with his metro card. His wallet was not in his pocket. Midas swiveled around, patting his other pockets as he turned.

No wallet. He started to run back towards the stairs.

FOURTY SIX

Midas poised himself to sprint up the stairs after his would-be Samaritan turned assailant when he saw an elderly lady bend down to pick up a black object from the floor. He looked again, it was his wallet. He stopped and asked her if he could see it. He opened the wallet and showed her his driving license. She matched the photograph to the face and smiled, "You are very lucky; be careful young man."

Midas guessed it had fallen from his pocket when he fell and slipped beneath the step overhang.

Midas started to walk towards the Metro. *How quick we are to judge, how fast we make conclusions that are wrong, really wrong. I thought he had taken it when he helped me up and bumped into me. How we stereotype and put stations on people, he mused.* Midas thought that if the guy had been clean-shaven, suited, smartly dressed, then maybe he would have first looked at the floor to see if he had dropped the wallet; because the guy was scruffy, unshaven, unkempt and shuffling, he assumed he had been robbed.

Midas did not feel happy. He thought that he had a good perspective of life, and of people. He thought that he was sufficiently humble to be non-judgmental. But he realized how deeply ingrained in his psyche social stereotyping in particular situations had become. He realized he was no different from any other American, irrespective of race, color, creed, or background. *We all carry our interpretation of other people – without even meeting them and speaking to them. WOW, that was a powerful encounter. I have to work on that. I forgive myself and say thank you for the experience – it taught me a valuable lesson.*

Over the next twenty-four hours, Midas polished off the business plan. He had done a lot of research beforehand and structured the plan. He had recognized the advice that many writers and blogs had given him – too much, is too much. There is no case for writing up volumes of analysis in thousands of words, and frankly no one will read it. The research is necessary to get a perspective and intelligence – but a synopsis is all that is required.

There are key areas and topics that any start-up business model should cover, and Midas used the structure wisely:

- Opportunity: What's the idea?
- Innovation: What's new?
- Customers: Who is the user / payer?
- Competition: Who?
- Sales, reach customer: How?
- Marketing, create demand: How?
- Biz model: How do we make money?
- Time to market: How long?
- Product development: How much?
- Technical risk or market risk?
- Seed Finance: How much / source?
- Following Finance: When, how much?

He used the headings to summarize his ideas in five pages. Admittedly, there was a twenty-page version behind it, but he knew that the Viking would never plough through a long document. He emailed the summary to Vanessa, asked her to print it and put it on the Viking's desk. He waited.

Vanessa called Midas a couple of hours later. Could Midas meet the Viking the following morning? Midas confirmed a time, ten o'clock.

The rest of the afternoon passed in routine chores and Midas headed to the East River. He found that the promenade behind Gracie Mansion was a cool place to be. He sat on one of the benches and reflected.

He pulled out his phone and messaged Lynn. "Moved north, as planned, settled in New York, where are you, how are you, what are you doing?" Given the long intervals between their communication, Midas was embarrassingly brief. But Lynn did not admonish him and replied in a long message – giving Midas chapter and verse of the recent weeks. She signed off, "Miss you, I want to come to New York!"

The following morning Midas presented himself at the Viking's office.

Today the Viking's demeanor was different. He was friendly and affable but concentrated; this was business.

He had read Midas's summary and he probed and prodded, commented and questioned, asked for clarification here and clarification there. He pushed Midas hard on the downside risks, and also why anyone would choose Midas's proposed service over, for example, Skype. This question took up some time, and Midas had to reiterate the positioning of his service as a secure, reliable high-quality visual communication application – which was suitable for business, and not aimed at the consumer and friend-to-friend market. He was providing accessible video conferencing at an affordable price, with no investment, to businesses of any scale. The features and functions Midas's application would provide were beyond Skype's capability and the capability of any other consumer-grade app.

The Viking accepted Midas's explanation and moved on to financing. How much money was required? Midas had guessed that he would need to initially invest around two hundred thousand dollars to get the service into the market. He would bootstrap, of course, but the Cloud had to be established which meant a small inventory of servers, located in rented space at data centers on both sides of North America, and on the other side of the Atlantic and Pacific. He would need to pay for software licenses. Midas's application used a secure access into the Internet so communication charges were negligible. As the service expanded, additional licenses and capacity would be needed, but this would be funded from revenue. He would need two staff initially, one on technical support and one to work with Midas on selling.

The Viking talked again about the maritime industry and gave Midas a couple of contacts to talk to. He liked what he read, and he applauded Midas for his ability to see the opportunity; he liked the way Midas had thought laterally from the visit to Lausanne and scaled the vision of the business beyond a few screens in one hospital. Actually, the Viking was doing Hans a disservice; Midas had heard that Hans was rapidly expanding across the hospital sector in Switzerland.

The Viking looked at Midas and asked him if he had the funds to invest. Midas said he had – his proceeds from the sale of First Integrated Marine were safely and securely 'locked away'.

"Have you the funds to expand?"

"To a point, yes," answered Midas. "And I believe revenues will start to cover expansion. I should be cash breakeven in three to four months, as contract payments are generally in advance of the service".

"Do you want a partner?" the Viking eyed Midas and watched his reaction.

Midas hesitated for a moment. It was Midas's baby, he wasn't thinking of taking anyone else on board, but he remembered how powerful the partnership with Mike had been.

"Have you some ideas?" asked Midas.

The Viking was quick to respond. "I really don't need another business, I have too many already. But I like your idea, I really do and I think that visual communication is the way to go – I can see my screen on my desk talking to my ships and to my yacht," the Viking laughed. "More seriously, I am not a – what do you say – a techie. But I can see how technology can change how we work and I think you are onto something."

The Viking took a sip of the tea that Vanessa had placed on his desk, "On a different matter, I always am careful who I go into business with, and you impressed me down in Florida. You struck me as someone who would go a long way. I back people, not ideas. Ideas are ten a penny; good people are rare."

Midas was astounded. This conversation has taken a turn that he could never have imagined.

Over the next half-hour, they discussed how to implement Midas's plan. The Viking would open his contact list, which was extensive, to Midas, and that would immediately give the new business a strong pipeline of prospects. Midas said he would work from his apartment for the time being, but the Viking offered a small office on E96th Street, between Lexington and Park. A basement office conversion, which was part of a building he had acquired in another transaction and was presently empty. It was formerly a hardware shop. It was fifty yards from 96th street Metro station.

After an hour, they shook hands. Midas would go ahead and put everything in place and the new company would start to change how the world communicates!

They also had a name: Metasys Visual Inc. Why? 'Meta' implied a higher level of abstraction; 'Sys' as an abbreviation of systems; and 'Visual' referring to visual communications: A system for a higher level of visual communication. Clever!

Midas stepped into the sunshine on 42nd Street and looked up.

You never cease to amaze me!

He was addressing his thoughts to the invisible universe.

What do have for me, next?

FOURTY SEVEN

In January 2012, Midas quietly launched their service into the market.

The Viking took an equal stake in the business. They would both fund the business, as necessary, on a dollar for dollar basis; the LLC shares were allocated 50-50 to the Viking and Midas.

They got some early traction. The benefits of visual communication and data sharing and collaboration were not lost on business people who had previously avoided video conferencing on a widespread basis due to its prohibitive cost. Midas's business model, which represented video as a service, was priced competitively, with the additional benefit that the user could use their existing personal computing and mobile devices. It was a win-win and he started to gain a portfolio of good customers.

He would have to recruit a team; he was reliant on some goodwill from the software vendor for support and was doing most of the selling himself. In his sparsely furnished small office acquired from The Viking on a nominal rent, he wrote contracts, figured out pricing, reached out to prospects and set up demonstration after demonstration, it was a bootstrapped start-up.

A friend set an accounting system up, another friend looked over the legals. He was working 14 hours a day. While he knew that he could sell their visual communications service anywhere, he initially restricted their 'territory' to the NY area and the East Coast, focusing on businesses in New York State, New Jersey, and Connecticut.

He quickly recruited a Sales VP, an ex-Avaya guy, called Ted. Ted was a typical road warrior, with a strong background in communications. Ted and Midas focused on businesses that were geographically diverse, where visual communications was a major benefit to reduce costs of travel, but whose decision makers were in the North East.

Midas and Ted were gaining customers. They were also stretching the capabilities of the software and infrastructure; Midas would need to invest to increase capacity.

What Midas had created was becoming known as a Platform as a Service or Video as a Service business.

The 'Platform' was the software and infrastructure that Metasys owned; customers could access and use the Platform for a regular payment (monthly or per user, or per call). Each customer had their own unique secure and discrete space on the platform and the software provided them with visual communication or video conferencing at low cost. This was an innovation in so many ways – ease of use, no capital cost, quality, reliability, flexibility, and security, all in a normal desktop computer, laptop, or computer.

Although the idea of creating a cloud (computer processing resources) across the globe by linking computers (from giant processors to glorified PC's referred to as servers) had been talked about for decades, it was the Web and the Internet together that spawned Cloud Computing, potentially for the masses, around 2000. It was another decade before this concept accelerated into the mainstream to provide a phenomenal range of services 'on demand'. Business-grade visual communications was a late adopter of the cloud, and Midas was one of the first to pioneer this sector.

Metasys Visual was trailblazing in a new niche sector, but... and there is often a "But".

No matter how appealing, innovative and creative an entrepreneur may think their idea to be, as soon as a new innovative service or product is launched, something will happen to diminish the prospect of success and create vulnerability. This was the case here.

Midas was trawling through some technical journals when he read of Google's acquisition of a company called GIPS in 2010. GIPS had developed computer code that allowed developers and engineers to create video and voice applications inside a web browser. Imagine being able to click on to a button on your favorite supplier's website and speak to someone without leaving that webpage: that was the concept, that was the vision.

After acquiring GIPS, Google quietly released the GIPS software as freely available open-source code. This meant that any developer /

engineer could use the code to create voice and video chat applications that operate in a web browser – say in Chrome, or Firefox - without users needing to install additional software layers known as a 'plug-in'.

These so called plug-ins had been necessary to date, and the reason why almost all companies refrained from this complex process.

The GIPS software was basic and incomplete, but it pointed in a new direction. The take-up by developers had been slow, and real-time communications was a backroom research play for just a very few academic and research departments and avid geeks.

Midas read more, and watched Google videos and realized that there was a seismic shift that was going to happen and it was almost top-secret. It was so far out of the mainstream that it was invisible. It remained that way despite, in mid-2012, Google famously announcing that something called Web Real-Time Communications would change the way the people communicate.

The more Midas probed, he found that engineers from a select group of top technology companies had picked up Google's initiative and alongside Google and Mozilla, they were also influencing the direction of what would be called 'real-time communication in the web'. This small group of engineers was proposing something that would eventually work and become stable. At that point there was the potential to revolutionize global communications.

The catalyst arrived, for Midas, when he read a comment from an eminent analyst[1] that stated: "Potentially, Web Real-Time Communications could enable the same transformation for the communications industry that the original browser did for information".

If true, in a few years, the manner in which businesses, consumers, suppliers, professionals, educators, doctors and patients communicate would start to change – maybe very quickly. Midas's new cloud-based visual communication platform would be rendered obsolete. Application developers will create whole new ways of communicating from within a web page, or from a mobile application.

Midas sat down with the Viking in his office, and outlined what he had discovered. Midas knew that the Viking was not a 'techie', but he

---

[1] Phil Edholm in No Jitter April 26 2012

was perceptive and had an agile mind. While not understanding all of the technical detail, he could visualize the impacts of changes on a large canvas. Things that could disrupt industries fascinated him.

The Viking understood the principles of what Midas was talking about, but also recognized that the in-browser communication technology was in its infancy, and it was a dream of some engineers. The fact that Google had acquired the expertise and the intellectual property gave the idea of web-based communication credibility. With Google's resources it was possible that something as far-fetched as looking at a supplier's webpage, clicking a button to discuss the contract with the supplier, or using an immediate and newly-opened video window in the web page, could become a reality. This could have repercussions across so many industries: from health care to education, from engineering to e-commerce, from transport to energy exploration, the list was endless.

The Viking warned Midas that creating such a disruptive technology was a long road, and an expensive road, to walk.

Midas's excitement was palpable. He wouldn't let it rest. He could see the communication taking place between mobile devices and call centers, and on web pages; he could see remote drilling sites contacting a distant operations center to 'show and tell' the details of a breakdown and get a solution faster. He could even see a shopping mall with the video wall that became interactive in a two-way conversation as a customer walked towards it. Midas was not short of imagination. A ship can communicate with the shore. He knew that had the Viking's attention.

Midas's small team continued to build the Metasys Visual communication business. It was starting to generate good revenue, and without the knowledge of Google's initiative, Midas could be easily convinced that his new business had significant promise over the next ten years. He and the Viking had invested a reasonable sum to set up the new company, but Midas still had significant reserves from the sale of the marine business. Midas's view of banks was unprintable, verging on paranoia. He had placed his funds in the custody of a small private boutique fund manager who had a stellar reputation, which Midas had researched extensively and thoroughly before he engaged them.

Midas was working hard at his business, but he found that his thoughts were preoccupied with real-time communications.

Once more he discussed it extensively with the Viking. He was counseled to check it out and then make a decision, "But do not lose focus on the new cloud visual communication business."

Midas found two engineers at MIT who were heavily into video and communication tools. They had built a number of experimental visual communication platforms. When Midas explained the significance of the Google acquisition he found that they were already aware of the technology initiative, and trials and tests were taking place in academic research establishments and in labs at the likes of Google, Ericson, and AT&T.

They told Midas that the basic code to communicate via a browser available for any developer to use only provided a simple and very partial solution to what Midas saw in his vision for future communications. They explained that the effort required to provide a fully commercial, reliable, secure global communication platform, which major businesses would consider adopting, from the source code that Google had released, was akin to the first ascent of Everest.

Ascending Everest did not deter Midas. He was passionate in his belief; he was convinced of his vision, and he started to research the field of networks, telecommunications, the internet, applications, visual communications software, digital and social trends, and future scoping. Every step that he took, every time he talked to experts, he became more confident that he was on the right track.

He reminded himself to retain the big picture, the grand vision, and be prudent and measured in the 'new' Metasys Visual direction. He was sure they should take advantage of the disruption in communications that he saw coming.

From his research Midas knew that he had sufficient knowledge, at a technical level, to have sensible discussions with the MIT engineers, but he could not let himself get drawn into the architecture and intensive technical discussions that they would have with others researching the same field.

It was clear that going down the path to bring a completely new technology to the market had to be done in stages. The Viking warned it was not for the faint-hearted. Very deep pockets were required, and there was considerable research required with uncertain outcomes.

Midas was faced with a massive opportunity: could he disrupt such a massive industry as global communications?

From tiny beginnings in a basement in Upper Manhattan, could Metasys Visual become a major player in changing how people communicate – forevermore?

FOURTY EIGHT

Midas and the Viking stepped into the latter's favorite Italian restaurant off 5th Avenue. The Viking walked over to a quiet table at the far right-hand side of the room. There was a quiet buzz as the diners who had arrived earlier talked quietly over the best Italian lunchtime menu in this part of town.

They sat down; a crisp white tablecloth, china and silverware had been set on the table. This restaurant was very Italian – family owned and run. Luigi's sons, daughters, wife, and cousins, populated the place. He had four eateries in the space of one hundred meters of storefront – a deli bar, a Japanese bar, and a salad bar. Today they were in the fourth, more up-market restaurant, named No Menu, from the custom of the dinner choice being Luigi's choice, with limited room for negotiation. There was a quietly stated elegance.

Luigi's daughter greeted them, the Viking chose vitello tonnato, for starters, and Midas chose the antipasto of cured meats. For a main Midas ordered a salted sea bass sauce and some vegetables on the side. The Viking took the arrabiatta penne. Midas declined wine. The Viking took a glass of Friulano.

Midas was ready to launch into the latest news but the Viking spoke first.

"Midas, I have been down the road of R&D projects before. Not tech ones, but R&D nevertheless. You know the multi-billion-dollar silicon plant we have in Arizona, that was a major breakthrough in silicon technology and in production methods, a first in the industry, one of the biggest plants in the world, cutting-edge in every way. But it cost us tens, if not hundreds, of millions overestimate. The engineers came in with a budget that was attractive to the Board, you will recall that I am on their Board - but that was only the beginning.

Costs soared; we were going into the unknown, just like you want to do. I don't expect your project to be any different. How much are you budgeting for research to get this web thing into a state when you can sell it?"

Midas explained that he had already had this conversation with the MIT engineers. There were many unknowns, many variables. One was Google and Mozilla, and, in a different way, Microsoft. Each different browser, be it Chrome, Firefox, or Internet Explorer, had to have "web real time communications code" embedded inside it, so that developers could write the browser to browser communication functions. But today, in Chrome and Firefox, the embedded experimental communications code was very unstable, and Microsoft was waiting in the sidelines and not releasing a browser with the necessary functionality. The technology was also subject to standards being worked through by the Internet Administration body called W3C (World Wide Web Consortium); the standard would not be completed for another year or two. To get a real estimate was very difficult.

At best, they could get a working proof of concept up in a three or four months, but how far that was away from commercialization was anyone's guess. And the number of engineers required to build products and a platform would start to rise. Both the market and the technical end game were unclear at this time.

At every level, the story was vague. Midas winced. He knew from the Viking's look that he was not convincing him, and to be honest Midas was not sure he was convincing himself about the accurate timescales.

Midas held on to his vision, held on to his belief. He knew deep down that this emergent technology would revolutionize communications. And he was not alone. He had talked to other experts who had followed this technology, they had concurred. But no one seemed to be able to articulate exactly how, and when, the commercial impact would be felt.

Everyone acknowledged that, as a technology, it would impact all aspects of how people engage with each other at a personal and business level. Midas reflected, it was more certain to bet in a casino – there you knew the odds and the parameters.

They talked about the processes that were needed to get to, at least, a working prototype of a product or service. The Viking was not technical and Midas knew that, so he carefully articulated the story in a way that was business-speak and not tech-speak. The Viking grasped the concepts but, and he admitted it, he did not understand how engineers function – or what the build and development process was.

The Viking did have a very good brain for plotting a future landscape, for seeing trends, and seeing opportunities. He was blessed with a strong instinct. He had made a lot of money in shipping and logistics by the consolidation of container lines; he had seen the demise of the bulk cargo and switched into containerization well ahead of the rest of the industry. He had seen the potential of renewable energy and invested heavily in solar before it became fashionable. He was incredibly well connected and watched global trends carefully. He was on the board of ten international businesses, and Chairman of two, so the type of conversation that they were having was not new to the Viking.

He was skeptical but healthily so. He was trying to probe Midas's thinking.

The discussion went back and forth for an hour. It was clear that the Viking had been doing his own research. He had his network of people, some of whom were active in the communications world. He was very close to the board of directors in two major Telcos. He had been quietly reaching out across boundaries to Europe and China to check out the awareness of this new technology and its impact.

Finally, they sat drinking coffee, the Viking's advice to Midas was clear.

"We need to get something working, to see if this is real, and how difficult it is. If it is very difficult then there are not going to be many players at this time, most businesses will sit back and wait for others to break ice and drown. If it is easy then everyone will rush in and you have a crowded market with no differentiation. Go and engage these MIT guys if you can. If we are going to do this, we need the talent, the best talent, and we need them locked in. We cannot invest tens or hundreds of thousands of dollars for them to get to a point of viability and then walk off with the family silver."

Midas noted that "We" had slipped into the conversation. They had both invested in the visual communications cloud business, but now they were moving into a different field and it was clear to the Viking, although he had not said this yet, that the new business needed his experience, gravitas, network and money. How true that statement was would be proven over time!

Entrepreneurial ventures, and entrepreneurs, need heavyweight mentors, sponsors, and supporters.

Midas walked back to the subway; the Viking had given him a lot to think about.

The office that housed the small team that supported the cloud video communication business was housed in up town premises owned by one of the Viking's companies. The office was in what had been a hardware shop previously and was in a street that was being given over to trendy starter offices, restaurants, and cafes. Slightly beyond the bootstrapping stage, Midas was still being frugal.

For the current Metasys Visual business, there was the team that Midas had put in place: a Sales VP, and a technical support guy, and, the latest addition, one technical project manager who dealt with commissioning of the systems and upgrading and maintenance of the servers. Midas had been amazed at the simplicity of the business. The technology risk had been removed by using proven software from a vendor of good reputation, so now it was all about marketing. Contracts were for two or three years, and an annual renewal thereafter. This created a long-term income stream. While the monthly subscriptions were modest and affordable for any business, they mounted up and, as more contracts were being signed, the monthly recurring revenue was on an upward path.

It had been six months since he had signed his first contract and he was signing on average two a month. The latest forecast showed they would reach breakeven next month, and cash surplus the following month. He wanted to get this to the point where anyone could go online, register and start with a free service, then upgrade to a paying contract. This was a model favored by the consumer end of the business, but it was proving to be difficult to implement in his business. Businesses seemed to want to deal with someone, and to do a proof of concept, however lightweight. And there were multiple levels of approval authority to navigate. He resigned himself to having to expand the sales team and lead generation.

The positive aspect of this business was that it was already disruptive in its own market. The idea of low-cost, high-quality video conferencing, without a capital outlay, and no significant communications charges appealed. There were no heavy communications charges because all the calls were carried, encrypted, over the Internet. Midas could see that the upward trend could continue with incremental investment in additional server capacity and support. He was confident, that with the appeal of recurring revenue he had a business capable of being built and then sold in a couple of years' time.

This suited his big picture strategy. He believed that it would take the MIT guys, if he could persuade them to join, that period of time to get to a viable and commercial solution to provide embedded real-time communications in web and mobile applications.

Midas was still concerned. His meeting with the Viking was timely; they needed to make a decision on whether to, and how to, go forward. It was a big bet, bigger than he had imagined. He would, once again, be staking his total available resources on a gamble. He reminded himself that this was what entrepreneurship was about.

There were some hard questions to be asked.

FOURTY NINE

Midas had read widely about entrepreneurship, particularly in the tech space. The question of failure was widely debated and argued; wild statistics were thrown around – many without any proof. That start-up businesses fail was a given, and how many fail was more debatable.

In the failure category, the top three reasons are nailed to the wall:

- First, *no market need* is the top of most lists – irrespective of industry – ideas that have no place in the minds, or wallets, of consumers.
- Next comes *the cash crunch:* funding runs out and an idea, however well intentioned, dies – starved to death;
- Then comes *the wrong team* – strangling the business with petty politics and ineptitude.

Beyond these top three reasons, there is another cauldron of evil waiting to snare the unwary entrepreneur:

- Business ineffectiveness, poor marketing, bad processes,
- Price and cost issues, loss of focus,
- Disharmony among team and investors, burnout, failure to pivot.

The list builds to liken the Entrepreneur's Journey to the Labors of Hercules.

Midas had to navigate these dark waters and come out unscathed. He had another investor – a demanding one, but a knowledgeable and experienced partner nevertheless. He was not alone.

But this was one of those times when he needed to think.

He sat on his favorite bench overlooking the East River. He was thinking about Metasys Visual and what they had achieved and what he had found.

As he thought about the place where the business was today, Midas realized that they had arrived at a classic management situation where significant alternative strategies had to be chosen or discarded.

On the one hand, they were successfully building a cloud-based visual communication business which, over time, would provide a sustainable and growing revenue stream from his subscription model, but could also have low barriers to entry, and be threatened by a completely new technology – real-time communications on the web. It may be short-lived.

On the other hand, he was going to dive into a completely new and untried and unknown technology, which – if delivered in line with the promises of Google and other proponents – would completely transform the way people communicate, all over the world. But when there would be wholesale adoption, and what that meant, was unknown. Being an early mover and building up a reservoir of unshakable experience and talent would be an incalculable asset when the market starts to adopt. But it would take money and time, in quanta that were unknown.

Midas was torn, his thinking intense. He had got up from his seat and was striding along the promenade. His thinking was often at its best when he moved. He walked one way and then another, he turned and retraced his steps. He turned again. It was as though each direction represented one of the seemingly conflicting strategies. He was measuring each one as he paced. After twenty minutes of to and fro, back and forth, along the quarter mile route, he returned to his seat.

There was no doubt that to run both tracks in parallel was the best course – for now. But Midas had to be ready to pivot as outcomes became clear.

The following day Midas was to meet with Chad and Dave. The two MIT researchers had said that they were starting to see breakthroughs and could put a simple demo together. That was encouraging, but Midas made it clear that their intention should be to extend beyond their simple demonstration and they needed to be prepared for it.

That evening, Midas rang the Viking and explained that he had a meeting planned for the following day, and that he wanted to put a proposition to the MIT guys.

He felt that Dave would want to remain at his university lab but Chad might be persuaded to cross over the great divide into the real world of business and technology start-ups. Midas had figured out that it would take at least one year for them to get a stable platform and product that could be taken to market. Even if Chad could be persuaded to work in part for equity, they were going to need a substantial budget to get through the twelve months. At the end of twelve months he could not guarantee of a useful outcome or one that could be commercialized.

Midas calculated that they would need a minimum of half a million dollars, possibly one million. At the point of time when that money was consumed and spent they should be approaching the stage where they had a sufficiently strong story to be able to go to a wider group of investors. They could sketch out a future strategy and the basics of an organization that would grow, in time, to in excess of 100 people. Once more Midas was going to empty his bank account.

The Viking's reaction was as anticipated, Midas was lectured on the risks of R and D – it was a bottomless pit that swallowed money with an insatiable appetite. The level of uncertainty, and the whole idea was, in the Viking's words, a crazy venture.

The Viking added, "Have you heard of Hofstadter's Law?"

Midas stated he had not.

"Hofstadter's Law – it always takes longer than you expect, even taking account of Hofstadter's Law?

"Do you get it?

"So, I can tell you now, whatever timescale you are thinking, double it, and double it again and then you might be fifty percent of the way there."

Midas had resigned himself partway through this tirade that he was going to have to run the course alone, but then at the end of the outburst, the Viking said that he would meet Midas dollar for dollar and that he should start to pull the venture together.

That evening Midas did not sleep; he was wondering what he had done.

He was about to flip the 'On' switch on what, to some, was a foolhardy venture. It was clear from the research he had done that a few companies, including big ones with significantly deeper pockets than theirs, were holding off on committing vast resources, or any resources, to this particular sector of technology.

Midas rationalized that being ahead of the pack would place them in a good position to be acquired once the rest of the world had woken up to the opportunity, but did not want to create the expertise all over again.

Being ahead of the pack might be a good thing, thought Midas, *but what monster was chasing him?*

FIFTY

The following morning Midas sat in Starbucks at the corner of Lexington and E96th Street, and waited for Chad and Dave to emerge from the Subway exit directly outside the coffee shop. He met with Ted, his Sales VP that morning and the forecast of the cloud visual communication business was looking solid. He told Ted that he would need to step back from some of the day-to-day management of the VC business, and Ted appeared to be very relaxed and said that he could continue to build the business provided there was access to Midas for advice on closing some deals, and to provide networking support. Part-time accounting and administration was being taken care of by one of Midas's old friends who had left the audit company that she worked for, and had gone freelance.

The conversation between the three would-be disruptors of the communications industry was animated and excited. Chad was plugged into the thinking amongst the close group of very eminent engineers from different companies who were the core of the web real-time communications movement. The development of this technology was being accelerated by the incredible level of cooperation between engineers in different companies who saw their mission in technology terms: pushing new horizons, and creating commonality of standards and approach which would allow the wholesale adoption of web real-time communications, irrespective of which companies would finally use the technology.

Chad demoed a real-time web call back to his lab, with voice and video out of a simple webpage on his MacBook.

"See? It can work", he said. "And this is just a one-to-one-person call."

Midas's responded, "That's fine, but how many more people can I bring onto the call?

"What I what to know is what are the constraints when sending over the Internet, what is the infrastructure, how is it working?"

A barrage of questions hit Chad and Dave, all of which they answered in a manner which gave Midas confidence that they had researched and built one of the very early prototypes of something that would ultimately change the world.

Midas outlined his vision for how their company would take this technology and commercialize it. He needed a commitment from one or both of the outstanding architects that sat in front of him. He told them that it was going to be a challenging journey – at times it would be fought with compromise between their technical, engineering, and research engineer's mindset and the needs of getting something into the market that was a product or service. He told them that they had very limited budgets to recruit a small team of engineers and there was an expectation that they would work, in part, for a small stake in the business.

As expected, Dave quickly declined, in a manner that confirmed his position was non-negotiable. He wanted to stay within the MIT environment, to work in his lab, and to be in contact with the future edge of research in a number of fields, which today was his primary responsibility. Chad was more receptive to the idea. He had never seen himself as a career MIT person. His primary interest was maintaining his reputation as an architect and engineer on the leading edge of emerging technologies. He thought that this opportunity was well within his capability and interest. Providing that he could be assured of a moderate level of monetary compensation, he had no difficulty in trading his time and sweat for equity.

They planned to start in earnest, with the new business, in a month's time. The current development work that Chad and Dave were immersed in would continue; as they done over the recent weeks, they would move the simple prototype forward and, at the same time, keep abreast of all the technical changes and developments that were emerging in this field.

Two days later Midas had breakfast with the Viking on Brave New Horizons that was now moored in North Cove Marina, NYC. He briefed him on the discussion with Chad and Dave. Midas said that Chad was willing to come on board and lead the architecture, design, and build of the commercial platform and a range of products and services which could be taken to market.

The Viking asked what Chad had asked for in terms of compensation.

The Viking was concerned about the risks associated with having one person at the center of this dive into an unknown world and a new era in web communications. Midas also understood the risk.

Chad had been offered a modest salary and the potential of a small part-ownership in the new business, which would be granted to him by way of options. Midas had hoped that this offer would act as an incentive not to rock the boat, not to leave, but be part of the team that could ultimately be seen to create an organization with substantial value. Chad had accepted the offer with an understanding that it would be reviewed at a future, appropriate time.

Midas was quietly confident that if they could solve the technical issues and deliver a platform and service there was no reason why a company worth hundreds of millions of dollars could not be created. But today he realized that the only thing they had was a very simple, unreliable and incomplete demo.

At the end of breakfast, the Viking and Midas shook hands to the future success of this his brave enterprise. Midas stepped ashore and watched the Viking's crew cast off. The Viking's yacht pulled off its berth, and turned her bow to port and navigated through the marina's narrow entrance towards the center channel of the river. Then it swung to the right and Midas watched 'Brave New Horizons' set sail down the Hudson River towards the Statue of Liberty. Towards an open sea and opportunity.

How very fitting, thought Midas as he read, not for the first time, the yacht's name.

FIFTY ONE

Midas exited the subway at 96th Street, and walked west along the street towards his hardware store as he usually, and jokingly, referred to their office. The original shop had been refitted at some point to create a decent small office. The name was appropriate given the premises' history.

He stood outside their glass-fronted office; it was four steps lower than road level. Wrought iron railings separated footpath from the windows: they looked old and decorative. Square chamfered newels, and hexagonal balustrades supported the top handrail, and the supports were in filled with scrolls. The wrought iron continued down the steps to the entrance.

The brick pillars of doorway remained; the original wooden split door was pushed open at each side, showing a new glass entrance, through which the inside of the office could be clearly seen. Flanking the front door were the original tall narrow windows of the shop; those had been re-glazed with a single panel of glass. The two wooden doors were painted in deep red, which contrasted with the white brickwork to give an appearance of a solid structure.

Looking through the open doors, the contrast was striking; a light beech-colored wooden floor stretched back into the shop. White dividers separated the four workstations, beyond which a white conference table sat in the center of the narrow space at the back of the room.

When he was in the office Midas preferred to work from the conference table; it gave him a large surface on which to spread pages from a large artist's sketchpad. Midas was a very visual person; he would sketch ideas, concepts, and relationships. He drew mad, complex, and circuitous line diagrams, explaining and describing his route map to the future.

This morning he entered the door to the left of the hardware shop. He climbed five steps to a small landing, entered the door, walked forward and then descended eight more steps to where a plate glass door accessed the room behind the hardware store. Midas had rented this rear area of the building's basement as the development office for the new web real-time communications business.

He pushed open the door, and stepped into the open space. No walls, no furniture, no dividers, just eighty square yards of bare wood. A substantial door was set into each of the front and rear walls, a smaller door was set into the side wall that led to a small kitchen and bathroom. The only natural light came through ceiling height wooden shuttered windows at the rear of the building and a small timber sash window set in the wall next to the bathroom. The door at the front end of the room could be opened to the existing office and this was a modification the landlord had promised to do in the next week. There would be a thoroughfare from front to back offices, avoiding the need to go outside and into the adjoining entrance.

On the floor lay sixteen flat packs of furniture. Later in the week, or during the weekend, Midas would open the boxes and assemble the furniture. He would enjoy opening boxes, and creating visible evidence of a new venture. It was tangible, it was real, and it was physical.

This afternoon and he would meet with Chad and Dave again. He hoped to see some more movement on the demo and he would also discuss the contract for Chad, which he presently carried in a folder in his backpack. The contract set out the terms that he hoped Chad would agree to.

In his dealings with Chad so far he found him to be somewhat aloof, and he gave the impression that he felt his capabilities and intellect and inherent genius was far above lesser mortals and day-to-day engineers. Midas smiled to himself when Chad adopted his superior attitude and joked and commented in a light sarcastic manner about his superior demeanor. Most of the time Chad recognized Midas's response and comments, and moments later he was laughing at himself, as he had climbed from his lofty perch. Sometimes he didn't – then he was obnoxious.

Midas had used his intelligence network to check out the two MIT guys. Technically, they came back with outstanding credentials. Dave was recognized as being the pure academic, most at ease in the university environment, whereas Chad was more likely to drive his own road, and would be comfortable working outside MIT, under his own direction. Chad would be good at architecting the embryonic real-time communication software platform that Midas envisaged to power a range of services from unified communications to embedded voice and video in applications on smartphones and tablets. Midas was warned, however, to give Chad enough rope, but not too much – in the latter case he would become difficult.

He returned to the front of the building and went into his hardware store.

Greeting the three guys that were in there, he headed to his table at the back of the room. As he sat down Ted approached him and said that he needed to speak.

"Midas, I had the software guys from White Plains on the phone. They gave me a hard time."

Midas listened as Ted shared the details of a call from the software licensor. They had become aware of Midas's visual communication cloud and his increasing client base.

"It's simple," added Ted, "They want a greater share of the action."

"Really? And what's your take on it?"

Ted answered, "They can see we are doing something no one else thought of and now they want to push the same model out to other licensees."

"What's started this, I wonder?"

"I can tell you," answered Ted, "When one of their guys approached Masterstore Shipping – remember they were the first guys you signed – Masterstore told them they were not interested as they could get what was being offered at a fraction of the price, from us.

"The guys from White Plains started checking and found that Masterstore are not our only customer. Our big cheese licensor wants to met with us."

"Ok Ted, let's wait. But I want you at any meeting."

"Right boss," Ted went back to his desk.

Midas's agreement with them was clear; he had purchased a number of software licenses that enabled him to use the software to power visual communications in whatever manner he wished. But the vendor now declared that the license was intended for internal corporate use only, not to be used to provide services to a wide range of other clients. They claimed that Midas supplying visual communications via the cloud was in contravention of his agreement. Furthermore, Midas's actions stopped the software vendor from selling to those companies that were Midas's clients.

He remembered, very clearly, when he had negotiated the software license he had explained his business model, that there would be multiple servers geographically located around the world; Midas's clients and users would access those servers from any country, whether it was the United States or elsewhere. This business model had received no objection from the vendor; they applauded Midas's creative use and, in short, wished him well.

The usage of Midas's system was climbing steadily. The vendor was looking at the fine print in the agreement to see if they could curtail Midas's growth, replicate Midas's business themselves, and generate revenue on the back of Midas's creativity and initiative.

With the new real-time communication business about to kick off, a legal case restricting the continued growth of his original business was the last thing that the business needed.

Midas trawled through twenty pages of legal text, the vendor's claim only had minimal substance. Nevertheless, he would need to spend a few hundred dollars on getting a legal opinion. He wrote an email explaining the situation and sent it to his lawyers.

It was eleven thirty. He took a prepackaged Caesar salad from his backpack, along with fresh orange juice, and placed them in the refrigerator in the tiny kitchen. He stepped into the bathroom and changed into his running gear. When they moved into the hardware store, he had a shower installed in the small water closet so that anyone who wanted to exercise had the luxury of a hot shower albeit in very cramped conditions.

He stepped out of the front door, turned left on E96th, and started to jog; he crossed Park Ave., Madison Ave., and 5th Ave., and entering Central Park, he cut off to his left. He ran diagonally to the central reservoir and hit the Shuman Running Track which circumnavigated the water. Although parts were still under restoration, it was accessible and provided a one and half mile circuit. Midas ran the circuit three times and returned to the office the same way he entered the park. It was a forty-minute jog. He found that running had a meditative effect on his mind and it was time that allowed him to reflect and turn things over and perhaps gain another perspective.

Today it was the vendor's attempt to hijack his current business that was one thing that preoccupied him. Intuitively, he also felt that he would have something else to think about after this afternoon's meeting with Chad.

FIFTY THREE

Chad and Dave arrived a little after two o'clock, backpacks over the shoulder and coffee in hand. Dave knew that he was attending only for the demo and technical discussions, after which he would leave and Midas and Chad to talk through Chad's engagement with the new company.

Chad connected his laptop to a forty-inch monitor on the wall, opened a webpage in a Chrome browser, and inserted an IP address in the address space. He also opened up a JavaScript window which revealed the browser code which was normally unseen by the everyday user. He typed in a few lines and hit return. A connection was established with their lab on the other side of town and a video window appeared in the browser and displayed another of their MIT colleagues waving at them from miles away. They were seeing another simple demo. The voice and video quality were excellent and Midas asked if it was possible to add additional people to the call.

Chad smiled and said, "You asked about that last time: just watch."

A few more lines of code and he hit return. A second video window opened in the browser, with another person.

"Now we're doing a three-way call," said Chad. He pointed to some statistics that were being generated in the small code window. Chad pointed to some numbers.

"Here you can see the bandwidth usage; you can see what it was when it was two people, and when there are three it consumes more bandwidth, naturally. And this creates a limitation on the number of people that you can add onto a call. We can solve that problem but it will take us quite some time. We're lucky today, it's stable. It's been very unstable over the past week."

Chad closed the Java script window and the Chrome browser took the full screen and showed the two other parties on the call. Although it was simple, it was revolutionary. They were looking at the future.

"The video window is small, can that be changed?" Midas asked, and the added, "And can you tweak the webpage so it looks like the real thing? You know what I mean, what it can ultimately look like. Today, looks are not important, but some work will need to be done to make the demo look appealing, as well as being technically accomplished."

It was at this point that he realized that some engineers are often interested only in function; form had no relevance. Midas was looking at the simple demo as something that would be shared with a number of people and therefore presentation was very important.

Chad thanked the guys on the call, and switched off the demo.

He turned and glared at Midas, "I am not an artist, you want me to build something I build it; you want it pretty – you can do that."

Dave looked embarrassed at this outburst. He swiftly packed his backpack, shook hands, and left Chad and Midas to discuss whatever they needed to deal with.

Midas outlined the offer to Chad. He would become the Chief Technology Officer (CTO) and have the responsibility, and the funds, to build a small development team; he would have carte blanche to research, develop, and build a working platform delivering visual and voice communication and data transfer on both web and mobile devices.

Chad looked at Midas. "Do you realize what you're asking for? You want something that the likes of Ericsson, AT&T, Google, Mozilla, and all the big boys are searching for?"

Midas looked back at Chad and said, without blinking, "Yes I know what I'm asking for, I'm asking that we change the world."

There was no doubting Midas's vision and he was now face-to-face with Chad, challenging Chad to deliver.

Chad acknowledged, "Okay, I can build you a Platform; it will work, it will be solid, it will be Telco or enterprise standard, but I need staff to work with me. And if you want it to look pretty you need to get someone to do that. I don't do fancy websites. They don't matter anyway."

Midas let the last comment pass. He didn't rise to the bait. Midas moved to outline the terms and conditions under which they would work together.

Chad would become an employee; he would be paid the rate that Chad had quoted earlier as being his requirement. But it would be paid in share options and cash.

Chad nodded his agreement and looked around. "When do I start? Which is my desk? I'll start now. You can give me the paperwork when you feel like it. I'll trust you on that."

Midas laughed, "Your office, your desk is in a flat pack in the back room."

Chad shrugged, picked up his backpack put his laptop in. "It's not a problem, I can work in a coffee shop until you're ready, just tell me."

In one way, it was not important, but Midas and noted the absence of any offer from Chad to join himself and Ted on the furniture assembly project.

He had received a reply to his mail from their lawyer. It was the lawyer's 'two-step dance' – one the one hand this, and on the other hand that - which is normally a prelude to a large quotation for legal fees.

They commented: "The agreement is not completely watertight. While the license agreement does not preclude you doing what you do, providing a cloud service to third parties, it does clearly say that the software is to be used for internal purposes only. When the agreement was written, it was never envisaged that it would underpin a global cloud service offering such as yours. We think that you are best advised to meet with the vendor and to find an amicable agreement."

Midas sighed. Previous dealings with the vendor had been both friendly and frustrating. Their sales rep was a nice enough guy, but he clearly lacked imagination and creativity. He was effectively a postbox between Midas and the vendor's head office.

"Ted, can you do something for me?"

"Sure."

Midas gave Ted a copy of the email. "We needed to bypass the local guy. Can you call our contact in White Plains and set up a meeting?"

Ted nodded. Minutes later he came back "The meeting's set for tomorrow morning."

Fifteen hours later, Midas and Ted were walking through Grand Central to catch the train to White Plains. It was a simple enough commute and as Midas walked, once again, into the splendor of the Main Concourse, he looked up; then he looked at Ted,

"What do you think of this place Ted?"

"It always amazes me, I think every time I have to stop and look up, I'm not sure what I am looking for, but it is just beauty, pure beauty."

They had stopped to marvel at one of the most inspiring buildings in New York. Grand Central had been a rundown building, devoid of its grandeur, occupied by itinerants and people seeking a place to sleep rough. Its facade had been blackened over the decades and no attempt had been made to reveal the splendor that Midas was now looking at. It'd taken millions of dollars and a number of projects over twenty years to reveal and renovate the core of the building: the concourse, the ticket hall, the ticket booths, the platform entrances, the passageways, and the canopies that greeted passengers in the early 1900's, in the golden age of steam.

Midas and Ted stepped out at White Plains Station, jumped in a cab for a five-minute ride to Tarrytown and minutes later they were pulling up outside a nondescript building that had the number 560 above the canopy over the entrance lobby. He entered the building and found the vendor's offices, which, apart from a small eight inch by four inch sign, was devoid of identity.

Their meeting with the vendor's Commercial VP and their COO was cordial enough; they applauded Midas's initiative and the growth of his business and freely admitted that they had not expected their software to be used in the manner that Midas had deployed it.

Their COO spoke, "You are breaking your agreement. You are using it beyond the scope of the contract."

"I don't think so," answered Midas, "my lawyers are happy enough that what we are doing is legal."

The COO became emphatic, "Not so, the agreement is for internal use, and you are doing something different."

"What we are doing is 'internal', internal to our business. We are not passing your software off to the market, you are getting paid for every user we add, I don't see your problem."

"We need a supplementary agreement, the COO went on, "you need to pay us a premium for global usage."

"Oh, you want a royalty on our business?"

"Yes, I guess that's one way to put it," answered the COO.

"How much?"

"Here's a calculation," the COO showed Midas a calculation and the new royalty proposal.

Midas scanned the paper and placed it in front of him. He said nothing. There was a long period of silence. Midas maintained eye contact with the COO, he did not blink.

After what seemed an age, the COO said, "Of course, it is negotiable around that figure."

"I understand," was Midas's reply. "We will have to do our calculations, but that number is not acceptable."

The conversation went back and forth, inconclusively.

Fifteen minutes later Midas looked at his watch, "We have a train to catch in twenty minutes. Is it possible someone could call a cab?"

The VP stood up, and put his head through the door and asked a colleague to make the arrangements.

He came back to his seat; "There'll be a cab in five minutes."

Midas stood up. "Is there a toilet?" The VP opened the conference room door, and pointed across the passage.

As Midas stepped out, Ted looked at the VP, he leaned across the table and asked quietly, almost conspiratorially, "Between you and me, how negotiable is negotiable?"

"Umm, we need a fifty per cent royalty, maybe forty."

"It's not going to fly; you guys need to go to five per cent. If you don't, we all lose," answered Ted,

"We are getting customers you will never win. And we pay you for the increased customers, today. Think about it." Ted stood up as Midas entered the room.

Midas thanked them for the proposal, thanked them for their time and said he would most certainly consider their proposal, he understood exactly their position. And he would need to look at the economics of his venture before he could respond.

On the train back from White Plains Midas asked Ted, "So, what was their range?"

"Ten per cent, fifty to forty."

"How did he respond to five per cent?"

"He went white!" smiled Ted.

"Good job," responded Midas, "We will see how serious they are. If they don't move, we'll freeze the business. Very soon we will have twenty customers, all paying monthly recurring income that would finance a support person and pay the monthly maintenance charge."

Ted added, "We could propose that future enquiries be directed to them so they could offer whatever service they thought appropriate."

Then Ted paused, "Freeze? What happens to me? I was just enjoying myself."

"Let's wait and see." Midas replied.

Midas liked Ted and he could see that there could be a benefit in keeping him in the new real-time business – if Chad moved fast enough.

They headed to Grand Central. Had any more crises emerged?

FIFTY THREE

It was Saturday morning. Midas had been out the previous evening and had bought a cordless, rechargeable drill and a selection of small tools. Ted had called off because his wife was sick.

Midas was in the back room. For the next three hours he unpacked boxes, fitted locating plugs, screwed screws, and tightened nuts. By lunchtime the room had a suite of self-assembly furniture.

The implications of the previous day had not been lost on Midas as he was on his knees in the back office. The guys working on the Visual Cloud business may have to go, space would be freed up. He now had a lease for the two significant rooms. Some of the space may not be needed for some time; it all depended on the pace of Chad's recruitment drive for engineers.

The problems with the company at White Plains had not been anticipated when Midas signed the lease. Now that the space was available, Chad would use it.

Monday came and Chad appeared mid-morning, Midas made no comment about timing knowing that engineers work on a time schedule that suited them and not him. This was generally an acceptable and constructive way of working. Going forward, Chad, as the CTO, may need to be mindful of others' schedules; Midas would see if this was to be a problem.

Midas and Chad sat around the new table with its white, scratch-free, pristine surface. Two new white coffee mugs sat on two new red mats, filled with hot black coffee from a new coffee machine that sat in the corner, incongruously on an upturned box. Midas congratulated Chad on the demo the previous week and Chad responded with a thank-you for Midas's support and his faith in him, giving him the opportunity to do something that was serious engineering – leading edge.

Chad passed across three résumés. These are some young engineers I know; they're good, very good, and I believe this project will excite them. I would like your permission to interview and recruit. Midas nodded his agreement. He knew that they would have to build a team rapidly and now was not the time to challenge the speed at which Chad was working. Midas just had to plug the cost of three more engineers into the cash flow and estimate when he and the Viking would need to make another contribution to the corporate purse. It would be in the upcoming quarter.

The next two months passed without too much excitement.

Midas met with the Viking every ten days, if he was in town. At this time, the meetings were routine, although Midas sensed the Viking's impatience to see some early indications that research and development was going somewhere.

Midas spoke to Ted about the discussions with the vendor, which went nowhere. And they both had agreed Midas's strategy to curtail new sales and offer to pass leads to the vendor was a tactical means to step back from what could have been an expensive confrontation.

One afternoon Ted asked Midas if he had time for a beer in the evening. Midas willingly agreed.

Later they were sitting in the Barking Dog on 3rd Ave, three blocks from the office.

"I understand where we are," Ted was saying, "and I can see what we can deliver in the next couple of years. I have an idea."

"You have?" Midas looked at Ted, he was a good man.

"Yes, I want to be part of the long haul, but you cannot afford me. What if, I work part-time helping you define the service offering from a customer and user viewpoint and design something that could go to market? I can't build it, but I can give some valuable input."

Midas nodded, it could make sense.

Ted continued, "I am ok financially, I started a personal training business, as a sideline and it's taken off, my partners could use my time to handle the increased enquiries. Win-win, right?"

"I like it, let me get back to you."

The two friends had another couple of beers and chatted about work, family, travel and New York, typical of any bar conversation.

A couple of days later, Midas mentioned the plan to Chad and received a lukewarm response. Midas was perturbed and put it down to being premature: they were in the early stages of development and he could understand Chad's argument that Ted's contribution would not be relevant for months. Midas accepted that, and agreed with the need to manage Ted's entry into the new business when the time was right, to be clear on his contribution

Nevertheless, Midas would have liked Chad to see the ultimate need and be a bit more enthusiastic.

The week after talking with Ted and Chad, Midas was in Canada to meet up with some friends he had made when he looked to explore expanding the cloud visual communications business in the north. They had a strong visual communications business that supported the Federal Government. The business model was similar to Hans' in Zurich: a neat, versatile platform operating in the confines of a large business.

He enjoyed good personal relationship with them and he used the time to test out the real-time communications project with them. One of his friends, Simon, was reputed to be one of the strongest technical people in the whole of videoconferencing, visual communication, and collaboration space in North America. He was relieved to get an overwhelming and totally positive reaction, with the caveat that while both believed that he was on a very promising track, it was a difficult one.

Midas did not yet realize it, but this friendship with Simon would prove to be a valuable asset in the new company.

FIFTY FOUR

The silence in the office was deafening. Engineers, heads down, earphones in, created a silent air of productivity. It was nine months since Chad had joined Midas and Ted had moved to his Personal Fitness Business. While Ted had planned to come back on a part-time basis, he had been so successful that he was running his own entrepreneurial start-up now, and doing well. He still maintained contact with Midas and was avidly interested in progress.

Chad had brought three more Engineers in and the Engineering team was now six in total, split into infrastructure, web and mobile iOS and Android. There were significant signs of progress towards a stable and working visual communication platform that could operate in a web page and on mobile.

It was a normal day in the office.

Midas was at the Chrysler Building. He was drinking coffee in the Viking's opulent office. He had just been listening to the stories of a recent sailing trip to Maine. But now the Viking had switched to business.

"Midas, I don't understand, if Google have put this code, as you call it, in the Chrome browser, why do we have to spend so much money to make it work?"

It was a good question.

Midas answered this way, "The code in the browser allows that browser to receive and send voice, video and data, but that's all. It, I mean the browser, does not have all the 'plumbing' necessary to create a communication experience. It is as though the code is reaching out, begging to be connected to something, an intermediary – which we call servers - so that it can say hello to another browser, and to recognize what signal it should send, and what kind of signal it can receive. This is where the engineers come in, they write other programs that allow that handshake, and the communication experience to take place. The engineers create the 'plumbing'. Now, if it is just a single instance of one computer to another computer, then that is easy, but that's not the real world."

The Viking listened intently.

"For effective business use, the browser has to be able to say hello to any one or more of tens of thousands of other browsers, and may sit on a call together with six, eight, or even ten other browsers. And while it is sitting on that call, another browser in the same business is doing the same, and then there could be thousands of calls all happening at the same time. This is called scalability. Scalability has two dimensions; a single call can scale – from two to four to eight to ten or more people. And the whole infrastructure in a business can scale to have thousands of concurrent calls at any one time."

The Viking interrupted, "And those calls can be anywhere in the world, in one international organization, like mine, for example?"

"Yes, or it could be an international bank, or a university, or a remote health care provider, all of these have hundreds and thousands of clients, many of whom want to use the system at any one time."

"Can I do all this on my phone?" asked the Viking.

"Great question," answered Midas, "the answer is yes, and your laptop, and your tablet. But here is the clever part. As a telehealth supplier, your patient might call from a computer or from a smart phone. On the computer they can use the telehealth web page but on their phone they use the telehealth app. And the app behaves in the same way as the web page, it has the special code built in and it is part of the web real-time communications infrastructure of the telehealth provider."

"Ok, I think that's enough for today. The Viking was smiling, "I know you are trying to make me a techie, and I fear you will not succeed. All I want to do is to be able to explain it to my business colleagues or someone I meet, so they can understand what wonderful things we are doing."

The Viking added an afterthought, "And I suppose all this complexity is the reason Chad is taking so long?"

"Yes, you can say that," answered Midas.

"Well, tell him to hurry up."

Midas returned to the office.

Demos were not an issue these days, and it was possible for an interested visitor to be shown a working prototype at a moment's notice. The cosmetics of the screen still frustrated Midas, and he found it very difficult to get Chad to understand that both form and function were important.

Google and Mozilla were constantly making modifications to the code, and a solution that Chad's team built and demoed today, might not demo tomorrow, because of an overnight change by Google. Chad had warned about this, and said that the situation would resolve itself over time as the web real-time communications initiative became more mature.

At this stage there remained a considerable risk. The black hole that the Viking warned about was opening up. It was still a big R&D project with no certainty about timescales. There were still uncharted waters ahead.

It was going to be at least another year before Midas could confidently say that a product or service may be in the marketplace and generating revenue. And the business was consuming money.

The Viking had asked Midas what would happen once the technology platform become stable enough to launch a product or service. When will that be? What were the service fees? It was far too early to answer.

The cash burn had increased significantly and both the Viking and Midas had topped up the account. Thankfully, the first foray into the cloud visual communications business was contributing to day-to-day running costs. But it would start to tail off in the next year.

The Viking and Midas started to discuss bringing in external investors. It was too early for major seed funding to be attracted, and they agreed that the next round of funding must come from 'Friends and Family'. This was a traditional route for Entrepreneurs to follow. Having made a significant commitment themselves, the founding shareholders could, with credibility, go to a group that was close to them to offer them very favorable terms to be the next group to commit funds to the business.

Midas had countless discussions with Chad, with Dave, with Ted, with Sherwin, and many other people who were close to the web real-time communication movement to help formulate a strategy to go to market. One favored route appeared to be to create a web and mobile voice, video, and chat application that would include aspects of collaboration, and can be branded in a number of different ways. The other option was to avoid the product route completely, and create a platform that others could use to underpin their applications on the web or on mobile devices.

The former route required considerable investment in the front-end design and in the user interface. No matter how good the technical platform was that supported what the customer used, if the user interface (i.e. what the customer or user experiences) was not attractive, user-friendly, responsive, and comprehensive in the functions and features and benefits that it offered, it would not be adopted.

Midas had brought Ted back into the business on a consulting basis; Ted had considerable experience from the cloud business and understood what businesses required from a communications application that would sit on their webpage or in their mobile device. He had documented this carefully, extensively and completely.

A few days ago there had been a meeting between Midas, Ted, Chad, and Dave to discuss probable directions. Midas was in favor of creating an independent application that could be branded in different ways, and also sold as white label product to anyone who may wish to use it internally or externally. Midas had argued that, in any event, the platform that had to be built to support this product was the same platform that would be built to service developers and organizations that wanted to incorporate real-time communication in their own web pages and applications, but did not want to build the substantial infrastructure required. These people would pay someone to provide the infrastructure, a business proposition known as providing a 'platform as a service', that met their requirements and was robust, proven, reliable, secure, and attractively priced.

In Midas's mind, creating both the platform and the product was gaining two revenue streams for the price of building something once. Chad argued assiduously against the strategy. His main argument was that the resources that were required to build the product were different from those required to build a platform, and his current headcount did not allow or provide the capacity that he needed. Midas also suspected that Chad had no interest in anything that required a sophisticated user interface – or something that was 'pretty' as he had described it one time before.

Midas argued that with a round of the financing coming in from the friends and family initiative there would be sufficient funds for the platform team and to recruit more engineers and build a product. Midas was not convinced that he was winning the argument.

Ted's presence at the meeting had been counter-productive. Whilst Ted did an extremely good job in articulating all the features required in the web and mobile products, together with the pricing mechanisms, he was at loggerheads with Chad.

Midas had to adjourn the discussion with a request that more work be done on understanding the resources required for products and continuing to go at max speed on platform development – which was business as usual for Chad.

The following day, Midas shared the content and tenor of the meeting with the Viking. They were discussing the draft of the first fundraising prospectus, and had to describe the market entry strategy as being first a platform as a service, with the potential to add already unique branded products to the portfolio.

The Viking's counsel was too not push Chad too hard on the products side and allow him to build up a significant and reputable platform. It was clear that the platform play was a technically sophisticated and ambitious project if it was to meet the requirements all corporate customers on the one hand and users on the other.

Over next few days they honed and sharpened their pitch; revenue projections were at best educated guesses. But the overall pitch was one of great optimism in a newly emerging sector where competition was extremely limited and opportunities were unimaginably huge. Of course, given the nature of the project and, being still in the mid-stages of and R and D, those investors who did come in would realize that, at best, their investment was a punt. If it paid off, it should pay off handsomely, but the was a chance that they might lose whatever they invested; it was the nature of very early stage investment.

It was a week after the Viking's web real-time communications tutorial; it was seven a.m. Midas had finished his run, showered, and was emerging from the small closet at the back of the office and heading to the coffee machine. He was usually the first person in the office by a long way; the engineers tended to come in mid-morning, but they would work through into the evening or overnight depending on the task at hand.

The door opened and Chad walked in. Midas could never remember a day when Chad had appeared so early.

"You need an early coffee, Chad?" Midas asked. Chad nodded as he sat down at the table normally occupied by Midas.

"We need to talk," said Chad, as Midas handed him a black coffee.

"Sure," said Midas, "what is on your mind?" Already Midas was sensing this was not going to be a good day.

"You will have heard of TenCent?" said Chad

"Yes," answered Midas, He knew of the fearsome reputation of the Shenzhen China-based company, one of the giants of web technology and much more besides.

"I know their engineers," announced Chad, "they were at a conference here a few months back."

Midas remembered the event, although he did not attend.

"Well, we got talking at that event, and we have had a few conference calls since."

"I see, and …?" Interjected Midas,

"They have offered me a job," said Chad. "I have received the offer last night."

"And, what is your plan?" asked Midas. He was quiet in his tone, as he was already assessing the implications should Chad leave at this critical juncture.

"It depends," answered Chad. "I like the work I do, but they are offering big money, multiple what you are paying me."

"So what's on the table?" asked Midas.

"From TenCent?" said Chad,

"No, what are you looking for here?" answered Midas.

Chad leaned back, he put both hands on the table, and he was striking an arrogant pose. He was trying his best to look down at Midas, which was difficult given the relative heights of the two men. He lifted his chin and looked down his nose.

"OK, I will tell you. There are number of things that are not acceptable," said Chad. "First of all, Ted needs to stop telling me how to do my job. In fact, it would be better if you fired him, but do it properly this time. Second I want a free hand in product decisions. I will decide what services we offer."

Midas interjected, "That's not your decision Chad, that's a combined decision within the team and at the end of the day it is my call as CEO."

"That is up to you," said Chad. "But I'm quite sure I am not going to sacrifice the integrity of the platform for some harebrained scheme that you and Ted have dreamt up."

Chad's tone was aggressive and brazen. He knew that he was in an almost unassailable negotiating position. He continued,

"I want my share options converted to shares immediately; if I stay I will not ask for a raise today, but I want to see a considerable increase in compensation within the next four months. I am thinking of a fifty percent raise. I suggest you and your rich buddy start thinking, and putting something in writing that I can respond to. If not, then I'm going to China."

Midas recognized that it was futile to appeal to Chad on the grounds of a shared cause, or common purpose, or a shared vision to change how people communicate.

"I think you need to leave this with me. You know the implications of what you're saying to me. You are aware of the pivotal role that you play, and the investment that had gone into this business so far."

Chad nodded, "It's up to you."

He finished his coffee and walked out of the office without saying another word.

Midas knew his next step.

FIFTY FIVE

Midas called Vanessa, the Viking's PA, to see if he was in town. The Viking was at a breakfast meeting in the Waldorf Hotel. Midas said that it was urgent that they met, and Vanessa promised a call back in the next few minutes. Five minutes later she called, Midas had an appointment with the Viking at ten a.m., in ninety minutes' time.

Midas closed the outer office door, and headed to 96th Street Metro.

Inside he was furious; he had been held to ransom by a guy he recruited and who had been given the opportunity to learn and lead a completely new technology, develop leading-edge skills, and who was critical to the business at this time. *These are the risks of small technology start-ups,* he thought.

He was not in a much better frame of mind when he sat down with the Viking in the lobby of the Waldorf. He related the short conversation with Chad verbatim. The Viking listened without making a comment. He had a frown on his forehead and he was stroking his chin, a mannerism that Midas had not seen before. He picked up his teacup, sipped his Darjeeling, and let out sigh.

"Midas, I have been here one time before. A long time ago someone tried to do to me what Chad is doing to you, and to me. I place the highest value on trust and loyalty, and the trust and loyalty goes both ways in any organization. We are all engaged on a mission, there can be no wavering, there can be no doubting, and there can be no hesitation. Of course, there is discussion and debate - that is healthy. But no one person is entitled to hold the company to ransom. Today, Chad believes that he holds a hand full of aces, and indeed that might be true. I am disappointed that he appears not to have the maturity to understand the immediate and longer-term implications of his demands."

Midas was about to interject, but the Viking held is hand up. "Excuse me Midas, but I'm not quite finished. I was about to ask if you believe that the TenCent offer was real, but then I realized it didn't matter. If it is a bluff and we call it, where does that place us? No further forward."

"What happens if we lose Chad at this time? Is there anyone that can take over? I think I know the answer," added the Viking.

Midas confirmed that no one in the company could take over. Dave could be candidate, but he would not leave MIT. There were very few people who knew anything about this emerging technology and a replacement would be almost impossible to find.

"What about your friend in Canada?" Asked the Viking.

"Possible, but it would take a while for him to exit his present company and get up to speed," answered Midas.

"We are about to solicit funds from our friends and family, we need those funds, and we cannot destabilize that initiative. So if you will allow me, Midas, I would like to suggest a way forward.

"For the time being, sideline the product discussion, formally offer Chad a thirty percent increase in salary effective from today, and decline the share issue.

"If, as I expect, he continues to insist that he gets his shares immediately, then you can tell him that I am not prepared to countenance anything more than issuing half of his entitlement in ordinary shares at this time. You can say that I was against any share issue at all, and that you persuaded me to grant some. You can be seen as the good guy. After all you have to continue working with him."

"I agree, although I don't like it. I would like your agreement to take some other actions," said Midas.

Midas continued, "I would like to bring in Simon as deputy CTO. There is a justification, which is that we need a strong architect on mobile and integration with applications. This is Simon's specialty. He is familiar with real-time communication and he would get up to speed quickly. I would also like to bring in a senior development manager who would take charge of all the engineers. In this way Chad will be only be in charge of his own research and this ring fences his influence.

His research is still vitally important, but he will have to share his content with two more senior people. It will cost us money but, after today, it will be an insurance policy. We will need those two people in due course and I'm just bringing their appointment forward."

The Viking nodded and said, "I agree and I have something else for you to consider. You, Midas, have one of the most agile and innovative and perceptive minds that I have come across. You have an amazing ability to see opportunity way ahead of anyone else. I saw it in Florida, and I saw it with the visual cloud thing you picked up in Zurich, and I have seen it with real-time communications.

"You have great talent in the way you do articulate the vision to anyone that will listen, but I know from experience that there will come a time when you and I need a hard-nosed, execution-focused CEO, who has been there before and built big technology companies. I have been sniffing around in my network and, if you agree, I would like to introduce you to a couple of people. There is no rush. We do not have to do this tomorrow morning, but we should keep it in mind."

Midas knew that the Viking's thinking was sound; the business could soon grow at an exponential rate, resources would need to be taken on board, major contracts negotiated, and while Midas believed in his personal ability, he would be happy to defer to a much more experienced mind.

He shook hands with the Viking and left. The meeting showed the value of having a partner who was accomplished and had been there before and could provide advice based on knowledge, experience, and a successful track record.

It was lunchtime when Midas got back to the office; everything was normal, Chad was at his desk and greeted Midas in a manner that was devoid of any untoward emotion. It was as though that early morning meeting had never taken place.

Midas suggested that Chad and he go outside for lunch, Chad agreed. They stepped out the door and walked to The 3 Guys Restaurant two blocks along 96th. When they were seated, and had ordered, Midas was making his very best efforts to be cordial, and said that he and the Viking had met in the morning.

Midas conveyed the same offer that the Viking recommended; he quoted the salary increase, he said that the Viking had declined to convert his options. Midas acknowledged that the Product vs Platform discussion was shelved and that Chad had gotten his way; the focus would be as he, Chad, had recommended. Midas added that the implication was that Ted would not be needed in the near term. Privately, Midas thought that such a step would not bother Ted. He was happy and busy doing what he was doing.

Midas added words to stroke Chad's ego, about how important he was, and what a tremendous position he was in, with far more autonomy than he could get anywhere else. He added that everyone associated with web real-time communications looked up to Chad as an authority.

Chad listened, acknowledging the points that Midas outlined.

Midas finished talking. Chad looked at him; he placed his knife and fork at the side of his plate, sat back his chair and said, "Is that everything?" His arrogance was palpable.

Midas nodded, "Yes, that's as far as we can go."

Chad leaned forward, picked up his utensils and started to eat, barely acknowledging that Midas was at the table. Midas decided not to say anything more.

Halfway through his lunch, Chad threw his napkin on the table, pushed his chair back, and stood up.

He looked at Midas, and said "Okay I'll stay."

He turned on his heel and walked out of the restaurant.

Midas thought to himself, *for how long?*

FIFTY SIX

The aft deck of *Brave New Horizons*, the Viking's pride and joy, looked like a photograph from the New Yorker or like something from a James Bond film, with an expectation that the hero would make a dramatic entrance at any time. It was crowded with beautiful people. The ladies, young and less young, wore the smallest, yet most elegant of bikinis or chiffon wraps, and the men's' attire would be suitable to grace any beach party on the beaches of the Hamptons, Long Island.

The crew wearing whites, and the serving staff in black, circulated discretely, and trays of canapés, Champagne and the finest wines were being served. Captain Joe was observing the proceedings discretely, quietly giving directions to the crew when needed.

The Viking was working the gathering, shaking a hand here, a pat on the back there, a joke with these people, a serious comment with those people; at all times beaming in an avuncular manner. There were around forty people: bankers, Wall Street types, media types, doctors, lawyers, and a sprinkling of very wealthy tech entrepreneurs. Midas had seen the guest list, in fact, he had helped to draw it up – it was impressive.

It was a long time since he first had to attend such a gathering. He still did not enjoy them; but now he was able to put on a brave face and network as well as anyone.

He winced, his feet were hurting, he had bought himself a new pair of deck shoes for the event, and they were giving him blisters. He wore blue shorts and the red and white striped shirt. He fitted in with the guests perfectly. He had drawn a line at buying an ascot tie or cravat, although he noticed that some of the men had added an ascot tie to their dress.

At the Viking's suggestion, Chad had accompanied him to the gathering. Midas had reservations about Chad's attendance as he was inclined to be less than diplomatic with his comments on occasions. Midas would admit that Chad had behaved himself recently, but at less august gatherings.

Midas sipped iced Perrier water and wished that Chad was doing the same as he noted that he was consuming champagne at an embarrassingly frightening rate.

After about 20 minutes of chit chat the Viking tapped his glass and called for attention. "Ladies and Gentlemen, you're all invited into the main salon where I would like to say a few words."

The assembled guests moved through the open center glass door into the interior, into a spacious polished teak floored lounge. Midas stood at the rear of the afterdeck watching them enter the luxurious interior and smiled when he recalled how different it was from the times when he and Mike sat on the afterdeck of Bolero, in Florida, drinking beer; nothing could be so different. Chad had gone in and was standing at the rear corner of the lounge. Midas made his way to the front to be near the Viking.

Once again the Viking tapped his glass, "My friends, I have something to share with you all, a short speech," he smiled and looked over the assembled group.

"I am sure that some of you had an inkling as to why you're here. I gave a clue on the invitation when I remarked that we're going to communicate with the future. No, no, not like that," he smiled, an elderly lady near the front gasped at the last remark, "I hope that none of you thought that we were going to hold a séance." This comment drew a grimace from most of the men.

The Viking continued, "As you know, I have been involved, with young Midas here," the Viking nodded in Midas's direction, "in a company that is, and I will not exaggerate when I say this, that is going to be a company that will change the way you, me, our children, and our businesses and institutions communicate with each other in the future. That is a bold statement. But I believe it to be true; if I did not believe it I wouldn't have invested a cent, as many of you know."

More laughter.

"I have invested several hundreds of thousands of dollars in this venture, and so has Midas, because we believe in the vision that we have, and in the capability of our team," he looked in the direction of Chad, "led by Chad, one of the best software architects in America."

"It is a vision and an opportunity that frankly I want you, my friends, to share. I am not begging for charity; I am offering you the opportunity to get in on the ground floor of something that may, who knows, become as big as Facebook, Amazon, or one of the Telcos, AT&T, Verizon, who knows? The opportunity is there."

The Viking had them in his hand, they were listening, they were engaged, they were thinking about the future.

"I will now ask Midas to explain what we're doing."

Midas swallowed hard; he could feel the palms of his hands and he hoped that the sweat that was there was not running down and dripping from his fingertips. He had already put down his glass, fearful that it would slip through his wet fingers. The back of his shirt stuck to his spine. Thankfully, the guests could not see.

Midas stepped forward; he nodded to the Viking, and faced what must have been a group that represented billions of dollars in net worth. He took a deep breath, wiped his hand unconsciously on the seat of his pants, put his hand in his pocket, and took out a smartphone.

He started, "Ladies and gentlemen, you all have one of these, you use it many, many, times each day. But it is, along with your laptop or computer, one of the most frustrating and inconvenient communication tools ever invented by man. And we are going to change that.

"Let me explain, I want you to imagine that you wish to contact your bank, or it could be your dentist, or your doctor, or your stockbroker, but for this example I'm going to use a bank."

Midas opened his phone and said, "I go to an application, one of these little buttons that seem to increase in number overnight, the next time you look there are more and more," a few people nodded and others chuckled.

Midas held out his phone and those at the front could see a Blue City Bank icon.

"This is your bank, it could be any bank; you tap on it, it opens. You authenticate it. It asks you what you want to do. You choose 'speak to my banker' and you tap the box. Moments later, no more than a few seconds, your banker's PA appears in the window of your phone. She acknowledges you by name, she knows who you are. She tells you that your banker will be free in a few moments, and she occupies that time with little pleasantry and then says 'I will put you through'. The next moment your friendly banker appears on your phone you have a discussion. He pulls up a mini statement for you to view and then takes it down again, and you continue the conversation. You complete your business. You tap the screen and the app is now closed."

He continued, "That experience could be a student talking to a teacher, it could be a patient talking to the doctor, it could be you driving along the highway when your car splutters to a stop on the hard shoulder and you are speaking to your garage engineer, who – by the way – asks you to plug your phone into a USB slot on the dashboard so that he can diagnose the problem while you are online. This is the direction that technology is moving. It is a complex and sometimes difficult technology to get right. Bankers, motor manufacturers, universities, schools, health establishments, insurance companies, may have the capability in-house or with their partner software companies, to develop that experience that I just described, but what they do not have is the time, the resources, the money, the experience, or the expertise to build the underlying technology platform that can support the interaction I have outlined to you." He paused to allow that last statement to sink in.

"We have that expertise, and an amazing engineering team, right here in New York, led by our CTO." Midas nodded to Chad at the back of the lounge, a few people looked around and to acknowledge Chad's presence.

"The platform is well beyond an internal proof of concept. It is reaching something which engineers call Beta, which means that it can be released to developers in the companies that I have described and others, to start to experiment and build web and mobile applications which will change the world!

"As the Viking said, I hope that you want to be part of this amazing journey; one that has already started but it is just a few steps along its ultimate path. The time to join us is now. I thank you for your kind attention and I hand back to our host."

There was a ripple of applause as Midas nodded to the Viking.

The Viking shook Midas's hand, and looked to the stunned audience and said, "Ladies and gentlemen, you are now party to a great movement. This is the first time we have declared our vision publicly. We're proud of it. We believe it. We feel it. I hope you do too. I want each one of you to come to me and tell me that you too want to be part of our company. Please continue to enjoy your drinks and the food. Midas, Chad, and I are here if you have questions. Please do not hesitate to come up and ask questions, and of course, you know I will be asking each one of you to open your checkbooks. But I know that I can ask with faith in the future. Enjoy. Thank you."

The voices started to increase in volume, people were chattering. A few people took out their mobile phones or smartphones, opened applications and frankly look puzzled.

A lady walked over to Midas and said, "You mean I can press this little button-thing here on my screen and speak to my beautician and she can see me?"

"Yes," said Midas.

"Oh my God, that's wonderful, that will change my life." And she walked away.

An elderly gentleman came over to Midas and shook his hand. "My name is Warren Bufferton, I thought your short speech was very inspirational; here is my card, I am interested to know more. Do come to see me next week."

He nodded and walked away.

Midas saw the Viking shaking hands, nodding, patting people on the back, smiling. He felt that things were going well. Both ladies and men surrounded Chad. He was holding court, no doubt confusing everyone present by giving a technical exposé, or a CTO version of what Midas and the Viking had said. Nevertheless, it would be so unintelligible that it would be impressive.

Two hours later the last of the guests unsteadily made their way down the ramp and onto the dock. They waved, said their farewells, got into their Limos, and drove off. Midas, the Viking and Chad sat the table on the afterdeck.

The Viking said, "Okay guys, the show is over; you can go and have a beer, grab something to eat at the Marina's restaurant, on my account. You did an excellent job; I know I have some serious commitments from the people that I spoke to but we will connect during these next two weeks. Have fun." And at that moment the Viking's Mercedes drew up at the bottom of the ramp and he shook hands, and was gone.

Midas looked at Chad and was about to suggest they go to the restaurant. Chad said, "Well, that's over. Let's see if these flunkies can give us some cash. I'll see you in the office." And with that comment he walked off the yacht. Midas did not think there was anything unusual about Chad's remark or behavior; it was something that he had been tolerant of, despite that it was inappropriate and becoming annoying.

The next two weeks passed with the Viking calling Midas to meetings - to coffee meetings, to breakfast meetings, to cocktails, as they worked the crowd that had assembled on the yacht.

Midas had researched how to build a compelling Pitch Deck and Investment Flyer. He had his Business Plan drawn up. He had a decent assessment of the market he was heading for. He had prepared thoroughly.

However, he witnessed a consistent response, and after the end of all of the meetings, he talked to the Viking about it.

"Look, I really worked hard on all of this material, but it was hardly discussed." Midas continued, "I start with the simple deck, and by the time I am four or five slides in, they glaze over and ask questions which seem to be superficial. With a couple of exceptions, none of these people we are meeting are interested in the technology; it seems to be – who's the competition, why are we better, how much money do we need, how will we exit, what are the returns?"

"I know," replied the Viking. "Let me explain."

He continued, "The Friends and Family Round is one that, in many ways, is the most unpredictable. We gather some people together who we know reasonably well, and they are what we think are excellent prospects. We give them a good story. But these people are not necessarily sophisticated investors. They have a lot of money, they are loaded many of them, but they employ specialists to run their portfolios, or they are into sectors that they know well.

"When something like this comes along we need to remember that first of all, they are being courteous to me and to you, by giving their time to listen. They have no need to, but they are doing it because of our relationships.

"Second, they are going invest based on a gut feeling, that says a lot about how they feel about you and me. Remember, they asked a lot about how much we had put in, whether we were taking salaries and expenses, and if we were going to take salaries. They asked a lot about your background, which you handled well, by the way. They are testing our commitment and our resolve.

"Third, they are not going to invest anything they cannot afford to lose. This is what I call 'punt money'. They have a small fund that they dip into for risky projects and to have a bit of fun. They could buy a share in a horse, in a racing yacht, or punt on a small family business venture. They could give it away if they wanted to. They can afford to lose the investment in us. They might not like it if we failed, but they are not going to be destitute. But they are not going to take undue risks on our account."

"Unlike me," commented Midas.

The Viking looked at Midas. "Yes, unlike you – you are an entrepreneur, this is your dream, and mine, and you will risk and invest your money, your hours that you are awake, and your soul. Because you see it as your life's purpose to change how people communicate. Some people, many people, think you are mad. But, when we IPO, then the boot is on the other foot, right?"

The Viking continued, "Don't get me wrong. The people we have pitched to are not stupid. They have amassed wealth in their own right by being astute and clever and excellent investors. So, Midas, believe me, they might not appear to ask all the questions you are expecting, but they will have done their homework before they came, checked out what we claim to be doing. They would have met us with an open mind. If they had rejected the idea they wouldn't waste their time to see us. So, in a way, we had an open door when we sat down with the people we met these past ten days. They were, how do I say this, 'mindful to invest' if they got a good feeling from sitting down and talking it through."

Midas said, "I think we did very well, seven figures will see us through a few months before we go to Series A"

"Hey, slow down. Series A may be a long way off. Next step maybe to bring in some good angel investors, or a seed fund, or to up the Friends and Family investment," said the Viking.

"Remember, we have already mapped it out: Friends and Family, Angel / Seed or a second F+F, then we go to the Funds. Private Equity or VCs for a Series A. We will decide when we get closer. In the meantime, you have got to deliver!"

"Yes, Boss!" Said Midas jokingly. "One more thing. What about the Board of Directors? Are you going to bring any of these investors onto the board? Chad still thinks he should be on."

The Viking frowned, "OK, good question. Regarding Chad – no, it is not appropriate. He is a C team player; an important member, yes. But not on the board. It is a difficult one, because he is the key player in our success at this time and, going forward, the next round of investors will want to see him locked in. But I don't think a board seat is the way. Let's come back to him another time."

The Viking continued, "You will recall Stefan, the German lawyer?"

Midas nodded. He remembered him from one of the meetings where he had been grilled. Stefan had a lot to say about governance of the company and Midas thought that he only did a half-good job at responding to Stefan. However, Stefan agreed to invest a modest six-figure sum.

The Viking continued. "He's invested. He has a good head on his shoulders. He is a bit of a hard case sometimes, an iron fist in a velvet glove. But he would keep us on the straight and narrow and will be invaluable later on. I hope you don't mind, Midas, but I did sound him out. He knows a number of the investors who are coming in. They would feel comforted if he was on the Board. He is willing to join us."

Midas responded, "You know him, it's your call. If you recommend him coming on to the Board then I am ok."

They drew their meeting to a close. By the end of the two weeks they had received or had committed well into seven figures; they felt comfortable that they had funds for the next step of the journey.

FIFTY SEVEN

It was cold when Midas stepped out of the door of his apartment block and walked down the six stone steps to a frost-covered footpath.

It was 5:15 AM. He set off on his 45-minute jog that was becoming a routine.

Somewhere, he had read that an extra hour in the morning was worth three more hours during the day, and he now religiously set his alarm at 5 AM. Leaders and entrepreneurs set good habits, and exercise and an early start to the day was part of a successful agenda. Although he had never been a morning person, he was enjoying this transition.

He was starting the day when most people were as far from their waking hours as Kansas is from the Atlantic – it gave him an edge.

This morning he was feeling pleased with the way the funding round had gone. He had called Simon last night and talked about him coming down to New York to join the team as CTO. He wanted to increase the engineering team by another four people, and while Chad was a good thinker, he was not a particularly good leader.

As he jogged, he turned over in his mind the options for dealing with Chad.

Midas was talking to himself, *I can't afford to lose him; he is the key architect of the platform, yet he is having difficulty in delivering anything beyond a proof of concept.* Midas had his fill of excuses and Simon's arrival would give him the chance to take this problem head-on.

He thought that if he could persuade Chad to take a Chief Architect role, it would give Chad the status that he always craved. It ring-fenced his ability to direct the engineers, and it would give him status in the developer community. He hoped that Chad would see this as a win-win situation although deep down he felt that he would have yet another battle on his hands.

He reminded himself that Chad was recruited for his ability to architect and build a brand new technology that was still being developed; it was difficult and frustrating but that's what he was paid for. And he said that he could deliver what Midas and the Viking saw as the way people would communicate. At a design of a platform and infrastructure level, Chad was delivering.

From his intelligence sources, Midas realized that Chad received a grudging respect amongst engineers. There was great respect for his insights and ability despite many people being put off by his arrogance.

Midas was reminded of advice that he had received from other experienced entrepreneurs: when you hire, do not settle for less than excellence – if you do, you will pay for it. Technically, Chad fit the 'excellence' criteria, but his personality created stress that a young business could well do without.

Midas also believed that it was time to bring in someone on the sales and marketing side. Although the product and the platform was still in a beta stage, he needed someone who would take a customer view when building the user interfaces, and take a strong view of usability when the platform and the video chat application were in the hands of developers and customers.

By the time he had finished mulling over his new organization, he had arrived back at his apartment.

He showered and poured himself a coffee. He then sat at his desk in the corner of his living room and checked his mail. He noted that Stefan had accepted the invitation to become a director. Midas was relieved. There comes a point when the business has to have more expertise and an outside perspective to complement the founders' driving passion. A good non-exec director will encourage and nurture the founders' drive and energy and, at the same time, provide a nudge to maintain the trajectory.

Stefan was going to come to the office later today. He would meet Chad and the team and it was also planned that he would meet with another colleague of Midas and Chad, an accountant called Dan. Dan had been introduced to Midas at a networking event and he had just finished a stint with another engineering company in Florida.

Dan was pleasant, articulate, had a respectable résumé, and - importantly - had volunteered to work for a minimum of six months in exchange for a small amount of equity. This appeared to be a deal made in heaven for a small start-up and, after discussions with the Viking, Dan had started some eight weeks ago. In the time he had been working with Midas, he had put a simple account structure in place, reconciled historical accounts, which had been maintained by Midas and the part-time administrator, and he should be set for the meeting with Stefan later today

Midas had agreed that Simon would join the organization in about eight weeks' time. While Midas was confident of Simon's role and ability to move the company forward, he needed to respect Chad's position and to invite Chad to have a conversation with Simon and get his feedback.

That conversation had taken place with predictable results. Chad knew of Simon's track record and reputation in the industry and a lengthy conversation had singularly focused on engineering the new technology. After the conversation, Chad told Midas that Simon was good enough to work for him. At that point Midas had held his breath and kept his counsel.

His phone buzzed, and he was surprised to see a message from Lynn. She was visiting New York the following weekend and suggested they had dinner to catch up on old times and to share the news that had accumulated over the period since they were last in touch. Midas smiled and raised his eyebrows. He was pleased and excited to see Lynn again; he knew that it would be a different Midas that sat down in front of Lynn. It was a long time since they last sailed together in the Gulf of Mexico. Midas had changed.

FIFTY EIGHT

"Listen! This is a tech company. You can't have a tech company without an Engineering Director on the board." Chad was leaning across to the office and he was gesturing at Midas. "You and the Viking, now with this German lawyer, believe that you have everything sorted. Well, if I walk out of here you have nothing."

Midas looked that Chad, "Yeah you're right, Chad. And you will have wasted more than a year of your life and we'll all screw up. And everyone loses. Is that what you want?"

Chad leaned back on his chair, "No, I'm just saying. I suggest when the you have your next cozy meeting you make the other two aware that I'm not happy."

In his mind Midas could see that the conversation between Chad and Simon had been threatening for Chad, but it was difficult for Midas to do anything else but to appear to involve him in the decision.

Midas nodded, "Okay, we'll discuss it again; here's some résumés of engineers I would like you to take a look at."

"Where are these come from?" sneered Chad, "you have taken to recruiting my staff now?"

Midas retained his cool, "They are just applications which I've accumulated as people are writing to me and it's not my role to decide on which engineer is good or bad, that's yours."

"Yes it is." Chad scooped up some paper résumés and said, "You can send me the rest by mail," as he stood up and pushed his chair hard against the wall. He walked back to his desk in the back room.

Midas watched him walk away from the conference table; Midas was getting tired of Chad's behavior. He was mercurial. Most days he could be gregarious, vocal, supportive, excited and would participate with Midas on whiteboard sessions with enthusiasm. When he worked like this he was good, very good and the experience was motivating, exciting, and fun. Other times he could be moody, sulky, and objectionable.

Midas could only conjecture what it was going to be like when the team was much bigger. He would find out in a few weeks' time when Simon joined, and new engineers were in the office.

It would be three days now before Lynn arrived. She said she would plan to stay downtown and Midas was looking forward to spending some time with her. He was not sure what else she planned in New York, but he hoped that they would get some quiet, quality time together.

Dan walked over and stood at Midas's table, "When will the auditors be here?"

"They're here in ten days' time," answered Midas.

"Don't forget, you have a meeting tomorrow with Stephan," Midas added.

"I won't be here, I'll be out of town," answered Dan.

"Uh! Were you going to tell me?" asked Midas.

"Or was I was, like, to just realize you did not meet Stephan when you're missing."

"No, I was going to tell you," shrugged Dan.

"I would really like you to change those arrangements. You were aware that Stephan was coming in and wanted to see you, and his schedule has been fixed for some time." Midas was looking at Dan, and it was clear that Midas was not happy at this revelation.

"Well, maybe I can come in the morning," said Dan while he was looking feebly at his schedule.

"Okay let's plan on that," said Midas. "Can you let me have a trial balance or anything which sets out the financial position as you see it, before Stephan comes?"

"It's almost finished. I'll give you what I have." Dan said as he walked away.

An hour later Midas was looking at the financial information that Dan had sent to him; it made no sense. When Midas ran the business with Mike in Florida he taken great pains to learn the intricacies of accounting entries, ledgers, balance sheets, profit and loss statement; he could do basic double entry accounting manually. He knew enough to know when something was not right and what he had received did not look right. Dan's accounts, at best, were incomplete; at worst they were a mess, a jumble of numbers and entries that could not be relied on in any way.

Midas called Dan back to the table conference table.

"Dan, I'm not an accountant but I know enough to know that this is wrong," said Midas as he pointed to the printout of documents. "It's completely meaningless: the balance sheet is not showing all the investments from friends and family, the draft profit and loss has got omissions, what the hell is going on?"

Midas went on, "There's not many of us in this business today, all the expenses and expenditures to date were recorded and passed over to you. This is not rocket science; this is something a part-qualified accounts clerk could finish on Saturday morning."

Dan played with his phone, he pulled the papers across the table from Midas, looked at them and said, "Yes, I told you they're not finished. I'm entering all this into a new account system."

"What new account system? For the number of transactions we have, you could do this with a handwritten ledger the size of a two-dollar notebook," said Midas.

"Sure, but you want a proper system; the auditors will need to understand that we have a system that can grow with us," answered Dan.

"I hope you're right, we'll see in a couple of weeks."

Dan got up, gathered his papers, and dropped them on his desk as he walked out of the office. "I've gone for coffee."

"Does he know what he's doing?" asked Chad, who had heard the conversation and was now standing in front of Midas.

"At this point, I have to assume that he does. You've seen his résumé. He came with a decent track record."

"I hope so, but it's not my problem." Chad turned on his heel and walked back to his desk.

Midas had a suspicion that his two key hires were less than what he would have desired. He was frequently reminded of advice he had received – do not compromise on excellence when you hire; if you do, it will come back to bite you.

He reflected on the challenge that few people were attracted to high-risk start-up ventures. The pool of available talent was limited. As your business grows, and your reputation grows with it, and you are seen to be doing leading-edge and exciting work, then people - particularly engineers - will start to migrate towards you. But there is a point before the vision is starting to have substance that you are persuading or trying to persuade good people to join you based on your dream, your ability to articulate an amazing future, and your persuasive skills to get them to buy into a risky and uncertain journey.

In any expedition–– and high-tech start-ups are no different from an expedition into the wilderness – it is a journey for the brave and courageous, and sometimes foolhardy and adventurous.

You do your best to assemble the best people, and pray that you have the best talent and the best resources with you; and sometimes you do your best to make that assessment on limited information.

The entrepreneur has to be ever mindful of the performance of the people around him and continually build and expand a team with complementary skills and talent.

It was six o'clock in the evening and Stephan and Midas sat on the high stool in Earl's Beer and Cheese, two blocks from the office. Stefan had just spent the afternoon in their small hardware store and was relating back to Midas his thoughts.

"Before I came, I checked around the technical people that I knew, and you're onto something Midas or, rather, we are onto something, because I am part of the company too. You and the Viking are clever, smart, with great intuition; you saw something that, from what I can understand, not many are acting on. We just have to build a team, and it will be a rapidly growing team, who can not only see your vision, but also deliver it, both at a technology level and in the marketplace. I am looking forward to meeting Simon."

Stefan continued, "There is no doubt that Chad is very clever. He explained his ideas. He used, for the most part, words that I understand, although there were times when he came across as condescending bastard! I let that pass. Both he and Dave at MIT are maintaining close contact, and I think that they are really working hard with your engineers and some of the MIT team to build the platform beyond its current beta stage."

"One thing did bother me: Chad has an obsession. He wants to be on the board," said Stefan

Midas sighed to himself.

Stefan continued, "He took exception to you and the Viking not giving him shares and inviting him onto the board when he joined. I have a feeling this is a problem that is going to come back and haunt us. The guy's got unreasonable expectations. We have to manage those expectations in some way, I know its early days, but have you thought about some kind of ESOP[2]? I can help you with that as I've drafted a number of ESOPs."

Midas responded, "Chad's already got options, or maybe he didn't tell you."

Stefan raised his eyebrows. "No he didn't. That's interesting. All he whined about was *not* having shares and *not* being on the board."

Midas nodded, "I'll take your advice on the ESOP, I think you're right; let's talk to the Viking about it next time we meet."

Stefan looked at the waitress and ordered another round, "Dan seems to be very affable, friendly. He told me of all the things to be done, and he seems vastly overqualified for what we need."

"I know," answered Midas, "he came when he was looking for a gig; he's working for equity. He argues that as we get bigger we will need somebody with his experience. He works part-time, probably three days a week, which seems to be a lot, but he says he's setting up a new accounting system which we can use."

Stefan commented, "Okay, as long as he does the job accurately and thoroughly, we have a decent resource."

---

[2] ESOP: Employee Share Option Program

"Are you sailing with us on the weekend?" added Stefan.

Midas looked at him over his beer, "No, what's happening?"

"The Viking is going out and he's asked me to go, and said you are going to be there. He's not told you?"

"No, not yet, but then I guess he thinks I have nothing else to do as I spend six or seven days in the office. I guess he'll tell me on Friday evening." Midas laughed and then added, "But I have company in town this weekend."

Midas told Stefan about Lynn and her visit in a few days' time.

"I hope she's understands what she's getting herself into if she's dating you," laughed Stefan

"Yeah, we've known each other for a long time; it's not serious, just platonic." Midas thought that, maybe, he wished it would be different.

As predicted, the Viking called on Thursday and invited Midas to go sailing on Saturday.

Midas explained that he had visitors in town.

The Viking had already spoken to Stefan. "Bring your young lady with you. And tell her she won't be alone. We'll have lots of ladies on the yacht, and guys, and she'll enjoy herself. Bring her along."

Moments later Midas texted Lynn and received an immediate reply, "Sailing, yes please. That's great, cool. Do I need a bikini?" Midas smiled.

Would the weekend be as promising as he hoped?

FIFTY NINE

It was nearly three months since the weekend sail on Brave New Horizons – a weekend that had become special for Midas and Lynn. They had not realized that the Viking had planned a weekend cruise, and when they boarded his yacht on Saturday morning they found themselves allocated to a double cabin together. As time passed they found themselves relaxed in each other's company and behaving as though they had been a couple for a long time.

After dinner and drinks with the other guests, they retired to their cabin and talked well into the early morning hours until eventually they fell asleep. At one point they thought their laughter would disturb other guests, particularly when Midas, being the gentleman, volunteered to take the upper bunk of the two small yacht-sized beds, and had managed to fall out immediately he had climbed the small ladder and half-rolled onto the narrow bed. His fall was not graceful, and he landed in a crumpled heap, wrapped in a duvet on the narrow floor beneath Lynn's bunk.

After the yacht had docked on Sunday, Midas and Lynn called by at her hotel on 72nd Street, collected her bags and travelled to Midas's Upper East Side apartment. Lynn stayed for the next three nights. She commuted downtown each day to her editorial office and, unknown to Midas, one of the tasks that she had during those visits was to negotiate relocating from Chicago to New York.

Her negotiations were successful, but the timescale would be at least another 9 to 12 months before it would become effective. She thought that she would wait until the following springtime to tell Midas of the relocation.

She told Midas that she knew a number of their investors that came on board in the friends and family round personally, and at the right time, she felt that she could bring another group of potential investors to the table. It would only be an introduction and then it would be up to the Viking, Midas and the team to convert the potential investors.

Simon had relocated from Canada to New York and had started work; for the time being he was engineering director, with the knowledge that within a few months a further reorganization would see the separation of the chief architect role and the chief technology officer role between Chad and himself. Midas and Simon were unaware that this move would need to come sooner rather than later.

Another five new engineers had settled in, their recruitment process being handled jointly by Chad and Simon, and on Simon's assessment they were all top rated engineers.

New applications which used embedded communications[3], which the Metasys Visual platform enabled, were starting to find their way into the marketplace. Most of these were simple video chat applications. Some facilitated the move to web real-time communications in the contact center sector.

The beta platform was seeing a good uptake by developers and engineers and there was a steady growth in the number of minutes per week being delivered to developers around the country. At last weekend's count, over fifty thousand minutes had been logged on the platform across five thousand developers.

Simon's research of the customers on the platform revealed that there were a number of large organizations that had started to experiment with 'embedded real time communication in apps', which suggested that future uptake could accelerate.

After the meeting with Stephan, and the auditor's report, Midas had fired Dan. It was clear that his efforts were incomplete and inadequate. The auditors questioned his claims that he was a qualified accountant and that he previously ran large accounting departments. In Midas's book, even the simplest of accounting controls were absent and the accounting package was a waste of time and money. Dan had protested that the auditors did not understand what he was

---

[3] Company or vendors Web sites or Apps (that are downloaded to mobile devices) which allow secure voice and video commination and sharing data between two or more parties, due to the technology being embedded in the web site or application.

doing but reluctantly handed over historical records to a bookkeeper seconded from one of the Viking's companies. Within two weeks she had created a simple system, reconciled much of the earlier entries, produced a trial balance, and set Midas's business on a clear track.

Chad and Simon were sitting at Midas's table; he had a concerned look. The previous week the number of developers on the platform had seen a spurt in growth, but the platform became unstable and the two engineers who, in their part-time, ran support desk had become overwhelmed during the weekend.

"The concept of the architecture is OK," said Simon, "but there is a fundamental design flaw which is making the whole platform unstable when we get a rapid increase in usage."

"The concept of sound, it's the engineers who are not executing properly," said Chad. "Every time they complete a development module, they should check and test everything – again."

There followed a heated exchange between Chad and Simon. It was at a technical level that Midas chose not to involve himself in, although he understood most, if not all, of what was being said. It was clear that Chad objected to Simon's challenge that the scalability on the platform had not been thought through.

To add complexity to the issues, there had been increasing demand from developers for access to the platform by mobile devices that Chad claimed to be built. But it emerged that Chad had implemented a temporary fix that was not yielding the results. So there were two problems: scalability and mobile access.

Simon was much more pragmatic and disciplined in his analysis of the problems than Chad appeared to be. And Midas tended to trust his judgment. There was clearly a significant issue and, although both senior engineers agreed it was not showstopper, there was much work to be done as the meeting adjourned.

Midas saw a text message from the Viking. He was invited downtown to meet with the Viking and Stefan. Clearly there was some degree of urgency; the meeting had been set for later in the afternoon.

As he travelled downtown Midas tried to conjecture what the meeting was about. His instinct told him that he had another raft of problems, which had not been of his making.

What was it this time?

SIXTY

As Midas stepped into the coffee shop at the Carlton Hotel on Madison, he spotted the Viking and Stefan sitting at a table, which overlooked E28th Street. He went over and joined them, ordered a macchiato, and waited for the Viking to share the purpose on the meeting.

Stefan spoke first, "Midas, we have a problem. It's Chad."

Midas felt his stomach tense, *What's he done now, for these guys to be involved?*

"He is now writing direct to our shareholders, expressing a view that any technology start-up should have the chief architect, the chief technology officer, whatever term we want to use for him, on the board. This is clearly being done without your knowledge, without the Viking's knowledge, and it only came to light last night when one of my friends sent me a copy of his mail."

"The mail was long and rambling and therefore had lost any impact; it was clearly written in a wave of immaturity, naiveté, and misplaced frustration," added the Viking.

"Fortunately, our shareholders are experienced and mature people, and the ones that I have spoken to see this for what it is: a disgruntled employee behaving inappropriately.

"They remember him from the yacht, when, apparently, he did not make too many friends. They've ignored the mail other than to suggest, quite rightly, that we get our house in order.

"A question. I am aware that Chad is the architect behind the platform, what happens if he leaves? Are we vulnerable?"

"Some months back I would have said yes," answered Midas, "but

Simon is now on top of the architecture, understands it, and, in reality, he is driving the engineering team and directing what they're doing. Chad is maintaining his role as the architect and Dave from MIT is also contributing. Simon is well-established now; Chad is not indispensable."

The Viking held his hand up, "Despite his behavior, he has been with us since the beginning, and, as he has reminded us on many occasions, he has been responsible for us getting to where we are today; the fact that Simon has taken over a considerable part of the process is really a smart move on your part Midas. Any one person must never hold us hostage. We know that Chad tried this once before and I hoped he had learned his lesson but clearly he is as unstable as ever."

"We're going to go into a second financing round in the next two months," said Stefan, "We cannot have any evidence, or demonstration, of a lack of cohesion in the team or a level of disloyalty – anywhere. We have to make a decision very quickly with regard to Chad's future. If he is going to go, he has to go immediately, well in advance of any approach to the next round of investors. And then you need to be able to articulate the case why the new team under Simon is strong enough to take this forward."

"I'm going to move Chad formally to the Chief Architect role, and give the whole of the engineering team to Simon," said Midas. "That's going to be effective immediately."

"Do you want to speak to Chad about the shareholder letter fiasco or shall I?" asked Midas.

"No, you do it," said the Viking. He added, "Before you go, there is something else I want to discuss with you.

"You and I have discussed the need to boost our capability in selling to big-time accounts, to getting access into Silicon Valley, and to get access to serious funding. You raised with me the fact that you do not have that level of experience and you suggested that we might want to bring in an experienced and heavyweight who can carry us into Silicon Valley.

"We talked about a new CEO type."

"I remember the conversation and I am relaxed about it," replied

Midas. "You know I am totally committed to our vision; more today than I have at any time in the past. I believe that we will change the way the world communicates. But, I agree that to accelerate towards that vision we need someone who has been there and done it, who is taken a tech start-up to Series A, Series B, and IPO or even acquisition. I've not done that."

The Viking replied, "I know, and it's to your credit that you see the need for us to step forward and change the role that you are presently have. You are doing everything, and we need a top flight guy with good big ticket and platform sales experience, and we need another strong, big account guy with him. You might want to think about getting Ted back."

"I'm with you."

"I want you to meet someone. He's in town next week. He was introduced to me by one of our guests at the original fund raising event who jokingly calls him 'Bernie the Bolt', that's bolt as in arrow – straight as a die, on target, and fast." The Viking laughed at the joke.

"He's in town next week, you and I are having dinner with him."

The meeting adjourned and Midas headed back on the subway. His mind was going at WARP speed. *Just what did he think he was doing? The guy's more stupid and naive than I thought. Does he think the shareholders will listen to him, and petition the board and the other shareholders to take him on board? It's not going to happen. He's made an ass of himself.*

Midas got back to the office and suggested to Simon that they step outside for a coffee. He wanted somewhere quiet to talk through his plan with Simon.

They sat down at nearby Starbucks; Midas outlined the conversation regarding the shareholder letter to Simon. Simon's expression changed from amazement, through surprise to contempt. "What are you going to do?"

Midas outlined the plan. The following day he would meet with Chad and tell him that in the new organization he would be Chief Architect with no staff, and Simon would take over the whole engineering.

"At the same time as that conversation is taking place, Simon, you are going to visit Dave at MIT and you are going to negotiate a consultancy contract with him, on a retainer, reporting directly to yourself. Lock him in. Chad walks and I want all the bases covered."

Simon nodded, "I have to meet Dave anyway, so it will be a good time."

The following morning Midas invited Chad to the same Starbucks. It was relatively empty and they sat at a table towards the back of the cafe.

Midas opened the conversation. "I think there is something which you forgot to tell me," Midas looked Chad squarely in the eyes. "Something about a letter that you felt compelled to write to shareholders."

"Well?" Midas continued to look directly at Chad, who was avoiding eye contact but still maintained an arrogant pose, grasping his coffee mug, as though he was going to throw it.

"I'm tired, tired of telling you guys, but if it was not for me you would have nothing. And any tech company that you see in Silicon Valley, Boston, New York has their Chief Engineer on the board."

Midas let it pass. Midas then looked at Chad and explained, in as friendly terms as he could; it was like talking to a child. "When people are elected to the board, they are elected by the shareholders and they're elected because those shareholders have agreed that the individual has something to contribute at board level: maybe it is solid strategic insight based on years of experience, access to funding, or access to potential customer networks, or any combination. They're not elected to the board because of their own feeling of self-importance."

He paused,

"There is no doubt Chad that you've made a considerable contribution to this business, and of course, you're right, without you we might not be where we are today, although there may be other top-flight chief architects who can do what you do, I don't know. But let's be very clear, writing to shareholders has a number of very negative implications."

There was zero response from Chad; his demeanor had not changed.

Midas continued, "First off, it suggests I cannot control my staff;

second, it suggests that the founders might have made a mistake in some of their early appointments to the senior team; and third, when we go out for the next round of funding there's going to be questions regarding stability within the team. None of these are good for you, nor me, nor the company, and I really fail to understand why you thought it was an appropriate move to spray emails around our shareholders."

Midas continued, he was hyped up now, "This is what I am going to do. With immediate effect you are appointed as the Chief Architect, you are responsible for the ongoing high-level design and architecture of the platform. Execution? Is in the hands of Simon, who with immediate effect, is Chief Technology Officer and has responsibility for all the engineers. You can have the status that 'Chief Architect' gives you; you will have a public face, so that your contribution is acknowledged, internally and externally.

"But there will be no board position - ever. We are going to have another fundraising round, which will probably bring one or two new non-exec directors onto the board, which will be, in my opinion, a good thing."

"What about my shares? My free shares?" asked Chad,

"What shares?" asked Midas, he was looking at Chad in disbelief.

"I'm entitled to shares; I was the founder of this company," said Chad.

Midas looked at him, this guy is impossible. He has lost touch with reality.

"I acknowledged you were the first engineering employee of the 'new' web communications business, but the founder you are not. We, along with Chen and Yang, our two engineers, and Dave who we retained on a consulting basis, started the web real time comms business as a result of initial work done by the Viking and me.

"Also, as you will note, you haven't invested any money in the company, you've been paid a salary, and you will have a payout from the ESOP program when it is put in place in the next few months."

"That's it?" responded Chad. "So I get no free shares. Okay, I guess I need to go away so I can decide what I'm going to do. I was planning two or three days' vacation, so consider that I'm on vacation from now."

As was his habit, he stood up and stormed out of the coffee shop.

Midas wondered, once again, why he was being so tolerant. He had respect and a soft spot for Chad. It was true that Chad had brought Midas's idea to fruition, but not without a lot of painful interchanges.

There was something that Midas could not put his finger on. He thought, *I'm not a psychologist but there is one big underlying problem here.*

He finished his coffee walked back to the office. As predicted, Chad's desk was empty, there was no sign of this laptop, or his bag, so Midas assumed that he had 'gone on vacation'.

That afternoon Simon and Midas briefed the engineers of the new organizational structure. Simon had been successful in negotiating a consulting contract with Dave. Simon and this team went heads down to resolve issues that had emerged over the last weekend.

Simon had presented Midas with a product road map, which showed significant levels of functionality being built on the existing platform.

Simon had spent years understanding the move to web communications and the move to real-time communication in apps. Midas knew that he could be confident that product direction was going to be under control.

Unbeknown to Midas, something else was rapidly unraveling and spinning out of control.

It was eleven-o-clock at night when his phone rang. Midas was dozing; he thought it was going to be Lynn.

The voice on the other end said, "This is the Officer Russo of the NYPD, Central Park Precinct, we have a guy here who claims that he works for you, he's been picked up and he needs to be bailed."

"What's he done?" Midas was pulling on his jeans as he was asking the question. He was praying that the guy in police custody was not who he thought it was but that was futile.

"His name is Chad and he has been brought in for trying to break into a building in the Park, and he is also well under the influence."

Midas groaned, "Okay, I am on my way."

It was a long night; Chad was looking worse for wear, disheveled, dirty, his jeans and shirt both torn. He grunted an acknowledgement to Midas before slumping on the bench in the cell.

Midas completed the paperwork and took Chad back to his apartment. Thankfully, Chad had not lost his keys; he still had his backpack wrapped around his neck.

Midas struggled to open the door. A neighbor opened the door opposite. She was about fifty-five.

She said, "Oh my God, not again. You go, I will take care of this. I'm used to it. He's been a mess since his girlfriend walked out."

Midas asked, "How long has this been happening?"

"Around six months. Sometimes he is really bad. He can make his way back to the door, but then fails the key test; he spends ten minutes banging on the door of an empty apartment shouting for his girlfriend. So now I have a spare key to open the door." As she was speaking, she unlocked Chad's door and pushed him inside.

Midas grabbed a taxi back to his apartment and sat on the sofa; it was two-o-clock in a long night. *Chad had a girlfriend?* There had been no indication of that, and his reputation around bars, which had been picked up from Engineers' gossip, suggested that Chad was anything but attached.

He wanted to ring Lynn; he needed to share the events with someone sane but decided that he would keep the story for another day.

He thought that this was going to be one event he kept to himself.

Four days later Chad appeared at the office, made no comment about anything that had happened between the time he sat down with Midas at Starbucks and now, when he walked in through the office door.

Midas said nothing.

There was a management meeting scheduled for eleven in the morning with Chad, Simon, and himself. That meeting passed uneventfully; Chad volunteered a description of his new role and acknowledged Simon's position as CTO.

After the meeting Midas received a call from the Police Station, he was asked to pay a visit.

Midas walked into Central Park precinct police station and presented himself at the front desk. He was asked to wait and a few minutes, a young female Sergeant approached him and introduced herself, "Hi,

I'm Sgt. Darcy, I work in community policing. Thank you for coming. Let's step into my office."

Midas followed the sergeant into a small office that was big enough to house the table and two chairs, but that was all. The sergeant nodded to the chair and Midas sat down, Darcy sat opposite.

"I want to talk to about the guy that you bailed. We know him, although he's never been charged, and I'm not counting last night. He is a problem waiting to happen. We see all kinds in this station. Not only families, we get joggers, walkers, tourists, but we also get a small trickle of misfits, the misguided, the poor, the rich, the insane, and the downright crazy. Thankfully they are fewer numbers, we keep the place peaceful and safe for everyone so they can enjoy. Ask about the troublesome bunch? Frequently we have to hunt them up and kick them out of the park when we close at one in the morning.

"We noticed that your man, Chad, that's his name, wanders around in the late evening. Bit of a bush creeper – you know, in and out of the trees. Been a few times when we had to bring him in for a warning or cooling off. It's usually minor stuff, he's drunk or is high on something. Lately, although he's wasted, he has a habit of following people; he seems to have a tendency towards, how do I say this, to stalk younger ladies. We have never been able to charge him on that score, and I don't want to have to. Has he had ever been in rehab?"

Midas shook his head, "All this is new to me. He does his job, sometimes he is a bit off the wall and unpredictable but he's done a good job until very recently."

"It's in the last few weeks that we've seen more of him and the problem seems to be getting worse," said Darcy."

"Okay thanks for the heads up, I'll see what we can do, maybe I can persuade him to go to rehab."

As Midas traveled back to the office, sitting in the back of the taxi, he decided that this was becoming too serious for him to keep to himself and he rang Vanessa and asked for a meeting with the Viking and Stefan; the meeting became fixed for the following day. They would meet before the dinner at which Midas was going to be introduced to Bernie the Bolt.

Late the following afternoon Midas headed downtown. The meeting was on Madison, and Midas arrived just after 6 PM. He met Stefan in the lobby of the Carlton Hotel, between E28th and E29th; they exchanged pleasantries while they waited for the Viking to join them. He came a few minutes later.

Minus outlined the recent events relating to Chad, and his meeting at Central Park Precinct the day before.

"Can he afford rehab?" asked the Viking.

"It's doubtful," said Midas. "We have a barebones medical cover for our team and we may be able to get a contribution."

"It's going to cost at least thirty grand to get him into a place for three months," added Stefan.

"Midas, talk to him. See if you can get him to take some time out. Contact rehab, find out what's the financial position. We can contribute a small amount privately. See what you can get from the insurance but I think it's time that we moved on."

The Viking continued, "He certainly has some major issues and I don't feel that just kicking him out into the street is the right thing to do. He has contributed to this company, and while his reward might not be in the form that he wants or expects, it's the least we can do to see if we can help him through this terrible period. Just let me know, in time, what happens. I do feel that we will not see much of him in the future."

With that the Chad subject was closed.

It would transpire that Chad would agree to go into rehab, which would be successfully completed after three months, but he would decline to return, and he would move to San Diego. He would be offered a consulting attachment by Midas, which he would decline. It was to be expected that it was to be the last that anyone heard of him. Two months after he left New York, one of the engineers would pick up some gossip about Chad on the network. What he would hear was serious and he would seek confirmation, which he got. He would walk to Simon's desk to break the news.

SIXTY ONE

The news passed to Simon was brief. Chad had been jailed in Tijuana, Mexico. He had been in a drunken altercation where someone had been killed. He would be incarcerated in a Mexican prison for the next decade, at least.

Simon passed the news to Midas, the Viking and Stefan. It was a sad ending to a promising career that had spun out of control. No one would ever know what drove an intelligent guy, one bordering on genius, through episodes of increasingly destructive behavior.

Midas also sent a mail to Nestor; it was time for a chat.

Bernie the Bolt was a tall friendly European of Scandinavian origin. He stood six foot two and sported a dark head of hair, above dark set eyes and a prominent nose. He looked as though he could be cast for any role in the Pirates of the Caribbean.

He shook Midas's hand strongly, and looked at him intently. Bernie said, "I've heard a lot about your work, you've done great, you really are a visionary. I checked out the work and the platform that's coming out of your place. Your guys should be on the Honor Roll and if there's anything I can do then it will be a pleasure to work with you."

They went into the dining room and for the next two hours they swapped stories; stories of business and other adventures, about disasters, flops and successes. Bernie was a warm individual and his jocular manner belied a person of considerable experience and charisma. Midas took an immediate liking to him and felt that the team would work well with Bernie at the helm.

They talked at length about funding and Bernie suggested they do a quick top-up round from the friends and family and at the same time get the company to ready a Series A. Bernie believed they could get a valuation of around forty to fifty million dollars, pre-money, at this time. Bernie said, "This may appear high for a pre-revenue company, but you're in the innovation and tech space; I have been looking at various acquisitions that have taken place among some of your lower-level competitors and forty million does not seem to be out of the ballpark. It could actually be higher. We'll see when we start going into the market."

Midas couldn't help but do a mental calculation of the value of the Viking's share and of his part the company. Sure, their original 50% each had been diluted when the Friends and Family round took place, and would be diluted again on top up, and Series A, but they would still see a worthwhile increase in the valuation of their holdings. He might even be able to part with some of his founder's shares during the Series A and bring some cash in.

It was agreed that Bernie would start in three weeks' time. Until then, he and Midas would plan a transition and start the fundraising process. They needed a flyer, a pitch deck, and an Information Memorandum for potential investors. They would plan how to achieve a rapid acceleration to a new level in both resourcing, capacity, and capability in the business.

Midas met Simon the following morning to brief him. Simon got in first. He had his team resolve all the issues that a few weekends before had caused so much grief, and he laid out a product roadmap with the features and benefits of their platform today. This was set against the competition and, today, there was a small headway above the rest of the field. When Simon highlighted the rest of his development plan and the product road map, that platform would be so far ahead of the competition that they would become the go-to company as developers and organizations started to embed real-time communications in the websites and applications and, looking to the future, in devices, on the Internet of Things.

The product roadmap made compelling story and Midas was looking forward to pitching this to the current friends and family, and to inbound investors and VCs in the run-up to Series A.

Midas and the Viking had agreed with Bernie that he would come in as CEO and a board member; Midas would take the role of co-founder and board member, and within the company, the title of President. The Viking would remain the non-executive Chairman.

With Stefan, the board comprised four people. Anticipating a board member from Series A, five would be the optimal number.

Over the following weeks Bernie, Midas, and Simon rewrote the strategy of the company. The vision remained intact: the company would change the way the world communicates. The focus was on real-time communication embedded into apps on mobile devices, in webpages, and IOT Devices.

This time around, the strategy document was much more rigorous. It dealt with all the issues that Nestor raised in his email to Midas eighteen months earlier, which Midas had dusted off and which Bernie concurred with.

Their work on strategy highlighted one major and important transition for Metasys Visual.

Midas had read, and Bernie agreed, that depending on a company's focus, the risks are skewed to either success being driven from technological success or from market penetration (technology risk, or market risk). With their earlier Cloud Visual Communications business, the primary risk was market-centric; the technology was licensed and proven, success depended on the ability to penetrate the market. As Metasys moved to the web real-time communication technology space (which underpinned real time and embedded communications in web sites and mobile applications), the massive research and development project drove the business risk to being wholly technical, at least for a significant period – the company's survival depended on getting an embryonic and unproven technology to work. As the technology was now becoming proven and tested, the majority of the business risk would migrate to market penetration.

Bernie explained that many tech start-ups never understand the need to change focus; techie inventors just assume that their ideas will gravitate into the market by force of their technical prowess. It never happens. To mitigate the risk in Metasys Visual, Bernie proposed to bring in a top-flight sales VP who would base himself in the Silicon Valley, the home of most of their prospective early adopters. Midas concurred.

The strategy discussions were shared with the Viking and Stefan, it received a unanimous agreement. Now it was time to build this into a formal Information Memorandum. Heading into discussions with serious VC investors and substantial family offices required a considerably more robust approach than they employed in the first round.

An updated pitch was tested on the Viking and Stefan and had received a positive response. The Viking and Stephan immediately circulated it to the existing Friends and Family investors, which resulted in one-third significantly upping their stake. These incoming funds gave the team the financial breathing space to set the wheels in motion on a Series A funding round in six to nine months' time.

Midas was on the subway heading to the Upper East Side. It was not crowded. The train stopped at 68th Street and Nestor got on, he walked over and sat down next to Midas. "You wanted to see me?"

Midas laughed, "Hi, where are you going this time? Vacationing in New York?"

"Kind of."

The two men chatted and in no time they were at 96th Street. Midas said, "This is where I get off."

"I know, me too. Let's have a walk along the promenade, you know the one they call the Bobby Wagner Walk, on the East River – nice place."

They walked along the river, and Midas told Nestor about Chad. "What happened, do you think? Why does someone sabotage themselves so badly?"

Nestor replied, "We don't want this to turn into a pseudo psychological session, nor do I want to analyze Chad, I don't even know the guy. But can you remember the conversation we had in the bar, after you had lost the Airshef deal and been screwed by the bank? We talked about limiting beliefs."

"Yes, I remember. Go on."

"Limiting beliefs such as 'I am not good enough, I am not deserving of success, and I am not worthy'. We all carry limiting beliefs with us from childhood. In some people they are very, very minor, eliminated by confidence and positive self-belief. In others they are acute; they are the dominant mindset. Sure, if we have awareness, we can address those beliefs and then work to remove them and replace them to have a healthier view of ourselves. Are you with me?"

Midas nodded.

"If we do not remove them they will always be an impediment to our success. In some people they are so intense and so deep-rooted that without help they will never be uncovered, nor treated, and give rise to dysfunctional behavior and psychotic disorders."

Midas nodded, he looked thoughtful, "I often recall the times you have talked about mindset and skill set, I am starting to believe that there is further dimension, something to do with emotional awareness. An understanding of our mind and how it impacts our behavior and what we think. I am not sure what to call it."

Nestor replied, "I think you are right, Midas, and to be fair, the categorization between mindset and skill set is a great point to start to become self-aware and make your own assessment, but then you need to start to create more color and content in your perspective of how you think and behave. I think emotional awareness is essential to emerge from that latter process. You have a very good point. Also, having emotional awareness is part of the journey of self-discovery."

He added, "Let's have dinner soon, we can talk about it some more. I need to go, and I suspect you have a lot to think about."

Midas bid his friend good-bye as he turned and walked back towards 96th Street, Nestor carried on going upriver.

SIXTY TWO

Bernie and Midas started on the round of VC's and brokers. At the beginning they focused on friendly contacts in New York and Silicon Valley. They limited the exposure to a few companies, primarily to get feedback and to sharpen the pitch. A frequent discussion point was the exit strategy of the company; would it be an IPO or a trade sale? Bernie and Midas were not quite sure which would happen first.

In discussions with potential investors, Bernie and Midas received strong endorsement for the composition of the board and for the support from the Viking who provided excellent leadership and had acted as a mentor to Midas. Investors saw the Viking as a staunch advocate and flag bearer for the business, an articulate and experienced focal point on the board, a statement of credibility for business in dealing with external parties, and fund raiser. The Viking was the epitome of an outstanding Chairman.

They were getting other positive affirmations. They were clearly in the right space; their choice to be a platform supplier was acknowledged as a strategic winner. The task of providing real-time communications embedded in webpages or in mobile devices and IOT devices appeared to be deceptively simple, but the infrastructure behind the front end solutions that developers built was hideously complicated. Many companies had tried and aborted the attempt to do anything except a simple peer-to-peer call with limited capacity to scale.

Midas had seen from the outset that the enterprise market would demand scalability, security, reliability and a range of features that integrated not only web-based devices but also was capable of interacting and operating with legacy communications protocols such as a Telco infrastructure. Simon had done a magnificent job in building out the original platform; some of Chad's early work was still in the core of the platform, massively enhanced by developments architected by Simon and Dave.

The weeks went past and turned into months; the Series A round was gathering pace. A number of investors had indicated that they would come in with between one and three million-dollar tranches, in a round that had a minimum of a ten-million-dollar tag.

Alongside progress on the investment front, interest and sales were accelerating at a terrific pace. There were thousands of developers taking advantage of the free access to the Metasys Visual platform to develop ideas and experimental solutions using real-time communication in apps; a percentage of these were transitioning to paying customers, launching real solutions into the world in the fields of telehealth, banking, and education, disrupting the old inefficient ways of interacting with patients, clients, and students.

Simon had been recruiting like mad to keep up with the pace. He had twenty engineers on his books now. Sure, this was still a small team by big corporate standards, but when you have the best and most committed and knowledgeable engineers available, a modest team can deliver miracles. Miracles were almost a daily happening in Simon's team. At a technology level, Simon was now so far ahead of the competition that he was winning awards at major conferences for Metasys Visual and for the applications that it supported.

Midas and Bernie sat down with the Viking at his usual table in the Carlton hotel.

The Viking passed over a one-page note.

"These guys are a USA - China fund, they have just raised one hundred million in a fund within a fund and they're interested. I know them well; they're good guys. They drive a hard but fair bargain and they will be well respected by the other VCs who want to toss in a million or so into the pot.

"Their chairman, who I know well, has nominated one of his senior guys to lead a team to look at us; they will be here next week from Chicago."

The three men reconvened at the hotel the following week. Joining them was Michael, an American Chinese, who had graduated from

Stanford, and moved straight into the VC World. He had 10 years' experience in the US and China and he had put together some significant deals. He was quiet, confident, and assertive when he wanted to make a point that he didn't feel was being understood. He was a nice person to deal with.

Michael's team completed due diligence in record time. Stephan had already warned Midas and Bernie of the due diligence process and all the necessary documentation had been collected assembled in a data room to be made available to any serious investor. This was the first time Midas had done this and he was overwhelmed by the detail that was needed in the data room – every conceivable contract that the company had signed, details of security and IP protection, business and personal details of everyone connected with the business, banking details and accounts, insurances, leases, asset registers, the list was endless.

Once the USA China group had completed their first assessment, they provided a Term Sheet. At that point one of the big banks stepped forward. A number of their connections in Silicon Valley had heard about Metasys Visual and one in particular, a Family Office of a former executive of the biggest search company in the world, was clamoring for a share of the action. From that point negotiations on multiple fronts moved very quickly.

The $10m Series A fund had become $15m due to an oversubscription from consortium members.

Two months after the first meeting with Michael, final and agreed term sheets were on the table from Michael's parents' fund, three other well-known funds in Silicon Valley and the Family Office. Fifteen million dollars would now flow into the company at a pre-money valuation of fifty million dollars. The Viking and Midas would be asked to liquidate five percent of their stock to make room for the incoming investors. Neither had any problem in seeing some cash being returned for the last three years of their endeavors.

Michael's team was confident that Bernie's strategy of amassing large strategic accounts would continue and lead to a successful IPO, possibly as early as within twenty four months.

As the deal was going to close, Midas was invited to visit Chicago where he would meet an unexpected new acquaintance.

SIXTY THREE

Midas boarded UA345 at LaGuardia. The welcoming stewardess was not welcoming at all; she was a study of indifference as passengers walked on board. Her grey uniform appeared to be a size too small and Midas thought it had the effect of creating a rather peculiar body form.

He was squeezed into his 6C aisle seat. His knees touched the seat in front of him, and he prayed that the aircraft had fixed seats. If the passenger in front had the temerity to recline his seat, he would hit Midas in the face. Midas wondered just how many more seats United could possibly squeeze into the fuselage of this A319.

On this occasion, and unusually, Midas had checked his bags, so he was less concerned about fighting for the possession of a cubic yard of space in the luggage compartment above his head. He thought he had done his fellow passengers a good deed.

His soft laptop bag he had dropped in the pocket in front of him.

He wore a light blue short-sleeved shirt, which hung outside the latest Levi Commuter jeans. His favorite blue dock shoes completed his cool casual look.

In a little under three hours he would be arriving at Chicago; he texted Lynn and was happy to see that she replied with a 'See you in arrivals, have transport.'

The flight was full, every seat occupied, bodies crammed in the metal tube like Oreos in a cookie jar.

Moments after Midas was seated, the passenger next to him climbed over to occupy the middle seat, not even waiting for Midas to get up. As soon as he was seated, the twenty-something guy next to him started to play a highly audible game on his smartphone. He seemed to be oblivious to the peep, peep, peep, from his handset until Midas tapped on his shoulder on to get his attention and to ask him to either mute or put his headphones.

"Great game, but I don't want to have to listen to this all the way to Chicago," Midas said, as he tried to connect with the youth's eyes which were buried under a mop of hair that fell onto his face. The boy shrugged and connected earphones to the phone and went back to his land of oblivion.

As the aircraft pushed back Midas closed his eyes. He travelled enough to develop the ability to transcend to the land of sleep before the aircraft took off. Today was no exception

As United's service on anything less than three-hour sectors was between minimal and non-existent, depending on the time of day, he would not miss anything by sleeping.

The pilot announced that he was moving from cruise elevation, to descend to Chicago airport - that brought Midas out of his dreamland. Midas fully expected the next announcement to say that they were going into a holding pattern; he was not disappointed.

He looked at his classic Blancpain Watch and guessed that they would overshoot the 12:40 PM arrival time by about 10 minutes. Lynn was an experienced traveler in and out of O'Hare and she would have made allowances for the delays on approach, the time to taxi, and the time for the baggage to appear.

He glanced at his watch again. His Blancpain was a treat to himself on the third anniversary of their tech start-up. He had been saving for the classic black and stainless steel 'Fifty Fathoms Chronometer' for eighteen months and had bought it just before the company's birthday. It was a man's watch; a black dial, discreetly branded with luminous hands, and a casing that had a rotating bevel which allowed elapsed time to be set and read easily. The smooth movement of the sweeping second hand was mesmerizing. The black and stainless bracelet was solid enough to be present, but not ostentatious. The watch was an example of understatement - Midas liked that.

The pilot had pulled out of the holding pattern and was now down to around 3000 feet. In a few moments the wheels would touchdown and a five-minute taxi would take them to their gate, which today was C 31 in terminal one.

Midas left the aircraft and walked through the underground passageway to the baggage claim area in the main building. He waited for around fifteen minutes for his bags to arrive, threw them onto a trolley and headed to the arrivals area.

As he exited the automatic doors he looked around to see if he could see Lynn.

The first thing he saw was a giant, pink, heart-shaped balloon, the string of which was being held by a young lady dressed in a white. It was Lynn. Midas smiled as he walked towards the balloon.

Lynn's white outfit accentuated her slim figure and gave her a tall lithe appearance. Her white blouse had long buttoned sleeves that had been pushed up to reveal her forearm; a high collar rose up at the back of her neck, beneath her long black hair. White casual trousers tapered to her ankles; her feet were revealed in red open lattice shoes. She carried a white box-shaped Coach handbag. Her hair was pushed back over her ears to reveal her signature discreet Gucci diamond ear studs. She looked at him through the fashionable black-rimmed glasses.

She smiled and wrapped her arm around his neck, looked up into his eyes, and lightly kissed his cheek. "Hello, my wonder boy. Come, I have the limo on standby."

She beckoned to a man in a limo driver's suit who was standing nearby.

"This is Joe; he will drive us into town."

Joe was about 240lbs - most of it muscle. He stood six foot four. He pushed his hand forward. "Mr. Midas, welcome back to Chicago."

Midas shook hands, or rather allowed his hand to disappear into a giant clam of a fist that was Joe's attempt at a handshake.

Ten minutes later they were on I90 for a one-hour journey into the city.

"Where are we staying?" asked Lynn. Midas noted the "we" and smiled to himself. He liked the level of intimacy, which had developed over the last year, and this was like a homecoming. Returning to Chicago, being met by a beautiful girlfriend at the airport, and being whisked into town in the back of a limo. What could be better?

"Well *I* am staying at the Kimpton Burnham Hotel," he answered with a smile, "and you, dear Lynn, are welcome to join me."

She made a fist and lightly punched his chin, as she laughed. "You think I would let you stay alone in my city?" she said.

"My city!?" Midas looked at her. "I was here before you."

"Oh really, so when did you arrive in Chicago?" Asked Lynne pointedly.

"When I was born," smiled Midas.

"Okay, you're older than me so you win," and with that she shuffled her bottom to the other side of the big bench seat, with a little girl sulky look on her face. Moments later she laughed and moved back towards him.

The traffic at the junction with I94 was terrible. It was almost stationary, and they slowly made their way through the congestion before speeding up again towards the city.

It was exactly one hour from the airport when they pulled up outside the Kimpton Burnham. The hotel was in a National Historic Landmark building, reminiscent of traditional downtown Chicago in the early part of the 20th century. It had been very tastefully renovated.

Joe lifted Midas's bags onto the trolley that had been brought to the curbside by a bellboy. Joe said, "If you need me, Miss Lynn will give you my telephone number. Call me at any time, and I mean anytime. You have a good stay."

Midas and Lynn both ascended in the wrought iron clad elevator to the 12th floor. Michael had booked the hotel and, as he said, it was befitting an important client with whom they were about to close a major deal. He had Midas accommodated in a small suite that overlooked the Chicago River.

Midas was grateful, particularly when he remembered that seven years earlier he left a decrepit basement flat in South Shore that was so far removed from his accommodation on this visit, that he had to pause and convince himself that it was real. The journey since leaving Chicago on a Greyhound bus, to arriving back, had been tortuous, challenging at times, depressing at times, elating, and always exciting.

"What's your program?" asked Lynn.

"Meetings all day tomorrow and on Wednesday; signing of the deal on Thursday, and on Friday I have lunch with someone that the Viking wanted me to meet, but other than that I'm free."

"I see, our busy man as always. No time for Lynn." She pretended to sulk.

Then quickly she added, "It's okay, honey, I understand. You do whatever you need to do this week but you don't book anything for next weekend. Next weekend you're mine." She stood before him looking up into his eyes her feet slightly apart, hands on her hips, her eyes staring intently through her glasses into his face. "Got it?"

"Yes I do get it, I get it."

With that, he put his arms around her tiny waist, lifted her off her feet and planted a long kiss on her lips. Her hands fastened around his neck and it was as though she was entwined around his body.

SIXTY FOUR

The next morning Lynn left early. By seven thirty she was showered and dressed and stepping out of the door, she shouted, "Midas, call me."

Midas had noticed that she had a day bag with her when they got out of the limo. *Clever girl, so well organized*, he thought when he saw that.

Midas left the hotel at nine o clock, and headed to the Willis Tower on South Wacker Drive. It was a five-minute cab ride. Once he arrived at what was the tallest building in America prior to One World Trade Center being opened, he was directed to the 81st floor. Michael's firm had two offices in USA; this was the main office and they had a much smaller office in New York City.

Over the next two days the Viking, Bernie, and Stefan joined Midas. They pored over legal documents: shareholder agreements, warranties, declarations, guarantees, and an array of the other necessary legal paperwork. By Wednesday evening the final draft of all documentation was completed. Michael's team and their partners in their consortium had been present during the day to ensure that their interests were adequately reflected in all the documents.

Michael, his team and the lawyers had done a great job preparing for these meetings. The two days, although busy, and occupied with drafting and redrafting clauses in a myriad of documents, had gone very smoothly. The final meeting between Metasys Visual Inc. and the funding partners' representatives was to take place on the following day in the afternoon. At that meeting all the documents would be formally signed and within ten days the finance would be available to the company.

The Viking and Midas both negotiated to sell ten percent of their total equity, which yielded a low seven figure to both of them; while it reduced the cash going into the business, Series A had been oversubscribed and now stood at $15 million. The transfers to the two founders were incidental to providing funding for the next stage of Bernie's growth plan, which he could see would be accelerated across North America, Europe and Asia.

As the final meeting closed, the Viking took Midas to one side. "I have a very important person that I want you to meet. We will have lunch tomorrow. I can't tell you very much. He wants to outline a project to you himself."

"What is it about?" asked Midas

"As I say, I can't say very much because he wants to introduce himself, his project and the background, to you personally."

Stefan joined them. "So have you told Midas that he is going to be a farmer?" asked Stefan, looking at the Viking.

"I haven't a clue what you're talking about!" exclaimed Midas.

Stefan took the hint and went to join Michael.

"What was that?" asked Midas.

The Viking answered, "Nothing, I'm not sure where he's coming from; we haven't started celebrating yet. He was sober. Strange."

Midas decided that it was better to wait until tomorrow

The team held a celebratory dinner at the Metropolitan Club on the 67th floor of Willis Tower. The Viking stood and toasted Midas and Bernie. He toasted Stefan and the original investors. He toasted Michael, his team, and their investor colleagues. In their absence he toasted the engineering team. He toasted the customers. In fact, he toasted anyone and everyone who had been involved in the journey to this point.

The Viking continued, "A journey starts with a single step, we make that step, we do not know where it will ultimately take us; there have been twists, and there have been turns; there are been hills, there have been mountains, and there have been dark valleys. Our expedition has taken on new members, and we have lost some of our initial team along the way. We set off with the vision to change the way the world communicates. We are making that change."

He paused and looked at the assembled team.

"Today, as we stand here, major corporations, although just now they are few in number, are using our platform to deliver a whole new level of customer engagement, which they never thought possible nor envisaged a year ago. It is the movement that we have ignited. A movement that will not stop. Over the coming years more and more people will create more and more applications, and opportunities, to use real-time communications in applications, and on the way, it will also extend to the Internet of Things."

He paused again for effect. Now he drew himself up to his full height and continued.

"As a result of vision, tenacity, and bravery, coupled with some of the best engineering talent in the country, Midas and, latterly, Bernie, has led this revolution. The gentlemen around this table represent a new class of investors for the company, who have placed that our disposal a considerable war chest which we will use carefully, judiciously, but we will keep the brave hearts, the innovation, the drive, and the vision that has brought us thus far. I hope and pray that within the next twelve to twenty-four months we may be back at this table celebrating a public offering of this great company."

The toast, Gentlemen is, "Metasys Visual and success."

The Viking raised his glass, everyone at the table stood and raised their glasses, "Metasys Visual and success," they called out in unison.

Shortly after the meeting broke up, Midas excused himself. He confirmed with the Viking that he would meet tomorrow, and went to the lobby of the Willis Tower, many floors below.

As he exited the elevator he turned right and walked towards Argo Tea Shoppe. He pushed open the door and stepped inside the little tea house, he was looking for someone. As he walked around the glass pillar in the center, a voice said, "Hi Midas."

Midas swiveled around; a man stood up and held out his hand. "Good evening, Mr. Entrepreneur."

Midas laughed, shook the outstretched hand, "Good evening Nestor."

"Congratulations, you have come far, in so many dimensions."

"Thanks to you Nestor," said Midas.

"No, I have just been the messenger, the universe has guided you, as it will guide anyone who cares to listen."

Midas sat down, "Well Nestor, what's next."

"I don't know, but I suspect that you will surprise yourself. Let me know." Nestor was beaming as he got up.

Midas rose, "Hey, don't go yet, I have a lot to talk to you about, a lot to thank you for." He grasped his friend's hand.

Nestor paused, "I appreciate what you have said, now go to your room, Lynn's waiting for you. And when you are there, look in the mirror, and say thank you to the guy you see.

"I will see you …. somewhere, sometime, you know me!"

With a wave and a smile, Nestor walked out of the tearoom.

SIXTY FIVE

Midas arrived back at his hotel. When he got to the room Lynn was already there, lounging on the sofa wearing a big yellow T-shirt on which the words 'De Walt Power Tools' was rather incongruously printed on the back and front.

"Where did you get that shirt?" asked Midas, as he stared in disbelief.

"It's yours, I stole it a long time ago; did you not miss it?" Lynn laughed as she stood up and moved to kiss him lightly on the cheek. "Don't you remember? You had this on the boat in Florida and I was wearing it on the deck; I said I would take it to wash. Well, it's washed and I'm wearing it." She laughed again.

Midas showered and came out of the bathroom wearing a white hotel robe. He looked at Lynn and asked, "Do I get my T-shirt back, or do I have to take it?"

She laughed, pulled the T-shirt off and threw it at Midas. "There, are you happy now?"

She ran and jumped on the bed where she lay face down, giggling to herself, dressed only in the smallest of white lace panties.

The following morning, Midas headed to Passo's Italian restaurant on South Wacker Drive for his 11:30 a.m. appointment with the Viking and the mystery guest.

He walked past the tables that sat under the canopy in the open air and headed towards the back of the restaurant where he saw the Viking. The Viking was sitting with a silver-haired gentleman who was wearing a lightweight grey suit, and a pink shirt with an open neck. Smart, distinguished, yet casual. Midas was unsure of his age but guessed he was probably around sixty.

As he arrived at the table, both the Viking and his guest stood up to welcome him. Handshakes were exchanged and the Viking said, "Midas, allow me to introduce Peter Haines. Peter and I have known each other for a long time. You might know Peter's family name; they have been in Chicago for generations."

Midas sat down. Indeed, Midas knew the name very well. The Haines family was an institution in Chicago. A business was started by Peter's father, John Haines in the 1940s and had been the go-to destination for Ford vehicles, at any one of their six showrooms, for decades.

"I've heard a lot of good things about you, Midas," said Peter. "I must congratulate you on your latest accomplishment. It seems that you have not only built a solid and far-reaching business, you're making impact on people's lives. That is to be commended. The Viking tells me that the organization will change, and he has said that now that you have the additional funding, you may have some time available. I would like you to help me on a small project, a project which will bring benefit to thousands of people."

Midas, the Viking, and Stefan had already discussed the possibility of Midas standing down from the position of President and just remaining a non-executive director on the board. Midas was comfortable with that idea.

"Whatever it is, I'm sure it will be interesting," said Midas.

They took a break from the conversation to order lunch. The Viking ordered Calamari Fritte followed by Filet Mignon with Truffle Mushroom Ragout. Midas ordered Caprese Salad, followed by Grilled Salmon. Peter declined a starter but asked for a Hummus Flight to be served as a main. Peter asked if they could have a bottle of Barbera, a medium bodied red wine from the Piedmont region.

Fay, who took the order, said, "You know your Italian wines, that is one of the best regions for Barbera." Peter smiled and nodded.

Peter looked at Midas. "Were you here in 1999, in Chicago?" Asked Peter.

"Yes." Answered Midas, puzzled by the question

Peter looked at him intently, "Do you remember the cows?"

Midas paused. His eyes moved up and to the left as he tried to recall any images of cows.

"Do you mean the colored cows?" he asked.

"Yes," answered Peter. "Do you know the origin of that project?"

"No," said Midas, "Tell me more."

"Before Chicago, the Swiss had a festival in Zurich where they featured highly decorated and colored cows. It was intended to reflect the agricultural industry in Switzerland. They used the cows as a means to generate funds for charity. I was in Zurich at the time. And when I came back to Chicago, I discussed what I had seen with a good friend by the name of Louis Wattenberg, who at the time was a big wig in the city council. We decided that we could do the same in Chicago."

He looked at Midas and the Viking and leaned forward on the table.

In a low voice, almost conspiratorial, he said, "In 1999, we placed 340 cows all around the city, and we brought in 250 million dollars in tourist revenue to the city, and donated over three million to charity organizations. That was so much fun."

He sat back in his chair and continued the story.

"It was so good, it's been copied. Since then 'Cows on Parade', as it has become known, has been featured in cities as diverse as New York, Toulouse – France, Manchester – England, Bilbao – Spain, and Kansas City, to name just a few."

"An impressive track record," said Midas. "That's a lot of cows."

"There's much more to come," said the Viking.

"There is indeed," Peter nodded.

At that point lunch was served and the conversation changed to informal chitchat

After the main course was finished and cleared away, they ordered coffee and continued with a fine wine.

Peter said, "Let me return to the main subject."

Midas nodded. The Viking sipped his wine. And Peter leaned forward.

"In 2019, it will be the 20th year anniversary of the Chicago event. What I'm about to tell you is not public knowledge, and it must not be so, you must promise me."

Midas nodded in agreement, wondering where this conversation was going. He would soon find out.

"I want to do a special event for the anniversary," said Peter, "I want to have the biggest Cow Parade in history. We will have 1000 cows in cities all over North America. This time it will be different from previous events, which have been sponsored by the local cities and local organizations. We will organize, obtain sponsors, recruit the artists, find the venues, create the media attention, and build the whole event ourselves." His voice was rising in excitement. "My objective is to raise a minimum of $10 million for charity."

"This is a serious undertaking," said the Viking. "In fact, it is a massive media event. Today with the advent of social media we can do things in a very different way than it was done 20 years ago."

The Viking looked at Midas, "Oh, I said 'we'. Peter has asked me to join his Board of Trustees for the project. Not sure what we're calling it; I'm not sure how we describe a project involving 1000 cows without milking the subject."

Peter and Midas laughed. The Viking laughed at his own joke.

"Midas, you're going to have some time on your hands now that you're stepping down from your role in the company," said Peter, "I need someone with vision, with imagination, determination, unwavering commitment, to drive the first stages of this project, and the Viking has convinced me that you are the man who can do this. What do you think?"

Midas was stunned. Something like this never entered his mind. He could see the enormity of the task; it was a big vision, it was a major undertaking and he would have less than three years to complete it.

"I'm f…f…flattered," he stuttered. He could never recall stuttering at any time in his life, that too was a new, if temporary, experience.

"I can see the potential, I can see so much possibility, I can see it is a truly exciting opportunity. To be honest, I am shocked, I'm surprised that you would want me to take on such a big event."

Peter held his hand up. "I know that this is something which you could not imagine. You were invited for lunch with someone that you've never met before and now you're being asked to take on yet another adventure – with one thousand cows – I know it's a crazy-sounding idea, but it is not crazy, not for one moment. In its way, it will also change the world."

Peter paused and then looked at Midas, "I cannot expect you to agree, not now. I would like you to take this away. I know you're from Chicago, I know that you are very capable; you are among an elite group of entrepreneurs who have achieved a great measure of success. I know you're not taking your company to IPO yet, but I looked very closely at your company and your organization, I've read all the prospectus and if the Viking speaks well of you that is good enough for me."

He paused

"It's now your call, Midas. I am not talking to anyone else at this time. In fact, only five people know of my idea today, six including you. Why don't we get together next week and try to develop my ideas? Even if you decide 'no', I would welcome your thoughts."

They finished their coffee and wine and Peter stood up. "Gentlemen, thank you for listening I hope that we will continue our discussions. It has been a pleasure to see you again," Peter nodded to the Viking.

Peter looked at Midas, "Midas it has been a pleasure to meet you. I have been looking forward to seeing you in person, and I have not been disappointed. The lunch is on me, and I will say good afternoon."

With that Peter stood up, moved past the table, waved to the staff, and walked to the front of the restaurant and disappeared into the street.

Midas looked at the Viking. "And you knew about this?"

SIXTY SIX

For the first time that Midas could remember the Viking looked a little embarrassed. "Well, yes. I know Peter, and I know a little about the project, and I knew he was very interested in finding a young entrepreneur-type to build on his vision. He has got too many commitments here to give it his attention, but you'll find working with him a fabulous experience."

"OK, I understand. Thank you for giving me a good reference. I will think about it. I like the idea – it's crazy!"

They chatted for a few more minutes, and then Midas got up to leave, "Speak to you soon." He shook the Viking's hand and followed the same path that Peter had taken a few minutes before.

Midas was excited by the prospect of running such a big enterprise. And he would be back in Chicago, where Lynn was. He was ready to accept, but would wait until next week to tell Peter and the Viking.

Midas was sitting by the window of their suite as Lynn came into the room. It was his turn to be dressed in his yellow de Walt T-shirt. "I have reclaimed my shirt," Midas said, laughing.

"I can see," said Lynn, giggling, she added "I am pleased you didn't take my panties, your boxers suit you better." They both laughed.

They decided on a light meal in their room and Lynn ordered two Caesar salads from room service. She had bought some Italian sparkling wine and they had a casual 'carpet picnic'.

"What have we planned for weekend?" asked Midas, "Where are we going?"

Lynn laughed, "We are going nowhere, I am taking you back to my apartment. I am cooking dinner, you are going to relax, and I want to take care of you for the weekend. We are going to chill. Read magazines, watch a movie, drink coffee on Sunday morning and have a lazy weekend."

Midas smiled, he hadn't been to Lynn's apartment before, and this was a first. And he felt very comfortable with the idea.

He told Linda about the meeting with Peter. She was excited about the project, about the vision, but seemed to be reserved about Midas's involvement, which surprised Midas.

"Does this mean you will be moving to Chicago?" She asked

"If I take the project, yes," said Midas.

"Will you take the project?" she asked.

"I am thinking that I will," said Midas.

Lynn held her wineglass with two hands and stared, with rapt concentration, into the wine. She was very quiet. Midas looked at her, unsure of what to say or do at this moment.

Slowly, Lynn looked up from the glass. And then she glanced down again and said, "I have something to tell you. If you take this job you will be in Chicago, I will be in New York. Many months ago I applied for a transfer to New York. Honestly, I did that because that is where you are Midas. And now you tell me you going to be in Chicago."

"I've not said I will be in Chicago. I have not taken the job," answered Midas

"I know, but you will, you will not be able to resist; this is a massive opportunity. And I would not want you to refuse the job on account of me." Lynn's eyes started to fill, a tear started to run down her cheek.

Midas put his arms around her; she buried her head into his chest, and held him tight. She sobbed quietly. He continued to hold her, and then lifted her head, and with his finger, lightly lifting her chin, kissed her wet lips. "We will figure something out. I have an idea."

They said nothing for what seemed to be an eternity.

Then Midas lifted her up and carried her to the sofa. She lay back on the sofa and Midas was kneeling on the floor facing her. He took both her hands into his. "Let me tell you about my idea," he said.

Lynn nodded, her eyes still wet with her tears. Midas reached for a tissue from the side table and wiped her eyes.

"This is my idea. You know that I have cashed-in a percentage of my shares, I have reasonable amount of cash into the bank. What if you were to take a break from the WSJ? We could keep the apartment in New York and commute between the two places, as we want. I will need to travel on the new project and maybe you might like to help me because you have such an amazing network of contacts." Midas was looking at Lynn, searching for a reaction, but there was none.

Midas continued, "Dear Lynn, there is one other thing which I have been thinking about for a long time and maybe now is the time to deal with it. You know, but I have always had a problem with being shy about our relationship. I've not said very much, because I don't know what to say. But now I am quite sure and I want you to listen to me carefully.

"You know that I have the opportunity to bring 1000 cows into existence and to populate North America with colored cows. I guess that makes me a cowboy." He smiled at his little joke.

He looked at Lynn; she smiled a little smile but no more than that.

"I…I…I guess that I might need a cowgirl to help me."

He looked at Lynn seeking a reaction but she looked puzzled.

"What are you saying?" Asked Lynn.

Midas looked down. At this point Midas was holding Lynn's hands and he realized that they were wet with perspiration.

"Umm, well, what I am saying is that I am a cowboy. Will you be my cowgirl?"

Lynn burst into tears, in seconds she was sobbing. Midas put his arms around her again.

Lynn looked at him, her fists were clenched, and she was trying to hit him on his chest.

"Cowgirl, is that all you want?" she cried.

"I w…want you to be my cowgirl," stammered Midas.

"I don't want to be a cowgirl, I want to be a wife," sobbed Lynn. She was shaking and sniffing, and her sobbing wouldn't stop.

"W…w…well, that's what I mean," stammered Midas, he was sweating.

"What do you mean, 'that's what I mean'?" cried Lynn.

"I mean that's what I mean, like I want you to be my wife," said Midas.

"What?" Lynn pulled back from him. "Are you asking me to marry you?"

"Well, yes, I guess," said Midas.

Lynn pushed him away and stood up.

"Midas you are horrible. You are so incompetent sometimes!" she screamed at him. "That's not how you ask a girl to marry you."

She walked to the wall and started to hit the wall with her fists out of rage and frustration. Her t-shirt was soaked with perspiration, her make-up had run, her hair was a tangled mess. Midas came up behind her. He turned her around, and as he did so he fell onto one knee.

He spoke clearly and with sincerity, "Lynn, my darling Lynn."

He was holding her hands and looking up into her eyes.

"Lynn, I am not very good at this, but I want you to know that I love you. I have never loved anyone before like I love you, and I don't think I ever will love anyone else. I want you to be my wife, I always have, since the moment I first saw you in that coffee shop when you asked to sit at my table. I do love you so much. Please, will you marry me?"

Lynn looked into Midas's eyes.

"Whatever happens to us in our life from this moment onwards, know that I love you Midas. I so want to be your wife and yes, I will marry you. And I will help you chase your cows across America, all one thousand of them."

She leaned down and kissed his lips.

ABOUT BILL LEWIS

Bill Lewis is a writer, speaker, mentor, and motivator, who helps transform businesses and people. Bill is an experienced Corporate Executive, Non Exec Director, and a serial entrepreneur. He is rated as an outstanding leader with the mind of a seasoned high-level performer.

He has served on the Boards of five companies, including the Global Board of a major system integrator. He has also led major businesses in Fortune 200 companies, and was the CIO at one of the world's largest Aircraft Maintenance organizations. He is a consummate influencer and decision-maker at Board Level.

Prior to becoming an entrepreneur, he spent over a decade delivering turnarounds and substantial profit improvement programs, as well as consulting for blue-chip companies.

He co-created, with another business partner, a successful and disruptive digital technology start-up, and has in-depth experience of the demands of start-ups, from idea to exit, including: strategy, business creation, execution, talent management, governance, fund raising, and exit.

Bill has worked in visual communications, digital technology, and major enterprise-level application deployment. He has held senior positions in airline operations, airline maintenance, airline in-flight service, and the automotive, engineering, and maritime service sectors.

His international experience is vast – covering a significant part of the globe, with extensive experience of 'difficult' geographic locations.

He was educated at Harvard Business School (AMP), and Lancaster University (UK) where he was awarded an MA with distinction.

His current interests include sailing, cycling, reading, and writing; past or occasional interests include: golf, scuba diving, skiing, and display skydiving.

Bill has a small claim to fame (his words) for being a volunteer emergency medic in New York, building houses in Mexico, and being an expedition leader in Tar Desert, India, and western Nepal.

Contact
bill.lewis@midasand1000cows.com

RESOURCES

RESOURCES - CONTENTS

Why Resources	299
The Modern-Day Vince Lombardi	301
Courses	309

- Amazing Free Courses

Videos	313

- Videos on Mindset and Motivation

Websites	317

- The Heavyweights
- The Funders
- Advice for Entrepreneurs
- Blogs and Blogging
- Specialized

Books	327

- The Heavyweights
- Historical and Classics
- Personal Development
- Entrepreneur and Business

WHY YOU NEED ACCESS TO RESOURCES SUCH AS THESE

It is incumbent on all entrepreneurs to read and learn, not just your own technical specialty but on a wider front. Invest in your mind.

I have met many, many successful entrepreneurs, and what has struck me is their ability to converse on a wide range of subjects in an informed manner. If your gig is web technology, no one is expecting you to be an expert on (say) the Chicago School of Economic Theory or fall in the Venezuelan currency, but to have an opinion on a wide variety of topics, and appear to be 'well-read' is useful in those chattering networking events and, believe it or not, it gives context to your business, and your thinking about your (next) great idea. Keep abreast of what is happening in the world outside your box.

Your knowledge and experience is an amalgam of what you read, what you hear, and what you see. Keeping a flow of quality content will build and build and build your reservoir of 'good stuff'.

There is an incredible treasure trove of good information and advice on web pages, YouTube, and in online magazines. Subscribing to a small number of high-quality entrepreneurial-focused channels will provide you with a regular injection of good ideas. I emphasize *small number*; do not be an information junkie that gets nothing done, and be careful not to chase the links too far and for too long – it becomes counter productive.

Reading books – remember them? Reading books can seriously damage your image – as a cool, digital dude, who would not be seen with an ounce of printed word in their possession. Surprise, top entrepreneurs devour books – real ones, with printed matter, and some online. Build up your intelligence quotient and business knowledge by selective reading.

The following pages provide some recommended resources to get you going. From there on, build your own library of great information. Feed your mind.

You can also find the recommended resources, support, and other outstanding material on www.midasand1000cows.com .

THE MODERN DAY VINCE LOMBARDI

It was legendary NFL coach Vince Lombardi who was quoted as saying that, "Excellence is achieved by the mastery of the fundamentals." Some fifty years on, the Lombardi of his generation, Sir David Brailsford, demonstrates that the core principle remains the same. (With some Brailsford polish!)

Sir David John 'Dave' Brailsford is the top flight British cycling coach. He was formerly performance director of British Cycling and is currently general manager of Team Sky. He is credited as one of the principal architects in transforming Great Britain's track fortunes over the last decade and can now claim to have replicated that on the road with Team Sky. Before Brailsford, British cycling was in the Green Bay Packers of the Cycling World.

After a sensational season for British cycling in 2012 – which saw Team Sky capture a one-two finish at the Tour de France before going on to win eight gold medals at the London Olympic Games – Brailsford faced the task of sustained success in 2013.

The results followed, with a second consecutive Tour de France victory, ensuring Team Sky did twice in four seasons what they had originally set out to do once in five. A third Tour victory arrived in 2015, with the team racking up its 200th win during a highly successful year.

Often describing himself as an orchestra conductor, Brailsford oversaw the mammoth task of bringing the team together in 2009 and witnessed the squad go from strength to strength over six seasons on the road.

Having maintained an upward trajectory, the goal remains to keep winning the world's biggest races, with the elusive one-day Spring Classics a continued target.

"Sport is about continuous improvement, it's about getting better," said Brailsford. "It's about being better next year than you are this year. It's a bit like Formula One. You have a car, and the designers might say 'we can't think how we're going to make this any better'. But ultimately you can. And that's what we've got to do. We've got to keep looking, researching and working – trying things. And that's what it's all about.

"Everyone is back at square one. Nobody has an advantage because of what we did last year. No one gets a 10-mile start or anything. We're all absolutely back to zero. And unless you've done the work - unless you've put in and unless you've done what it takes - then you're going to suffer. There's no hiding place in this sport."[4]

Sir David Brailsford's 20 Lessons in Leadership[5]

1. Do the simple things excellently.

Brailsford is often quoted that the failed 2010 Tour de France team concentrated on the 'peas rather than the steak'. To explain, he told us that they spent hours focusing on all of the really clever touches (the peas) and missed really working on the basics of performance (the steak). The results were a poor and, in his words, a humiliating return from the race. *So many teams fail to really focus on doing the basics better than the competition. Those who do the simple things really well almost universally win the battle. This is echoed in analyzing successful teams (and businesses) throughout history.*

2. Optimize talent with a dynamic, fun and challenging culture.

David Walsh of the Sunday Times told us that he had never seen teamwork with the quality and professionalism anywhere in the world

---

[4] http://www.teamsky.com/teamsky/staff/article/7746#hbfZFbdacxvXfp9T.97

[5] "Sir David Brailsford's 20 Lessons in Leadership" retold by Tony Babb and published in Harrington Starr, in February 2014

that he witnessed when living with Brailsford's Team Sky. *Brailsford explained that it is "incredible what you can do with the right people" when you optimize your talent in a dynamic, challenging, fun and energetic culture.* He is adamant that people create the culture, and selection is therefore, essential to that process. Get the right people on the bus, in the words of Jim Collins in Good to Great, and your culture will be formed.

3. Behavioral change only comes when either the suffering or reward is great enough.

This was a key part of Brailsford's message. *He is steadfast in the opinion that change can only happen from within.* You can't force change on an individual; they have to drive that attitude, and it will generally only come when either the suffering is great enough or the reward big enough. As with many elite performers, he is driven by the terror of losing rather than the joy of winning. In his own words, he "doesn't do losing well." Avoidance of the suffering of losing, the "humiliation and incredible embarrassment" he felt in 2010, helps him to change his behavior. *In the corporate world there is a clear message when frustrated by a team member resistant to change. Discover what will make them tick, either through reward or suffering, and focus the communication around those factors.*

4. Give ownership and appeal to the mature side of the team.

Another feature of great leadership clearly espoused by Brailsford is the ownership that he gives. He talked of appealing to the mature side of his team. He does not try to tell. He continued that he "rarely likes to be told how to do things" and wouldn't react well to being shouted at. With that in mind *he focuses on respect*, not shouting and *being ready to prompt with questions* rather than preach with dictatorial commands. This clearly helps to *provide the culture of trust and ownership* so clearly prevalent in his teams.

5. Success can be corrosive and failure hugely motivational.

Few coaches manage to maintain their position at the summit. Brailsford has specialized in it. London Olympics Golds followed Beijing, Froome followed Wiggins. He is a master of the monopoly. *Planning for success is, in his mind, essential.* The complacency that surrounds success will be explored in the brilliant performance author Rasmus Ankersen's next book "Hunger in Paradise." *Too many fall away when they reach the top. Their attitude changes as they gain the trappings of success and an arrogance is born that wasn't there as they hungered to climb their Everest.* He touched on this as he spoke of the demise of England Cricket under the watch of his close friend Andy Flower. Again reverting to the power of avoiding loss driving him, the constant restlessness is very apparent in Brailsford. Success cannot be allowed to be corrosive. Failure is not terminal but a driver to drive forward and be used as motivation to succeed.

6. People like clarity.

Role clarity and task clarity are essential. An elite team needs absolute clarity in their position. Team Sky operates with absolute clarity in vision. Clear roles, clear boundaries, everyone in the team has a very clear idea of what is expected of them and what they are expected to do. *With this clarity comes engagement and flow. With flow comes exceptional performance.*

7. Help people to believe that they are the best.

Brailsford sees that *his role as a leader is to help people believe they are the best. That belief is fundamental to success. Winning is contagious and the fire is lit by the belief that that win is possible.* He works to ensure that the team believe that they have an advantage and it is a privilege to be a member. They know they have the best training, the best kit, the best support, the best structure. When that belief is alive in the individual, winning becomes that much more attainable.

8. There is a direct correlation between salary spend and performance.

The "Performance Investment Model" is clearly an advantage that Sky's huge investment afforded the team on tour. The same can be said with the Lottery funding for Team GB in the velodrome. *Brailsford is adamant that there is a clear correlation that the more money you spend on salary, the greater the return in performance.* He was uncompromising in his desire to bring on the best cyclists and the best leadership team. His investment in salary was returned in performance. Does this translate into the commercial world? There is a clear line of thought to suggest that the best talent secured at the highest cost will outperform those who hire cheaper alternatives. *Without vision, purpose and direction however, the results will be far from inevitable.*

9. The greatest marginal gain is a simple smile.

If you are a small start-up with limited financial resource or the richest investment bank on the planet, *one of the best marginal gains that you can give your team is a simple smile* ... "and it doesn't cost a penny!" Brailsford believes that when you are under pressure, a smile from a colleague asking "are you okay?" and "what can I do to help?" can mean as much as any significant investment. *Playing the game with poise and a smile on your face can make all the difference.*

10. If you want people to perform, make them feel valued.

If Sir Dave Brailsford were ever to return to the corporate world (he spent time as a management consultant some years ago) *the one biggest bit of advice that he would give is to make people feel valued.* Performance hinges on people feeling genuinely valued in an organization. This is clearly a subject area of real importance and significance to him. Intrinsic engagement can only truly exist if the team feel valued and have an ability to influence the group. Again, this is absolutely a critical feature of the groups that he has been associated with.

11. Make sure you hire the very best.

Team GB and Team Sky shared the standout fact that, under the charge of their performance director, they hired the very best in their field. From psychologist Dr Steve Peters (whom he described as his most important hire) through to Wiggins himself, he is *uncompromising in his drive to hire no one but the very best.* As compromises are made in the quality of those brought into the organization, so too does performance dip. Jack Welch has famously been quoted as saying you must *"hire people better than yourself."* Some task for Brailsford, but one he is committed to.

12. To be a great leader, you need to know yourself first.

Again reverting back to Steve Peters, he spoke of the importance of a leader first knowing themselves. *Leadership, he claimed, is about having an effect on others. You must know your impact on others and to do that you must first see how you impact others.* Dr Steve Peters was fundamental in helping him to see his impact. From that he could tailor his approach accordingly. The Harrington Starr leadership team was fortunate to recently spend an afternoon with the exceptionally talented former SAS man and author of the incredible book "Elite", Floyd Woodrow. *His total belief in Myers-Briggs tests echoes Brailsford's belief that communication needs to be tailored by knowing how you communicate with others. This becomes a great starting point for leadership.*

13. Understand how to win and then work back.

All of Brailsford's teams start with what winning looks like. Once they have defined that, they then work back and put the plan in place for how to get there. That compelling vision and goal becomes the catalyst for commitment, accountability and performance. Defining winning and building a common purpose around that goal is more difficult than it seems. An investment of time to define it brings excellent results. More work certainly needs to be done in business to define what great really looks like.

14. Find the optimal way to make the team perform at the optimum level.

It is widely appreciated that Team Sky are one of sport's most prepared teams in history. Whilst Brailsford seemed almost reluctant to talk about marginal gains, the theory has dominated any headline in which his success has been examined. *There is an inspirational intensity around the optimization of the teams that Brailsford prepares. He writes down the ideas, values and principles of the team. He starts with a big book of "how we are going to run this team" and is then relentless in exploring the "optimal way to make our guys better prepared to perform at an optimum level."* That sentence alone probably best sums up his philosophy on the role of a leader.

15. Be compassionately ruthless.

For Brailsford, *the performance standard has to come up to a certain level. You must find and recruit people who can come up to a clear and agreed performance level. Once an individual starts to struggle to perform to that standard you must support them but, if they still can't do it, you must let them go.* Another trait that he shares with Sir Alex Ferguson is he is a master of letting talent go at the right time. Brailsford is a key subscriber to performance science, and *when the performance level dips off, he has the courage to make the tough decisions. That courage is critical to leadership in an elite environment.* The key is to leave on good terms and he is confident that this has been achieved with all the staff he has cut over the years because the standards of performance were clear, the conversations continuous throughout, and the communication fair. When people know where they stand, the big decisions are both easy to make and easy to take. Far too often, these decisions can lack the compassion required and are shrouded with a perception of Machiavellian intent.

16. Build the right culture to get 30% more.

Brailsford believes that the same person can perform at a minimum of 30% better in one environment than they would in another, purely down to the culture. With that in mind, he sees it as essential to strive to build the right culture in a team to ensure every member is given the maximum opportunity to flourish.

17. Be massively driven to improve.

Another feature of all of the elite performers and world-class leaders that we have studied is *the constant desire to learn and improve.* In his early twenties, having left school at 16 wholly uninterested in school, Brailsford found an obsession with reading about what made people exceptional. *His thirst for knowledge saw him devour book after book in his quest to understand how to win.* You see the same habit echoed by the exceptional England Rugby head coach Stuart Lancaster in particular, who Brailsford joins in the P8 Summit of elite coaches including Mike Forde, Arsene Wenger, Andy Flower and Steve McLaren. All share that hunger to learn. *This can be directly linked to some of the great leaders in business who share that restlessness and desire to constantly educate and improve.*

18. Winning is contagious.

To quote Lombardi again, "winning is a habit." *You need to learn to win and absolutely believe that you are going to do so* in Brailsford's eyes. *Building a winning culture requires a team who believe that they are going to win and that comes from a conveyer belt of success.* Once that momentum is building, it can be very difficult to derail.

19. The team should create the rules.

Brailsford is not alone in saying that *the team should create the rules to gain maximum buy-in and engagement.* There are clear team rules that are pinned up in the famous Team Sky bus. Those rules were co-invented by the riders. *This is a philosophy that consistently springs up when reading about successful teams.* Clive Woodward championed the "teamship rules" written and upheld by the winning 2003 rugby team. He continued this with clear, team-led rules in the work he did with Team GB in London 2012. Relating back to his desire to give ownership to the team, this is a clear example of how *great leaders will involve the team in decisions to create environments of trust and accountability.*

20. Vision leads to understanding

The final piece of the jigsaw is the creation of a clear, compelling vision. Everybody in Team Sky and Team GB understands 100% what the team stands for. When you talk to experts in elite performance, people who have absolutely performed and worked at the peak, *the common theme of that team is the powerful vision of where it wants to be.* We have spent time discussing this with Floyd Woodrow, Olympic Gold Medallist Ben Hunt-Davis and the leading sports and business psychologist Simon Hartley. All are unanimous in their belief that vision is the starting point for a team or businesses success. Brailsford very clearly agrees.

COURSES

More information is available at
https://midasand1000cows.com/entrepreneurial-free-courses/

Amazing Free Courses

There are amazing free online courses covering almost every aspect of Entrepreneurship and Business delivered by top-quality Professors from top-flight Universities – and they are FREE.

Alison

This platform offers free online courses from some of the most well-known names on the Internet today, including Google, Microsoft, and Macmillan. With over 4 million users and over 600 courses already, it covers topics such as economic literacy, personal development and business/enterprise skills. Alison has an amazing course on Entrepreneurship delivered by Jeff Hawkins, Co-Founder of Palm and Handspring called "Characteristics of a Successful Entrepreneur".

Coursera

Much like MIT's Open Courseware, this site has 114 educational partners that provide free courses to almost 10 million users. One benefit to Coursera is that there are very specific courses that fit perfectly into particular niches, such as "Data Management for Clinical Research" from Vanderbilt University and "Innovation for Entrepreneurs: From Idea to Marketplace" from the University of Maryland. Its wide network of partners allows for a greater selection.

MIT Open Courseware

These are actual courses taught at MIT and offered for free on the site for viewing and reading at your discretion. The school put together an entrepreneurship page that lists over sixty available courses that are beneficial to start-up business owners. Courses include "Managing Innovation and Entrepreneurship", "Early State Capital" and "The Software Business."

VIDEOS

These videos are available at
https://midasand1000cows.com/mindset-motivation-videos/

Videos on Mindset and Motivation

Read and / or listen to anything from:

                Bob Proctor
                Joe Vitale
                Les Brown
                Napoleon Hill
                Tony Robbins
                Zig Ziglar

Recommended that you start with these -

Bob Proctor:

Words of Inspiration

How To Be Successful – Paradigms Explained

Joe Vitale:

Understanding the Law of Attraction

Expect Miracles (Audiobook)

Les Brown:

Dream – Motivational Video

Life Has No Limitations Except The Ones You Will Make:

Napoleon Hill:

Five Steps to a Positive Mental Attitude

The Law of Attraction

Tony Robbins:

Limitless Passion

Creating Unstoppable Self-Confidence:

Zig Ziglar

How to Get What you Want:

The Law Of Attraction: Believe In Yourself.."

WEB SITE RECOMMENDATIONS

These websites are accessible via
https://midasand1000cows.com/entrepreneurs-resources/

These are "Must-Bookmark" web sites and channels

(Disclaimer: this is a distillation of numerous different recommendation lists that can be found on the web. The comments may be from the original site, or the authors, or a mixture of both)

THE HEAVYWEIGHTS

AllThingsD.com	This is a must for anyone who needs to keep up to date on tech news that impacts entrepreneurs.
boss.blogs.nytimes.com	This *Times* blog is the ultimate tool for entrepreneurs and founders. The advice is current and easy to consume.
Forbes.com	Keeping up with business news is crucial. Forbes makes sure you're up to speed on the latest topics.
Forbes Woman	A compilation of insights on business, culture, entrepreneurship, and current events from a range of smart women writers.
ForteFoundation.com	The product of premier business schools and mega corporations, this site is meant to encourage women to pursue business leadership roles. It combines the best advice from the best resources around the country.
HBR.org	The Harvard Business Review blogs are a fantastic place to learn from the best. Features regular updates focused on entrepreneurs.
TheEconomist.com	This is not specifically for entrepreneurs, but the commentary makes it a requisite for any business professional. You need to stay up to date on all news, not just entrepreneurial news, to cultivate partnerships.

THE FUNDERS

AngelList.com	Do you dream of finding an angel investor? This is the platform for new companies to get equity from reliable investors.
CrunchBase.com	Everything you need to know about funding your start-up can be found here.
ForEntrepreneurs.com	This website is the result of David Skok's years of experience at Matrix Partners. Skok's approach to start-up techniques and financial modelling is user-friendly.
TheFunded.com	With more than 18,000 entrepreneurs and CEOs on this site, don't overlook this resource.
OneVest.com	One of the most reputable of crowd funding sites. If crowd funding is part of your start-up strategy, head to the site with a reputation in the field for making it easy.
Paul Graham	A legendary venture capitalist and founder of Silicon Valley incubator Y Combinator, Paul Graham's insights extend far beyond the technology and start-up communities.
VentureBlog.com	Features Dave Hornik and August Capital. Read their views of venture capital. For those seeking to invest, or want investors

SOLID ADVICE FOR THE WOULD-BE AND SEASONED ENTREPRENEAUR

500Hats.com	Dave McClure started this blog to share his pearls of wisdom on being an entrepreneur. It's enjoyable to read, and learning from the founder of 500 start-ups is a great way to get wisdom.

AllBusiness.com	This site is rich with advice and tips for just about everything an entrepreneur may need to know. From office etiquette to internet marketing, it's a favourite daily stop for many small business owners-to-be.
A Smart Bear	Serial entrepreneur Jason Cohen sold his last start-up in 2007, but he continues to mentor entrepreneurs and participate in the start-up community. His experience and behind-the-scenes knowledge is chronicled on his indispensible blog.
blog.guykawasaki.com	Kawasaki's "How to Change the World" blog is a comprehensive platform from one of the best. Some of the most common themes include human capital, management, and advice just for entrepreneurs.
ChicCEO.com	Designed for female entrepreneurs, you'll find plenty of downloadable resources here from a plethora of contracts to business plans. Even though it's meant for women, there are plenty of resources for both genders.
Design Sponge Biz Ladies	This blog spotlights insider advice and instruction on a variety of business topics, like building a wholesale business, promoting events, using Kickstarter to fund your company and initiatives. These guest posts, make sure you won't waste time reinventing the wheel.
Entrepreneur.com	Another obvious one, right? However, signing up for Entrepreneur's notifications or getting the app can help you stay up to date on the latest strategies and news affecting entrepreneurs. It's a must for founders.

Inc.com	The famous magazine has an excellent section for start-ups. Find out the latest in tips, news, and resources for entrepreneurs from one of the most reputable magazines in the industry.
Innerpreneur.com	The spirit of entrepreneurship is alive and well at this blog, where it's all about encouraging personal growth. It's something founders can put on the back burner, but it's crucial to be a well-rounded CEO.
Mixergy.com	The site that was built by entrepreneurs just for entrepreneurs showcases a series of interviews from start-up founders who were once in your shoes. Learn from the best, and know you're in great company.
Noobpreneur.com	Don't let the kitschy name veer you away from this reputable source for small business tips and tricks. It takes a user-friendly approach to dishing out advice, and it's easy to soak up the truly good information.
SaaStr.com	Web start-ups interested in monetizing can get started at this platform. It calls itself "curiously famous" and is renowned for helping entrepreneurs make passive income online. It sounds easy, but it's an art and skill that you need to learn.
Score.org	Whether you prefer your workshops in the real world or virtual, Score is the nation's leading mentorship platform for entrepreneurs. Find out how to grow your business smart by depending on the best.

SBA.gov	The Small Business Administration has been an invaluable resource for small business owners for years. There's a chapter in every major city, but the site itself is chock full of the latest news and information for entrepreneurs, too.
StartupDigest.com	A newsletter worth subscribing to? It's true when it's StartupDigest, which focuses on information for entrepreneurs without ever getting off course. If distraction is an issue for you, it won't be with this offering.
TheStartupDonut.com	A U.K. site, it's applicable to start-ups on either side of the pond. Find the tools you need and the articles necessary to get your start-up off the ground. It's especially useful if you have dreams of going multinational.
ysn.com	A business blog designed to suit every industry; this is where you can get the support and encouragement necessary to keep moving forward. Enjoy the latest entrepreneurial news as well as features that highlight how some of the most successful of founders made it to the next level.

BLOGS AND BLOGGING

CopyBlogger.com	You don't need to be a marketer to benefit from one of the best marketing blogs around. Get titbits of advice that apply to entrepreneurs and start-ups (and not just in the marketing realm).
MarieForleo.com	Forleo is an entrepreneur who's enjoyed immense success, but it's her personality and character that make this blog a must-see. She's optimistic, light, and bubbly. Many readers consider her a huge inspiration.

Medium.com	Ev Williams, co-founder of Twitter, created Medium as a chic platform for blogging. However, there are also fitting reads focused on careers from successful entrepreneurs providing first-person perspectives.
ProBlogger	You don't have to be an official blogger to benefit from Darren Rowse's site. Even businesses that are just aiming to use a blog as a promotional tool can learn a lot from this encyclopaedia of blog-related information.
QuickSprout.com	Need to learn the basics of search engine optimization (SEO) in a jiffy? The leader in entrepreneurial traffic, Neil Patel, is at your service. Whether you're an SEO newbie or a pro, there's something Patel can teach you.
TheBossNetwork.org	Join an online community of female entrepreneurs who encourage and support each other virtually. There's zero tolerance for flaming and trolling here, so you get just full support from peers and mentors.
Social Media Examiner	This blog on all things social media has articles for newcomers as well as digital natives. Plus, it's current and comprehensive in focus.
Under30CEO.com	Are you a young entrepreneur with dreams of making it big before the big 3-0? If so, then this blog is for you, but you don't necessarily still need to be a twenty-something to benefit from it. Advice for younger founders can be just as relevant no matter what your age.

SPECIALISED

Dutiee.com	The go-to site for social entrepreneurs, you can glean information on how to succeed as a non-profit and ways to incorporate social into any type of business. There's an emphasis on ethically made goods, too.
FTC.gov	The Federal Trade Commission has a section on the Franchise Rule that you need to get comfortable with. Find out all of the legal issues involved with franchise purchasing before you get in too deep.
News.YCombinator.com	Dubbed the techie Reddit site, Hacker News is where you'll find all things entrepreneurial with a coding edge. It's the product of Incubator Y Combinator and provides an insider's view on the industry.
Quora.com	This one's a no-brainer for many. Some of the most reputable entrepreneurs and leaders in the tech industry come here to dole out information, making it among the best websites to get your questions answered.
Reddit:startups	You might go to Reddit to distract yourself, but it's actually an incredibly useful website if you can avoid the time-suck spots. Head over to the start-up section to find truly helpful advice from those who have been there.

BOOKS

RECOMMENDED BOOKS FOR THE ENTREPRENEUR'S BOOK SHELF

These books are accessible via
https://midasand1000cows.com/entrepreneurs-resources/

THE HEAVYWEIGHTS

Name: **An Inquiry into the Nature and Causes of the Wealth of Nations**
Author: Adam Smith
Adam Smith's The Wealth of Nations was recognized as a landmark of human thought upon its publication in 1776. As the first scientific argument for the principles of political economy, it is the point of departure for all subsequent economic thought. Smith's theories of capital accumulation, growth, and secular change, among others, continue to be influential in modern economics.
Publisher: University of Chicago Press; Facsimile of 1904 ed edition
Date Published: 15/02/1977
No of pages: 1152
ISBN-10: 226763749
ISBN-13: 978-0226763743

Name: **Meditations**
Author: Marcus Aurelius
One of the world's most famous and influential books, Meditations, by the Roman emperor Marcus Aurelius (A.D. 121–180), incorporates the stoic precepts he used to cope with his life as a warrior and administrator of an empire. Ascending to the imperial throne in A.D. 161, Aurelius found his reign beset by natural disasters and war. In the wake of these challenges, he set down a series of private reflections, outlining a philosophy of commitment to virtue above pleasure and tranquility above happiness.
Publisher: Dover Publications
Date Published: 11/07/1997
No of pages: 112
ISBN-10: 048629823X
ISBN-13: 978-0486298238

Name: **Out of Crisis**
Author: W. Edwards Deming
According to W. Edwards Deming, American companies require nothing less than a transformation of management style and of governmental relations with industry. In Out of Crisis, originally published in 1982, Deming offers a theory of management based on

his famous 14 Points for Management. Management's failure to plan for the future, he claims, brings about loss of market, which brings about loss of jobs. Management must be judged, not only by the quarterly dividend, but by innovative plans to stay in business, protect investment, ensure future dividends, and provide more jobs through improved product and service. In simple, direct language, he explains the principles of management transformation and how to apply them.
Publisher: The MIT Press; Reprint edition
Date Published: 11/08/2000
No of pages: 507
ISBN-10: 0262541157
ISBN-13: 978-0262541152

Name: **The Prince**
Author: Niccolò Machiavelli
The Prince is a classic book that explores the attainment, maintenance, and utilization of political power in the western world. Machiavelli wrote The Prince to demonstrate his skill in the art of the state, presenting advice on how a prince might acquire and hold power. Machiavelli defended the notion of rule by force rather than by law. Accordingly, The Prince seems to rationalize a number of actions done solely to perpetuate power. It is an examination of power – its attainment, development, and successful use.
Publisher: CreateSpace Independent Publishing Platform
Date Published: 01/06/2011
No of pages: 92
ISBN-10: 1463573669
ISBN-13: 978-1463573669

Name: **The Richest Man in Babylon**
Author: George S. Clason
The ancient Babylonians were the first people to discover the universal laws of prosperity. In his classic bestseller, "The Richest Man in Babylon," George S. Clason reveals their secrets for creating, growing, and preserving wealth.
Publisher: CreateSpace Independent Publishing Platform
Date Published: 03/12/2014
No of pages: 100
ISBN-10: 1505339111

ISBN-13: 978-1505339116

Name: **Think and Grow Rich**
Author: Napoleon Hill
Think and Grow Rich by Mr. Napoleon Hill is a bestseller and one for all ages, a modern-day classic filled with ideas which have the power to change your life and set you upon the path of learning and self-development. This book conveys the experience of more than 500 men of great wealth, who began at scratch, with nothing to give in return for riches except THOUGHTS, IDEAS and ORGANIZED PLANS. Here you have the entire philosophy of money-making, from the actual achievements of the most successful men known to the American people during the past fifty years. It describes WHAT TO DO, also, HOW TO DO IT! It presents complete instructions on HOW TO SELL YOUR PERSONAL SERVICES. It will readily disclose what has been standing between you and "the big money" in the past.
Publisher: CreateSpace Independent Publishing Platform
Date Published: 06/03/2014
No of pages: 114
ISBN-10: 149617545X
ISBN-13: 978-1496175458

Name: **The Effective Executive: The Definitive Guide to Getting the Right Things Done**
Author: Peter F. Drucker
The measure of the executive, Peter F. Drucker reminds us, is the ability to "get the right things done." This usually involves doing what other people have overlooked as well as avoiding what is unproductive. Intelligence, imagination, and knowledge may all be wasted in an executive job without the acquired habits of mind that mold them into results
Publisher: Harper Business; Revised edition
Date Published: 03/01/2006
No of pages: 208
ISBN-10: 0060833459
ISBN-13: 978-0060833459

Name: **Walden**
Author: Henry David Thoreau

Written by noted Transcendentalist Henry David Thoreau, Walden is part-personal declaration of independence, social experiment, voyage of spiritual discovery, satire, and manual for self-reliance. Published in 1854, it details Thoreau's experiences over the course of two years in a cabin he built near Walden Pond, amidst woodland owned by his friend and mentor Ralph Waldo Emerson, near Concord, Massachusetts.
Publisher: CreateSpace Independent Publishing Platform
Date Published: 27/12/2013
No of pages: 206
ISBN-10: 1494812509
ISBN-13: 978-1494812508

PERSONAL DEVELOPMENT

Name: **Abundance: The Future is Better Than You Think**
Author: Peter H. Diamandis
Providing abundance is humanity's grandest challenge—this is a book about how we rise to meet it.
Publisher: Free Press
Date Published: 21/02/2012
No of pages: 400
ISBN-10: 1451614217
ISBN-13:978-1451614213

Name: **As A Man Thinketh by James Allen**
Author: James Allen
All that we achieve and all that we fail to achieve is the direct result of our own thoughts. As a Man Thinketh is a classic in the truest sense: few books have been so widely read, have stood the test of time so well, have had such an impact on generations of readers, and have carried such a simple, profound message: You are what you think. Og Mandino counted As a Man Thinketh among the top ten success books of all time--read it today and put its wisdom to work for you!
Publisher: Tremendous Life Books
Date Published: 01/06/2001
No of pages: 32
ISBN-10: 0937539562
ISBN-13: 978-0937539569

Name: **Conversation: The Gentle Art of Hearing**
Author: Gary Allman
Now, answer this question: do you ever feel your mind going BLANK during conversations? And then you think of all the things you could have said later on? Just imagine how great would it be to never run out of things to say during parties or meetings, with hot girls or with powerful men!
Publisher: CreateSpace Independent Publishing Platform; 2nd edition
Date Published: 19/06/2016
No of pages: 92
ISBN-10: 1534780750
ISBN-13: 978-1534780750

Name: **Finding Your Way in a Wild New World: Reclaim Your True Nature to Create the Life You Want**
Author: Martha Beck
Finding Your Way in a Wild New World reveals a remarkable path to the most important discovery you can make: the knowledge of what you should be doing with your one wild and precious life. It's the thing that so fulfills you that, if you knew what it was, you'd run straight toward it through brambles and fire. Life coach and bestselling author of Finding Your Own North Star, Martha Beck, guides you to find out how you got to where you are now and what you should do next, with clear instructions on tapping into the deep, wordless knowledge you carry in your body and soul.
Publisher: Atria Books; Reprint edition
Date Published: 01/01/2013
No of pages: 320
ISBN-10: 1451624603
ISBN-13: 978-1451624601

Name: **How To Win Friends and Influence People**
Author: Dale Carnegie
You can go after the job you want...and get it! You can take the job you have...and improve it! You can take any situation you're in...and make it work for you!
Publisher: Simon & Schuster
Date Published: 24/08/2010
No of pages: 128

ISBN-10: 0762462019
ISBN-13: 978-0762462018

Name: **Jonathan Livingston Seagull: A story**
Author: Richard Bach
This is the story for people who follow their hearts and make their own rules...people who get special pleasure out of doing something well, even if only for themselves...people who know there's more to this living than meets the eye: they'll be right there with Jonathan, flying higher and faster than they ever dreamed.
Publisher: Scribner; Reissue edition
Date Published: 21/10/2014
No of pages: 144
ISBN-10: 147679331X
ISBN-13: 978-1476793313

Name: **Mindfulness: An Eight-Week Plan for Finding Peace in a Frantic World**
Author: Mark Williams, Danny Penman, Jon Kabat-Zinn
MINDFULNESS reveals a set of simple yet powerful practices that you can incorporate into daily life to help break the cycle of anxiety, stress, unhappiness, and exhaustion. It promotes the kind of happiness and peace that gets into your bones. It seeps into everything you do and helps you meet the worst that life throws at you with new courage.
Publisher: Rodale Books; Reprint edition
Date Published: 13/11/2012
No of pages: 288
ISBN-10: 1609618955
ISBN-13: 978-1609618957

Name: **The Aladdin Factor**
Author: Jack Canfield, Mark Victor Hansen
We have the ability at our fingertips to achieve these things. It's the Aladdin Factor: the magical wellspring of confidence, desire--and the willingness to ask--that allows us to make wishes come true. Now, bestselling motivational authors Jack Canfield and Mark Victor Hansen introduce us to the Aladdin Factor--and help us put it into effect in our own lives.

Publisher: Berkley Books; Berkley
Date Published: 01/10/1995
No of pages: 277
ISBN-10: 0425150755
ISBN-13: 978-0425150757

Name: **The Attractor Factor: 5 Easy Steps for Creating Wealth (or Anything Else) From the Inside Out**
Author: Joe Vitale
Discover the secret to lifelong wealth and happiness! This second edition that includes an Attractor Factor IQ test, exercises for putting lessons into practice, new stories, and more. Dr. Joe Vitale presents his even more powerful and effective five-step plan for attracting wealth, happiness, and success to your life.
Publisher: Wiley
Date Published: 22/9/08
No of pages: 320
ISBN-10: 0470286423
ISBN-13: 978-0470286425

Name: **The Fountainhead**
Author: Ayn Rand
When The Fountainhead was first published, Ayn Rand's daringly original literary vision and her groundbreaking philosophy, Objectivism, won immediate worldwide interest and acclaim. This instant classic is the story of an intransigent young architect, his violent battle against conventional standards, and his explosive love affair with a beautiful woman who struggles to defeat him. This edition contains a special afterword by Rand's literary executor, Leonard Peikoff, which includes excerpts from Ayn Rand's own notes on the making of The Fountainhead. As fresh today as it was then, here is a novel about a hero—and about those who try to destroy him.
Publisher: Signet; 25 Anv edition
Date Published: 01/09/1996
No of pages: 720
ISBN-10: 0451191153
ISBN-13: 978-0451191151

Name: **The Power of Impossible Thinking**
Author: Yoram (Jerry) R. Wind, Colin Cook
The Power of Impossible Thinking is about getting better at making sense of what's going on around you so you can make decisions that respond to reality, not inaccurate or obsolete models of the world. This bestseller reveals how mental models stand between you and the truth and how to transform them into your biggest advantage! Learn how to develop new ways of seeing, when to change to a new model, and how to understand complex environments.
Publisher: FT Press; 1st edition
Date Published: 09/02/2006
No of pages: 352
ISBN-10: 0131877283
ISBN-13: 978-0131877283

Name: **The Secrets of As A Man Thinketh**
Author: Adam H. Mortimer
Achieve the ultimate in health, wealth, and happiness. This modern update on a timeless classic will teach you how to direct your mind to get exactly what you want in life. By applying the life-changing principles in this book, you'll discover how your everyday thoughts can open up a new and exciting world and ensure you a life of true abundance!
Publisher: Cedar Fort, Inc
Date Published: 14/08/2012
No of pages: 64
ISBN-10: 1462111432
ISBN-13: 978-1462111435

Name: **Thinking, Fast and Slow**
Author: Daniel Kahneman
Daniel Kahneman, the renowned psychologist and winner of the Nobel Prize in Economics, takes us on a groundbreaking tour of the mind and explains the two systems that drive the way we think. System 1 is fast, intuitive, and emotional; System 2 is slower, more deliberative, and more logical. The impact of overconfidence on corporate strategies, the difficulties of predicting what will make us happy in the future, the profound effect of cognitive biases on everything from playing the stock market to planning our next

vacation—each of these can be understood only by knowing how the two systems shape our judgments and decisions.
Publisher: Farrar, Straus and Giroux; Reprint edition
Date Published: 02/04/2013
No of pages: 499
ISBN-10: 0374533555
ISBN-13: 978-0374533557

Name: **True North: Discover Your Authentic Leadership**
Author: Bill George, Peter Sims
True North shows how anyone who follows their internal compass can become an authentic leader. This leadership tour de force is based on research and first-person interviews with 125 of today's top leaders—with some surprising results. In this important book, acclaimed former Medtronic CEO Bill George and co-author Peter Sims share the wisdom of these outstanding leaders and describe how you can develop as an authentic leader. True North presents a concrete and comprehensive program for leadership success and shows how to create your own Personal Leadership Development Plan
Publisher: Jossey-Bass; 1st edition
Date Published: 09/03/2007
No of pages: 251
ISBN-10: 0787987514
ISBN-13: 978-0787987510

Name: **You'll see it when you believe it**
Author: Dr. Wayne W. Dyer
'Our thoughts are a magic part of us, and they carry us to places that have no boundaries, and no limitations' In this bestselling thought-provoking book, Dr. Wayne Dyer stretches beyond self-help to self-realization. To do so, he embarks on a journey to activate our minds and shows us how to transform our lives by using our thoughts constructively: in other words, how to focus on a belief and see it. Using anecdotes and examples, writing with wit and compassion, and drawing on his own amazing life story, Dr. Dyer has, once again, written an inspirational self-help book that explores how to achieve personal transformation through the visualization of thought - and teaches us that believing is seeing.

Publisher: Arrow Books Ltd
Date Published: 03/02/2005
No of pages: 272
ISBN-10: 0099474298
ISBN-13: 978-0099474296

Name: **You Were Born Rich: Now You Can Discover and Develop Those Riches**
Author: Bob Proctor
Zig Ziglar may be the master motivator, Mark Victor Hansen of Chicken Soup For the Soul, the master storyteller; Anthony Robbins may be the guru of personal development, but Bob Proctor is the master thinker. When it comes to systematizing life, no one else can touch him. He is simply the best.
Publisher: TAG Publishing LLC
Date Published: June 26, 2014
No of pages: 207 pages
ISBN-10: B00LCDWF34
ISBN-13: N/A

ENTREPRENEUR AND BUSINESS

Name: **80/20 Sales and Marketing: The Definitive Guide to Working Less and Making More**
Author: Perry Marshall
Stop "Just Getting By" ... Master The 80/20 Principle And Make More Money Without More Work. When you know how to walk into any situation and see the 80/20's, you can solve almost ANY marketing problem.
Publisher: Entrepreneur Press
Date Published: 13/08/2013
No of pages: 230
ISBN-10: 1599185059
ISBN-13: 978-1599185057

Name: **Art of the Start**
Author: Guy Kawasaki
What does it take to turn ideas into action? What are the elements of a perfect pitch? How do you win the war for talent? How do you

establish a brand without bucks? These are some of the issues everyone faces when starting or revitalizing any undertaking, and Guy Kawasaki, former marketing maven of Apple Computer, provides the answers. The Art of the Start will give you the essential steps to launch great products, services, and companies-whether you are dreaming of starting the next Microsoft or a not-for-profit that's going to change the world.
Publisher: Tantor Audio; MP3 - Unabridged CD edition
Date Published: 19/01/2009
No of pages: 311
ISBN-10: 1400160634
ISBN-13: 978-1400160631

Name: **Blink: The Power of Thinking Without Thinking**
Author: Malcolm Gladwell
In his landmark bestseller The Tipping Point, Malcolm Gladwell redefined how we understand the world around us. Now, in Blink, he revolutionizes the way we understand the world within.
Publisher: Back Bay Books; 1st edition
Date Published: 03/04/2007
No of pages: 296
ISBN-10: 9780316010665
ISBN-13: 978-0316010665

Name: **Blue Ocean Strategy**
Author: W. Chan Kim
Written by the business world's new gurus, Blue Ocean Strategy continues to challenge everything you thought you knew about competing in today's crowded market place. Based on a study of 150 strategic moves spanning more than a hundred years and thirty industries, authors W. Chan Kim and Renee Mauborgne argue that lasting success comes from creating 'blue oceans': untapped new market spaces ripe from growth. And the business world has caught on - companies around the world are skipping the bloody red oceans of rivals and creating their very own blue oceans. With over one million copies sold worldwide, Blue Ocean Strategy is quickly reaching "must read" status among smart business readers. Have you caught the wave?
Publisher: Harvard Business Review Press; 1 edition

Date Published: 03/02/2005
No of pages: 256
ISBN-10: 1591396190
ISBN-13: 978-1591396192

Name: **Business Adventures: Twelve Classic Tales from the World of Wall Street**
Author: John Brooks
What do the $350 million Ford Motor Company disaster known as the Edsel, the fast and incredible rise of Xerox, and the unbelievable scandals at General Electric and Texas Gulf Sulphur have in common? Each is an example of how an iconic company was defined by a particular moment of fame or notoriety; these notable and fascinating accounts are as relevant today to understanding the intricacies of corporate life as they were when the events happened.
Publisher: Open Road Media; Reprint edition
Date Published: 12/08/2014
No of pages: 464
ISBN-10: 1497644895
ISBN-13: 978-1497644892

Name: **Built to Last**
Author: Jim Collins
Built to Last, the defining management study of the nineties, showed how great companies triumph over time and how long-term sustained performance can be engineered into the DNA of an enterprise from the very beginning. But what about the company that is not born with great DNA? How can good companies, mediocre companies, even bad companies achieve enduring greatness?
Publisher: Harper Business; 1st edition
Date Published: 19/07/2011
No of pages: 330
ISBN-10: 66620996
ISBN-13: N/A

Name: **Business Model Generation: A Handbook for Visionaries, Game Changers, and Challengers**
Author: Alexander Osterwalder, Yves Pigneur
Business Model Generation is a handbook for visionaries, game

changers, and challengers striving to defy outmoded business models and design tomorrow's enterprises. If your organization needs to adapt to harsh new realities, but you don't yet have a strategy that will get you out in front of your competitors, you need Business Model Generation.
Publisher: John Wiley and Sons; 1st edition
Date Published: 13/07/2010
No of pages: 288
ISBN-10: 0470876417
ISBN-13: 978-0470876411

Name: **Creativity, Inc.: Overcoming the Unseen Forces That Stand in the Way of True Inspiration**
Author: Ed Catmull, Amy Wallace
From Ed Catmull, co-founder (with Steve Jobs and John Lasseter) of Pixar Animation Studios, the Academy Award–winning studio behind Inside Out and Toy Story, comes an incisive book about creativity in business and leadership—sure to appeal to readers of Daniel Pink, Tom Peters, and Chip and Dan Heath. Fast Company raves that Creativity, Inc. "just might be the most thoughtful management book ever."
Publisher: Random House; 1 edition
Date Published: 08/04/2014
No of pages: 368
ISBN-10: 0812993012
ISBN-13: 978-0812993011

Name: **Emotional Appeal**
Author: Roy Garn
The Magic Power of Emotional Appeal: The Fine Art of Swaying Opinion in Any Situation [Hardcover] Roy Garn (Author). Only used copies available – get a copy while you can.
Publisher: Prentice Hall
Date Published: 13/05/1905
No of pages: 261
ISBN-10: 0135452449
ISBN-13: 978-0135452448

Name: **Enchantment: The Art of Changing Hearts, Minds, and Actions**
Author: Guy Kawasaki
Enchantment, as defined by bestselling business guru Guy Kawasaki, is not about manipulating people. It transforms situations and relationships. It converts hostility into civility and civility into affinity. It changes skeptics and cynics into believers and the undecided into the loyal.
Publisher: Portfolio; Reprint edition
Date Published: 31/12/2012
No of pages: 240
ISBN-10: 1591845831
ISBN-13: 978-1591845836

Name: **How to Get Rich: One of the World's Greatest Entrepreneurs Shares His Secrets**
Author: Felix Dennis
How to Get Rich is different from any other book on the subject because Dennis isn't selling snake oil, investment tips, or motivational claptrap. He merely wants to help people embrace entrepreneurship, and to share lessons he learned the hard way. He reveals, for example, why a regular paycheck is like crack cocaine; why great ideas are vastly overrated; and why "ownership isn't the important thing, it's the only thing."
Publisher: Portfolio; Reprint edition
Date Published: 26/05/2009
No of pages: 320
ISBN-10: 1591842719
ISBN-13: 978-1591842712

Name: **How we did it; 100 entrepreneurs share their stories**
Author: Mr. Anand Srinivasan
Aspiring entrepreneurs have a number of concerns that stop them from launching their own business - How do you pay your monthly bills when you are not making money? How do you find the right manufacturer so that you do not get swindled? How do you find the right developer? How do you actually find customers? What happens if you fail and do not find a job again?
Publisher: CreateSpace Independent Publishing Platform

Date Published: 15/04/2014
No of pages: 254
ISBN-10: 149759975X
ISBN-13: 978-1497599758

Name: **Influence: The Psychology of Persuasion**
Author: Robert B. Cialdini
Influence, the classic book on persuasion, explains the psychology of why people say "yes"—and how to apply these understandings. Dr. Robert Cialdini is the seminal expert in the rapidly expanding field of influence and persuasion. His thirty-five years of rigorous, evidence-based research along with a three-year program of study on what moves people to change behavior has resulted in this highly acclaimed book
Publisher: Harper Business; Revised edition
Date Published: 26/12/2006
No of pages: 336
ISBN-10: 006124189X
ISBN-13: 978-0061241895

Name: **Lucky or Smart: Fifty Pages for the First-Time Entrepreneur**
Author: Bo Peabody
At twenty-seven, Bo Peabody was an Internet multi-millionaire. He has co-founded five different companies, in varied industries, and made them thrive during the best and worst of economic times. Through it all, the one question everyone asks is: Was it his smarts that made him an entrepreneurial leader, or was it just plain luck? The truth is, Bo was smart enough to know when he was getting lucky. With proven methods for success and a witty, conversational voice, Bo takes the reader through the lessons his experiences as an entrepreneur have taught him.
Publisher: Book Surge Publishing
Date Published: 11/11/2008
No of pages: 78
ISBN-10: 1439210101
ISBN-13: 978-1439210109

Name: **Money and the Prosperous Soul: Tipping the Scales of Favor and Blessing**
Author: Stephen K. De Silva
CFP and CPA firm owner offers a unique, holistic approach to money and finances that combines financial philosophy, biblical truth, supernatural deliverance and prophetic teaching.
Publisher: Chosen Books
Date Published: 01/09/2010
No of pages: 192
ISBN-10: 0800794966
ISBN-13: 978-0800794965

Name: **My Life in Advertising and Scientific Advertising**
Author: Claude Hopkins
Gain a lifetime of experience from the inventor of test marketing and coupon sampling -- Claude C. Hopkins. Here, you'll get two landmark works in one, and discover his fixed principles and basic fundamentals that still prevail today
Publisher: McGraw-Hill Education; 1st edition
Date Published: 01/02/1966
No of pages: 336
ISBN-10: 0844231010
ISBN-13: 978-0844231013

Name: **Outliers**
Author: Malcolm Gladwell
His answer is that we pay too much attention to what successful people are like, and too little attention to where they are from: that is, their culture, their family, their generation, and the idiosyncratic experiences of their upbringing. Along the way he explains the secrets of software billionaires, what it takes to be a great soccer player, why Asians are good at math, and what made the Beatles the greatest rock band.
Publisher: Back Bay Books; Reprint edition
Date Published: 07/06/2011
No of pages: 336
ISBN-10: 0316017930
ISBN-13: 978-0316017930

Name: **Peak: How Great Companies Get Their Mojo from Maslow**
Author: Chip Conley
After fifteen years of rising to the pinnacle of the hospitality industry, Chip Conley's company was suddenly undercapitalized and overexposed in the post-dot.com, post-9/11 economy. For relief and inspiration, Conley, the CEO and founder of Joie de Vivre Hospitality, turned to psychologist Abraham Maslow's iconic Hierarchy of Needs. This book explores how Conley's company "the second largest boutique hotelier in the world" overcame the storm that hit the travel industry by applying Maslow's theory to what Conley identifies as the key Relationship Truths in business with Employees, Customers and Investors.
Publisher: Jossey-Bass; 1st edition
Date Published: 21/09/2007
No of pages: 274
ISBN-10: 0787988618
ISBN-13: 978-0787988616

Name: **Positioning: The Battle for Your Mind**
Author: Al Ries, Jack Trout
The first book to deal with the problems of communicating to a skeptical, media-blitzed public, Positioning describes a revolutionary approach to creating a "position" in a prospective customer's mind – one that reflects a company's own strengths and weaknesses as well as those of its competitors.
Publisher: McGraw-Hill Education; 1st edition
Date Published: 03/01/2001
No of pages: 224
ISBN-10: 0071373586
ISBN-13: 978-0071373586

Name: **Precision: Principles, Practices and Solutions for the Internet of Things**
Author: Timothy Chou
You may not be sure why your coffee pot should talk to your toaster, but precision technology powering an Internet of Things has the potential to reshape the planet. To help clarify, Dr. Timothy Chou has created Precision to introduce us to the basics of the Internet of

Things (IoT) for the enterprise. The first part Precision: Principles and Practices introduces a vendor neutral, acronym free framework. Dr. Chou then discusses the framework's fundamental principles and these principles put into practice. The second part Precision: Solutions puts Dr. Chou's IoT framework into practice highlighting 12 real world solutions for manufacturers who are building precision machines and companies utilizing these machines to receive precision enhanced business outcomes. Case studies discussed span a number of industries such as power, water, healthcare, transportation, oil & gas, construction, agriculture, gene sequencers and mining.
Publisher: lulu.com
Date Published: 16/05/2016
No of pages: 294
ISBN-10: 1329843568
ISBN-13: 978-1329843561

Name: **Reality Check: The Irreverent Guide to Outsmarting, Outmanaging, and Outmarketing Your Competition**
Author: Guy Kawasaki
For a quarter of a century, in his various guises as an entrepreneur, evangelist, venture capitalist, and guru, Guy Kawasaki has cast an irreverent eye on the dubious trends, sketchy theories, and outright foolishness of what so often passes for business today. Too many people frantically chase the Next Big Thing only to discover that all they've made is the Last Big Mistake.
Publisher: Portfolio; Reprint edition
Date Published: 22/02/2011
No of pages: 496
ISBN-10: 1591843944
ISBN-13: 978-1591843948

Name: **Rich Dad Poor Dad - What the rich teach their kids about money**
Author: Robert T. Kiyosaki
Rich Dad Poor Dad, the #1 Personal Finance book of all time, tells the story of Robert Kiyosaki and his two dads—his real father and the father of his best friend, his rich dad—and the ways in which both men shaped his thoughts about money and investing. The book explodes the myth that you need to earn a high income to be rich and

explains the difference between working for money and having your money work for you.
Publisher: Plata Publishing; 1 edition
Date Published: 16/08/2011
No of pages: 274
ISBN-10: 1612680011
ISBN-13: 978-1612680019

Name: **Surely You're Joking, Mr. Feynman! (Adventures of a Curious Character)**
Author: Richard P. Feynman, Ralph Leighton
Richard Feynman, winner of the Nobel Prize in physics, thrived on outrageous adventures. Here he recounts in his inimitable voice his experience trading ideas on atomic physics with Einstein and Bohr and ideas on gambling with Nick the Greek; cracking the uncrackable safes guarding the most deeply held nuclear secrets; accompanying a ballet on his bongo drums; painting a naked female toreador. In short, here is Feynman's life in all its eccentric—a combustible mixture of high intelligence, unlimited curiosity, and raging chutzpah.
Publisher: W. W. Norton & Company; Reprint edition
Date Published: 17/04/1997
No of pages: 352
ISBN-10: 0393316041
ISBN-13: 978-0393316049

Name: **Switch: How to Change Things When Change Is Hard**
Author: Dan Heath, Chip Heath
The primary obstacle is a conflict that's built into our brains, say Chip and Dan Heath, authors of the critically acclaimed bestseller Made to Stick. Psychologists have discovered that our minds are ruled by two different systems—the rational mind and the emotional mind—that compete for control. The rational mind wants a great beach body; the emotional mind wants that Oreo cookie. The rational mind wants to change something at work; the emotional mind loves the comfort of the existing routine. This tension can doom a change effort—but if it is overcome, change can come quickly.
Publisher: Crown Business; 1st edition
Date Published: 16/02/2010

No of pages: 305
ISBN-10: 0385528752
ISBN-13: 978-0385528757

Name: **Team of Teams: New Rules of Engagement for a Complex World**
Author: General Stanley McChrystal, Tantum Collins, David Silverman
When General Stanley McChrystal took command of the Joint Special Operations Task Force in 2004; he quickly realized that conventional military tactics were failing. Al Qaeda in Iraq was a decentralized network that could move quickly, strike ruthlessly, then seemingly vanish into the local population. The allied forces had a huge advantage in numbers, equipment, and training—but none of that seemed to matter.
Publisher: Portfolio
Date Published: 12/05/2015
No of pages: 304
ISBN-10: 1591847486
ISBN-13: 978-1591847489

Name: **The $100 Startup: Reinvent the Way You Make a Living, Do What You Love, and Create a New Future**
Author: Chris Guillebeau
Still in his early thirties, Chris is on the verge of completing a tour of every country on earth – he's already visited more than 175 nations – and yet he's never held a "real job" or earned a regular paycheck. Rather, he has a special genius for turning ideas into income, and he uses what he earns both to support his life of adventure and to give back.
Publisher: Crown Business; 1st edition
Date Published: 08/05/2012
No of pages: 304
ISBN-10: 0307951529
ISBN-13: 978-0307951526

Name: **The 4-Hour Workweek: Escape 9-5, Live Anywhere, and Join the New Rich**
Author: Timothy Ferriss

Forget the old concept of retirement and the rest of the deferred-life plan–there is no need to wait and every reason not to, especially in unpredictable economic times. Whether your dream is escaping the rat race, experiencing high-end world travel, earning a monthly five-figure income with zero management, or just living more and working less, The 4-Hour Workweek is the blueprint.
Publisher: Harmony; Exp Upd edition
Date Published: 15/12/2009
No of pages: 416
ISBN-10: 9780307465351
ISBN-13: 978-0307465351

Name: **The 15 Commitments of Conscious Leadership: A New Paradigm for Sustainable Success**
Author: Jim Dethmer, Diana Chapman, Kaley Klemp
You'll never see leadership the same way again after reading this book. These fifteen commitments are a distillation of decades of work with CEOs and other leaders. They are radical or provocative for many. They have been game changers for us and for our clients. We trust that they will be for you too. Our experience is that unconscious leadership is not sustainable.
Publisher: Dethmer, Chapman & Klemp; 1st edition
Date Published: 10/01/2015
No of pages: 374
ISBN-10: 0990976904
ISBN-13: 978-0990976905

Name: **The E-Myth Revisited: Why Most Small Businesses Don't Work and What to Do About It**
Author: Michael E. Gerber
In this first new and totally revised edition of the 150,000-copy underground bestseller, The E-Myth, Michael Gerber dispels the myths surrounding starting your own business and shows how commonplace assumptions can get in the way of running a business. He walks you through the steps in the life of a business from entrepreneurial infancy, through adolescent growing pains, to the mature entrepreneurial perspective, the guiding light of all businesses that succeed. He then shows how to apply the lessons of franchising to any business whether or not it is a franchise. Finally, Gerber draws

the vital, often overlooked distinction between working on your business and working in your business. After you have read The E-Myth Revisited, you will truly be able to grow your business in a predictable and productive way.
Publisher: HarperCollins;
Date Published: 03/03/1995
No of pages: 268
ISBN-10: 0887307280
ISBN-13: 978-0887307287

Name: **The Entrepreneur Mind**
Author: Kevin D. Johnson
To achieve unimaginable business success and financial wealth—to reach the upper echelons of entrepreneurs, where you'll find Mark Zuckerberg of Facebook, Sara Blakely of Spanx, Mark Pincus of Zynga, Kevin Plank of Under Armour, and many others—you have to change the way you think. In other words, you must develop the Entrepreneur Mind, a way of thinking that comes from learning the vital lessons of the best entrepreneurs
Publisher: Johnson Media Inc.
Date Published: 22/01/2013
No of pages: 268
ISBN-10: 0988479702
ISBN-13: 978-0988479708

Name: **The Fire Starter Sessions: A Soulful + Practical Guide to Creating Success on Your Own Terms**
Author: Danielle LaPorte
As the creator of DanielleLaPorte.com--deemed "the best place online for kick-ass spirituality" - Danielle LaPorte's straight-talk life-and-livelihood sermons have been read by over one million people. Bold but empathetic, she reframes popular self-help and success concepts.
Publisher: Harmony
Date Published: 18/02/2014
No of pages: 368
ISBN-10: 0307952118
ISBN-13: 978-0307952110

Name: **The Four Steps to Epiphany**
Author: Steve Blank
The Four Steps to the Epiphany launched the Lean Startup approach to new ventures. It was the first book to offer that startups are not smaller versions of large companies and that new ventures are different than existing ones. Startups search for business models while existing companies execute them.
Publisher: K&S Ranch; 2nd edition
Date Published: 17/07/2013
No of pages: 370
ISBN-10: 0989200507
ISBN-13: 978-0989200509

Name: **The Hard Thing About Hard Things: Building a Business When There Are No Easy Answers by Ben Horowitz**
Author: Ben Horowitz
Ben Horowitz, cofounder of Andreessen Horowitz and one of Silicon Valley's most respected and experienced entrepreneurs, offers essential advice on building and running a startup—practical wisdom for managing the toughest problems business school doesn't cover, based on his popular ben's blog.
Publisher: Harper Business
Date Published: 04/03/2014
No of pages: 304
ISBN-10: 0062273205
ISBN-13: 978-0062273208

Name: **The Innovator's Dilemma: The Revolutionary Book That Will Change the Way You Do Business**
Author: Clayton M. Christensen
The Innovator's Dilemma is the revolutionary business book that has forever changed corporate America. Based on a truly radical idea—that great companies can fail precisely because they do everything right—this Wall Street Journal, Business Week and New York Times Business bestseller is one of the most provocative and important business books ever written. Entrepreneurs, managers, and CEOs ignore its wisdom and its warnings at their great peril.
Publisher: Harper Business; Reprint edition

Date Published: 04/10/2011
No of pages: 336
ISBN-10: 0062060244
ISBN-13: 978-0062060242

Name: **The Lean Startup: How Today's Entrepreneurs Use Continuous Innovation to Create Radically Successful Businesses by Eric Ries**
Author: Eric Ries
Eric Ries defines a startup as an organization dedicated to creating something new under conditions of extreme uncertainty. This is just as true for one person in a garage or a group of seasoned professionals in a Fortune 500 boardroom. What they have in common is a mission to penetrate that fog of uncertainty to discover a successful path to a sustainable business.
Publisher: Crown Business; 1st edition
Date Published: 13/09/2011
No of pages: 336
ISBN-10: 0307887898
ISBN-13: 978-0307887894

Name: **The Millionaire Fastlane: Crack the Code to Wealth and Live Rich for a Lifetime.**
Author: MJ DeMarco
The mainstream financial gurus have sold you blindly down the river to a great financial gamble. You've been hoodwinked to believe that wealth can be created by recklessly trusting in the uncontrollable and unpredictable markets: the housing market, the stock market, and the job market. This impotent financial gamble dubiously promises wealth in a wheelchair -- sacrifice your adult life for a financial plan that reaps dividends in the twilight of life. Accept the Slowlane as your blueprint for wealth and your financial future will blow carelessly asunder on a sailboat of HOPE: HOPE you can find a job and keep it, HOPE the stock market doesn't tank, HOPE the economy rebounds, HOPE, HOPE, and HOPE. Do you really want HOPE to be the centerpiece for your family's financial plan?
Publisher: Viperion Publishing Corporation; 1st edition
Date Published: 04/01/2011
No of pages: 336

ISBN-10: 0984358102
ISBN-13: 978-0984358106

Name: **The Obstacle Is the Way: The Timeless Art of Turning Trials into Triumph**
Author: Ryan Holiday
Its many fans include a former governor and movie star (Arnold Schwarzenegger), a hip hop icon (LL Cool J), an Irish tennis pro (James McGee), an NBC sportscaster (Michele Tafoya), and the coaches and players of winning teams like the New England Patriots, Seattle Seahawks, Chicago Cubs, and University of Texas men's basketball team.
Publisher: Portfolio
Date Published: 01/05/2014
No of pages: 224
ISBN-10: 1591846358
ISBN-13: 978-1591846352

Name: **The Star Principle**
Author: Richard Koch
Richard Koch has made over £100 million from spotting 'Star' businesses. In his new book, he shares the secrets of his success - and shows how you too can identify and enrich yourself from 'Stars'. Star businesses are ventures operating in a high-growth sector - and are the leaders in their niche of the market. Stars are rare. But with the help of this book and a little patience, you can find one, or create one yourself.
Publisher: Little, Brown; Reprint edition
Date Published: 04/03/2010
No of pages: 272
ISBN-10: 0749929626
ISBN-13: 978-0749929626

Name: **The Startup Playbook: Secrets of the Fastest-Growing Startups From Their Founding Entrepreneurs**
Author: David Kidder
According to the Kauffman Index of Entrepreneurial Activity, more than 565,000 new businesses were created in 2010 in the United States alone—each one of them hoping to strike gold. The Startup

Playbook will help them succeed. Going insider to insider with unprecedented access, New York Times bestselling author and Clickable CEO, David Kidder, shares the hard-hitting experiences of some of the world's most influential entrepreneurs and CEOs, revealing their most closely held advice. Face-to-face interviews with 40 founders give readers key insights into what it took to build PayPal, LinkedIn, AOL, TED, Flickr, and many others into household names. The Startup Playbook is the go-to for entrepreneurs big and small.
Publisher: Chronicle Books
Date Published: 02/01/2013
No of pages: 292
ISBN-10: 1452105049
ISBN-13: 978-1452105048

Name: **Thinkertoys: A Handbook of Creative-Thinking Techniques**
Author: Michael Michalko
In this revised and expanded edition of his groundbreaking Thinkertoys, creativity expert Michael Michalko reveals life-changing tools that will help you think like a genius. From the linear to the intuitive, this comprehensive handbook details ingenious creative-thinking techniques for approaching problems in unconventional ways. Through fun and thought-provoking exercises, you'll learn how to create original ideas that will improve your personal life and your business life. Michalko's techniques show you how to look at the same information as everyone else and see something different.
Publisher: Ten Speed Press; 2 edition
Date Published: 08/06/2006
No of pages: 416
ISBN-10: 1580087736
ISBN-13: 978-1580087735

Name: **Work Rules: Insights from Inside Google That Will Transform How You Live and Lead**
Author: Laszlo Bock
From the visionary head of Google's innovative People Operations comes a groundbreaking inquiry into the philosophy of work-and a blueprint for attracting the most spectacular talent to your business

and ensuring that they succeed.
Publisher: Twelve
Date Published: 07/04/2015
No of pages: 416
ISBN-10: 1455554790
ISBN-13: 978-1455554799

Name: **Work the System: The Simple Mechanics of Making More and Working Less**
Author: Sam Carpenter
Work The System: The Simple Mechanics of Making More and Working Less, guides the reader in modifying his or her fundamental perception of the world, moving from an inaccurate vision of barely controlled chaos, to a more accurate one: that life is an orderly collection of individual linear systems each of which can be improved and perfected one at a time. The reader is guided through the process of "getting" this new vision, and then through the specifics of applying it via Carpenter's "system improvement" methodology.
Publisher: Greenleaf Book Group Press; 3rd edition
Date Published: 01/10/2011
No of pages: 304
ISBN-10: 160832253X
ISBN-13: 978-1608322534

Name: **Zero to One: Notes Startups, or How to Build the Future**
Author: Peter Thiel, Blake Masters
Thiel begins with the contrarian premise that we live in an age of technological stagnation, even if we're too distracted by shiny mobile devices to notice. Information technology has improved rapidly, but there is no reason why progress should be limited to computers or Silicon Valley. Progress can be achieved in any industry or area of business. It comes from the most important skill that every leader must master: learning to think for yourself.
Publisher: Crown Business; 1 edition
Date Published: 16/09/2014
No of pages: 224
ISBN-10: 0804139296
ISBN-13: 978-0804139298